VAN MORRISON

VAN MORRISON

Inarticulate Speech of the Heart

John Collis

LITTLE, BROWN AND COMPANY

A *Little, Brown* Book

First published in Great Britain in 1996
by Little, Brown and Company

Copyright © 1996 Brown Packaging Ltd

The moral right of the author has been asserted.

A CIP catalogue record for this book
is available from the British Library.

ISBN: 0 316 87640 2

UK companies, institutions and other organisations
wishing to make bulk purchases of this or any other book
published by Little, Brown should contact their local bookshop
or the special sales department at the address below.
Tel: 0171 911 8000. Fax: 0171 911 8100

Editorial and design by Brown Packaging Ltd
255-257 Liverpool Road
London N1 1LX

Printed and bound in Great Britain by
Hartnolls Limited, Bodmin, Cornwall

Little, Brown & Company (UK)
Brettenham House
Lancaster Place
London WC2E 7EN

Contents

Acknowledgements

My first vote of thanks must go to Graham Barrett, an authority on the work of Morrison and many other artists, who has given freely of his advice and encouragement as well as making available to me his collection of taped Morrison interviews. In particular, the discography could not have swelled to its present size and detail without Graham's help.

I have enjoyed reacquainting myself with three earlier books on Morrison, by Ritchie Yorke, Johnny Rogan and Steve Turner. I have also drawn on interviews conducted by Stephen Davis, Jackie Flavelle, John Tobler, Paul Vincent, Mick Brown, Paul Jones, Jonathan Cott, Happy Traum, Sean O'Hagan, Richard Williams, John Grissim Jr, Ian Birch, Dermot Stokes, Seamus Creagh, Anthony Denselow and Bill Morrison. These and all other sources are identified at the back of the book.

In Belfast my informative and companionable guides were George Jones, who played with Morrison in all the pre-Them bands, and Terry Hooley of Good Vibrations Records – I owe them a considerable debt of the dark stuff. I was delighted to meet legendary record dealer Dougie Knight, while Billy Harrison, Eric Wrixon and Jim Armstrong took a lot of time to help me piece together "The Story of Them".

Two dear friends from the days of that fine band Bees Make Honey were of great assistance – Rod Demick recalled Belfast during the days of Them, while my host in Dublin was Deke O'Brien – so hospitable was he that we never quite got round to talking about Them's rivalry with his band Bluesville. But the crack was good.

Thanks to the many others, quoted in the book, who were kind enough to take my phone calls, to Malcolm Southwood, Rob Steen and John O'Toole for temporarily plugging any gaps in my record collection, to John Gill for suggesting me for this project and to Ashley Brown for agreeing with him.

John Collis, London, March 1996

Introduction

Van Morrison is a member of an elite within the musical establishment, one of those artists who have broadened our experience of the music by chiselling out a highly individual niche in the rock face. They are too individual, perhaps, to have had a significant effect on the development of the music, but in their distinctive approach to the basic tools of the blues and country, they have enriched and influenced popular music immeasurably. And they are not entirely without influence – Morrison once claimed: "Springsteen's definitely ripped me off. He's ripped my movements off as well!"

Morrison himself consciously resists categorisation. "From the journalistic point of view," he says somewhat dismissively, "what I do is rock music, but what I actually perform and do on albums has nothing to do with rock. It's not played like rock music. It's a combination of gospel, blues, folk." And again: "I'm not really interested in pop or rock music."

More than most, Morrison has proved capable of speaking to successive generations. The latest in his weighty catalogue of records will be bought by many who were not even born when he cut *Astral Weeks*, and to whom the "beat boom" that gave rise to Them in the mid-1960s is as distant, strange and monochrome as Churchill's cigar and ration books.

Van Morrison's bedfellows include Randy Newman, with his pared-down parables and wry observations of the land of dreams from a man of Jewish European immigrant stock. The aching, jazzy, heroin-hippy music of Tim Hardin, whose music could be escorted up the pop charts by artists as diverse as Bobby Darin and the Four Tops, is another example. Ry Cooder, combining densely textured slide guitar with a determination to illuminate all corners of the American musical experience – whether it be a Depression lament or a German-imported south Texan polka – is a further candidate.

Among this company stands Van Morrison, steeped both in American folk music and his Irish ancestry. As Irish writer and broadcaster Shay Healy puts it, he "incorporated the Irish ballad into the tradition of American soul music."

One false approach to Morrison's work, is to regard him as a poet working within the rock framework. Poetry should be language in its most polished form, and as a distillation of the poet's experience. Sometimes Morrison aims at this and succeeds triumphantly, but he is more likely to repeat a phrase like a mantra, or burst into scat singing. The words may often be prosaic, and so can hardly be poetry. "I don't think of myself as a songwriter," he says. "I know songwriters and I'm not one. A songwriter is a guy who can come in at 9.30 in the morning and write a song on demand. I've never been able to do that. I'm an inspirational writer. So I'm not like a craftsman, which a songwriter is." By 1995, though, he had changed his tune: "Songwriter" on *Days Like This* finds him emphasising that his songwriting is a craft, but nothing more elevated than that.

The magic of Morrison's performance is not in poetry, much though he may draw on poets for inspiration. It lies in his ability to combine both the spiritual and technical possibilities of musical expression. On some occasions he may well enchant us with the strength of his imagery, but at heart he is a jazzman, using words and tonsils as his instruments. He was also, in his early days, a rock-'n'roller, seemingly identifying more with Little Richard's primal scream than, say, Roy Orbison's delicious melancholy.

That early expression of his genius, 1968's *Astral Weeks*, begins with the line, "If I ventured in the slipstream between the viaducts of your dreams." Even in the peace-and-love era that gave birth to this observation, it sounded dodgy. The late Vivian Stanshall, singing with the Bonzo Dog Doo Dah Band, charted similar territory in his doo-wop ballad "Canyons of Your Mind", when exploring "the wardrobe of your soul, in the section labelled Shirts."

And yet *Astral Weeks* overcomes this hesitant start to become a work of stunning musical – and, yes, lyrical – invention, one that still exerts a power to surprise and delight. Even *Astral Weeks*, though, delighted us in a self-sealed vacuum, barely affecting the sales of upright basses and flutes, let alone sending the river of popular music off on a new course. This major engineering was the work of others such as Buddy Holly, Chuck Berry, Bob Dylan, the Beach Boys and Jimi Hendrix.

These are among the select few artists who actually changed the course of the music, whose removal from the overall picture would significantly alter it as well as diminish it. After them, there could only be variations on a theme, revivals (ska, rockabilly, even the blues itself), and the harnessing of ever more clinical or ingenious gadgetry. Van Morrison was not destined to affect the music so profoundly but to adorn it, to suggest previously unsuspected potential and above all to entertain succeeding generations with a brand of music that hadn't quite been heard before.

He is, of course, an artist displaying contradictions of all kinds. This most introverted and jealously private of rock stars, for example, established his teenage showband reputation with explosive, alcohol-fuelled, on-stage acrobatics.

Harry Bird was prime mover of the Regents Showband until it disbanded in 1969. One of his reminiscences gives a taste of Morrison's potent stage image in the early 1960s. Morrison was briefly a saxophone player in the Regents, in the hinterland between his two formative bands the Monarchs and Them, deputising for the regular sax man who had broken his wrist.

"We were playing a young farmers' dance in Randalstown," says Bird. "A pretty culshy [yokel] affair it was. We thought of ourselves as a pretty trendy band at the time but this audience were all farmers, six foot two and built like elephants, with the shit still on their boots. We were booked for a five-hour dance and we were struggling, because normally we had two singers to spread the work and one of them was ill or something. Someone asked Van if he could sing a bit and he said 'Oh, yeah.'

"So he sang 'Blue Suede Shoes'. He was out in front of us and when he started to sing the whole hall just stopped dancing. 'Well, it's one for the money, two for the show…' It was as if they'd been mesmerised. They probably hadn't heard anything like this, and we were all behind Van wondering what the hell was going on. So I edged round to look at him – his face had gone purple! His eyes were stuck out like organ stops. He was freaking out, going crazy, and the crowd just watched in amazement, wondering if he was going to have a stroke or something. We couldn't let him sing any more – he was scaring the people!"

It is the contradictions inhabiting the shy extrovert, a man who insists that he has absolutely nothing to say when beyond the confines of the concert stage or the recording studio, that contribute to an enigma. And it may well be that he takes a certain amount of private pleasure and satisfaction in living up to this enigmatic reputation, moving from shyness to surliness. We can choose to be intrigued by it or not, to play the game by his rules – concerts and records are the only negotiable currency, and even then with the artist reserving the right to dismiss the effort – or to ignore him. One sometimes suspects that Van Morrison wouldn't care much either way. At least, that's what he would say.

"He's a cryptic person. Gentle and quiet at the best of times, but given to sudden fits of anger." This was a verdict on Van Morrison given by his friend and, for a while, intended biographer, the late

Donall Corvin. Corvin was an Irish journalist with intimate knowledge of the musical and social milieu that gave rise to Morrison's
music. But when it came to turning the conversation of friends into
a formal, chronological and accurate interview, Corvin was undone.
Morrison would prevaricate and provide misleading and conflicting
recollections of the same incident, even reportedly taking to his bed
when his old chum arrived in the USA specifically to interview him.

Morrison has thus frustrated every hope over the years that he
would co-operate in the charting of his life. However supportive
and laudatory the writer's motives, he will get no thanks and may
well get a writ instead. Such biographical writing as has managed
to tease out a few first-person quotes has largely had to rely on the
thin gruel of magazine interviews, orchestrated by Morrison's record
company. The artist has dug a moat of silence around himself, and
seems to take amusement in scowling from above his castle walls.

In private, even on occasions in the company of strangers,
Morrison can be in a mood to relax, to unwind, to converse
politely. Whether his more familiar reticence, particularly towards
journalists, is indeed a deliberate mystification or paranoia it is undeniable that Morrison has rarely said anything particularly illumi-
nating for publication, outside the grooves of a record. That's what
he does, makes records. He feels, not unreasonably, that anything
else is his own business, and that an ability to make music does not
imply an ability to fashion endearing or revealing sentences. When
he's been cornered, acceding however unwillingly to a record company's request for press publicity, he has usually been at pains to
confirm that view by saying little, if anything, of interest.

The very day after I agreed to write this book I read an article by
a previous biographer, Johnny Rogan, in the first (and only) issue
of the rock magazine *Encore*. It was a dreadful warning. The introductory "standfirst" to the piece said: "Everyone has a book in them.
But not if you want to write it about Van Morrison…"!

Sometimes, it seems, you might not even have a magazine article in you. Liam Fay of Dublin's *Hot Press* tells of an encounter with Morrison in the summer of 1989. An interview for a cover feature was arranged with the artist's management and Fay flew to London, where Morrison was then living. The meeting was to be in one of Morrison's favourite Notting Hill restaurants.

"He stormed in 35 minutes late and said he didn't want to do the interview there, he wanted to go to a cafe across the road instead," says Fay. "After he'd smothered his chicken and chips with ketchup he harangued me for 20 minutes on why he hated journalists. He believed that they all had what he called an 'angle', and he wanted to know what mine was. He also seemed preoccupied with the idea that the editor of the magazine must have been afraid to meet him for some reason, and so had sent a lackey in his place.

"After I'd asked a couple of questions he suddenly said, 'This isn't working,' and turned off the tape. He was also very annoyed that I was only 25. 'You know nothing.' I tried to ask a harmless question to calm him – why did he decide to call himself Ivan Morrison on the production credits to *Avalon Sunset*? He shouted at the top of his voice, 'Because it's my fucking name!'

"Then he insisted on having the tape. 'If you don't give me that tape you're a prick.' He made a couple of phone calls, one a long one to Belfast, and then demanded the tape again. I just gave up and walked away. I was really shaken up. About five minutes later I was waiting for a cab, because there was a tube strike that day, and I saw him appear over the hill. He saw me too, and what I didn't know was that I was standing right outside his house. Total coincidence – I didn't know where he lived. He came charging down the road at me and was flicking at me with his coat. He was shouting, 'Get away from my house.' Eventually he scuttled off.

"When I went through the tape later I realised that what answers he had given me were either monosyllabic or abusive, even though he'd switched off the tape for most of the ranting. He referred to the editor of *Hot Press* a few times, saying, 'You're not getting your pound of flesh, Niall Stokes!'

"I called up one of his people, John Rogers, who'd arranged the interview. He seemed very surprised – and concerned about the abuse. He understood that Van had wanted to do the interview. But I thought he was absolutely deranged on that day. Deranged and paranoid."

I recount Fay's meeting with his hero, with his permission, not to adopt a dreaded "angle" on Morrison, but because I believe it illuminates dramatically one side of his character, when shyness and a yearning for privacy can boil over into screaming fury. Other witnesses attest to the generosity and warmth of a complex man. Shay Healy, for example, in spite of following Morrison's least-favourite profession, says that during several meetings over the years he has "never had a cross word from him".

This reclusive artist is only part-way through a long, fertile and much-appreciated career that began when he was 15. He is, as we have noted, musically reborn for each generation. Inevitably, every now and again, someone is going to rise to the challenge of providing an updated assessment of his contribution to rock music, sadly aware all the time that the subject would rather he didn't bother.

This career has included a long love-hate relationship with all the elements that necessarily make up the life of a rock star, and yet it would seem that this is the only life he ever yearned for. He has confronted head-on not just the media but the demands of fame and success, the intrusive enthusiasm of his admirers, the loyalty of musicians and, more understandably, the machinations of the industry that disseminates his work.

Any number of reasons have been suggested for his swings of mood – maybe they are governed by whatever happens to be the current staging post on his religious and spiritual journey, maybe it springs from his working-class background. This is hard to credit, since the roots of rock in the blues were hardly the province of the plump middle class, and yet another troubled singer from comparatively humble origins, the late Del Shannon, always felt an element of guilt about his success, as if for some strange reason it shouldn't really be bestowed upon people like himself. He took comfort in alcohol and eventually, years after drying out, felt that his life had become such a hopeless knot of irreconcilable strands that suicide was the only option.

Maybe in Morrison's case he sets impossibly high musical standards for both himself and his musicians, hearing in his mind's concert hall something that he feels can never be achieved.

The fact that depression plays its part in Morrison's songs is made explicitly clear in his 1995 set *Days Like This*, by and large an upbeat, life-affirming collection of songs. Among the exceptions, however, are "Underlying Depression" and "Melancholia". In the first he notes that "outside there's a cavalcade of clowns but they're bringing me down," and he suggests that the problem has been with him all his life: "I was born with the blues and my blue suede shoes." And it was this assumed inheritance that bewildered, even frightened, the young farmers of Randalstown all those years ago.

As for melancholy, "it's in my blood and it's in my veins," and Morrison bemoans the fact that "every single day, it won't go away." In less skilled hands such introverted musings could only come over as self-pity, and it is a mark of Morrison's continuing power as an artist that he adroitly avoids the trap, one that at other times has threatened to ensnare him.

And so, for whatever reason or reasons, Morrison does indeed seem to have been "pursued by furies", and to have explored any number of philosophical avenues in search of peace.

"Whatever it is," in Corvin's phrase, was there at the start of his career – the storms of anger that sometimes overwhelmed a shy and otherwise civil man. Ever since, he has assembled and disbanded musical congregations at will, and sometimes a change of direction has, to the sympathetic outsider, seemed prompted more by frustration than eclectic curiosity.

And throughout all of this journey Morrison has adopted the stance of the beleaguered artist, hounded by impertinent critics and over-demanding fans, bruised by the collision of his artistic sensibility and the cigar-chomping business in which he has been forced to work. He has persisted in this pose in spite of the fact that the press has almost always been supportive and that, by and large, the sort of fans he attracts are far too polite to claw annoyingly at his trousers. Maybe they claw at his lyrics, but more fool them if they delve too deep – that would be like reading something more than delightful comic alliteration into a Dylan line like "The pump don't work 'cos the vandals took the handles." We're not talking Nietzsche or even Stephen Hawking here – it's only rock'n'roll, albeit at the more cerebrally nutritious end of the spectrum. And as for the means of disseminating his work: "I was never part of the record business, ever. I basically deliver tapes and distribution happens through the record company. We, my company, deliver the product and it's a distribution deal after that."

Morrison's stance could perhaps be prompted by cunning rather than distempered bewilderment. Given that press and fans alike are far more likely to celebrate his genius than to probe for shortcomings, the frown could be a device deliberately designed to elicit sympathy and respect, to keep everyone at a distance and pump up the mystique, to burnish that mystique as far as the fan is concerned, and to warn the hack fearful of unleashing a storm of Celtic wrath.

This hack, for one, offers only respect, and simply wants to get the amateur psychoanalysis out of the way at the outset. Van Morrison is entitled to fight for his privacy in any way that he can, just as others are entitled to preen and pose in the tabloid gossip columns if they wish, but once an entertainer has taken the punter's shilling he or she has entered a contract, and the contract states that he who pays the piper might wish occasionally to peek beyond the rim of the compact disc.

The paradox, of course, is that so confessional a writer should be so unforthcoming about his work, almost as if he knows he has something to say, has no obvious means of material support other than by saying it, but is fearful of being heard. Given some of the prattlings of far lesser artists there may well be nothing but wisdom in his stance. But what he does say, exclusively in his music, is such that those who have grown up with it sometimes bring so much intellectual and emotional weight to their response that they seem to be demanding a form of private dialogue with the artist. That can get silly, sending someone as intelligent as Morrison scurrying for cover.

When you are aware of your own fallibility, and of the often arbitrary nature of creative work lauded as carefully honed perfection, there must be a huge temptation to shy away from the dead hand of literary interpretation. And Morrison shares with many of his jazz and blues heroes a somewhat Olympian vision of the artist's role – not necessarily up there on the mountain top, but at least being left alone to do what he's meant to be doing. The marketing and press departments, a&r men, journalists and fans have no place in this view – they can simply accept or reject what he's up to. They live on different, lesser mountains.

And so, in his insistence that "I just do my music", maybe he hopes that those who would interpret, analyse or simply describe his work will just go away. This has only made his more diligent followers that bit more persistent and curious. And it is impossible to be sure whether Morrison is displaying naïvety or cynicism beneath the cloak of gruff humility. Former business colleagues have attested to his ability to act ruthlessly in those aspects of the music industry he affects to despise, while he clings to the romantic notion of an artist divorced from the dirty-hands aspects of the process.

In spite of his reserve and his insistence that the recorded work is the only text negotiable between artist and listener, he has of course chosen to conduct aspects of his private life very much in public, in the grooves of the disc and in concert. Some of his songs seem to be thinly veiled autobiography, certainly and consistently from the stunning "TB Sheets" onwards, springing from their author's own life-search, his considerations of love, ambition and spiritual yearning. Morrison would not wish it to be thought, however, that he is revealing too much. "Very few of my songs are biographical and even then it's fragmented. Some parts of your own experience you'll write into a song and the rest you'll make up. They're not generally about me." This rings true: writers in all forms of expression draw, consciously or sub-consciously, on past experience and current emotions, without the results being in any way identifiable as autobiography.

Even before "TB Sheets", he was writing little musical memoirs like "The Story of Them". Central to this slow, seven-minute blues, a smoky, improvised reminiscence, is the oft-repeated phrase "good times", as Morrison recalls with affection the excitement and hopes of the early Them days:

Barred from pubs, clubs and dance halls
Made the scene at the Spanish Rooms on the Falls
And, man, four pints of that scrumpy was enough to have you out of your mind
Climbing up the walls...
Now just around this time
With the help of the three Js started playing in the Maritime
That's Jerry, Jerry and Jimmy
You know they was always fine
And they helped us run the Maritime

When an artist writes clippings from his own fragmented

autobiography in song, whether it takes the form of this simple nostalgia for "good times" or a deeper, inevitably confused spiritual search, it is only natural that many of his admirers will search for clues in attempting to make sense not just of the music they admire but also of their own lives.

This must be at the heart of his continuing popularity, not just with those who are growing old with him but with the young. At the age when so much of their emotional life seems focused on sex and spirituality, they find that a middle-aged man is still wrestling with their problems. And the essence of the matter is there in the title of his 1983 album: he deals in the "inarticulate speech of the heart". In one phrase, he has summed it all up.

ONE

A Childhood in East Belfast

Bloomfield, the area of East Belfast where Van Morrison grew up, belies any straightforward image of a tough, working-class enclave these days. Hyndford Street and its surrounding maze of small residential roads is unassuming but spruce. Number 125 is distinguished by a discreet brass plaque, fixed at head height to the right of the door, like a solicitor's plate. When the plaque was unveiled in 1991, the obsessively private Morrison was predictably annoyed. This led to a memorable headline in the local *Sunday Life* newspaper: "Don't Blame Me, Says Van Plaque Row Man."

The hapless "Van Plaque Row Man" is paint-sprayer Leslie Brennan, living at 125. "I can't win," he said at the time. "It wasn't my idea, there's nothing in it for me. It's Catch 22. The Belfast Blues Appreciation Society approached me about putting a plaque up – I didn't even know it was Van's old house. Some of the neighbours were keen on the idea so I said OK. If I'd said no people would have said I was a scrooge. I said yes and now Van Morrison's unhappy."It was left to visiting American blues legend Buddy Guy, rather than the man himself, to perform the unveiling ceremony.

Just south of Hyndford Street, the refreshing, foliage-trimmed stream of Conn's Water bubbles under Beersbridge Road, and the map confirms the impression that Bloomfield is still hedged around by a necklace of green – playing fields, parks, even a golf course to the south-east, just beyond the Knock Road.

To the north of these streets, where the railway used to run in Morrison's childhood, a luxuriant nature walk has been established along the old cutting. The greenery of the area was even more extensive when Morrison was a boy. His childhood friend George Jones points out some houses in Orangefield, with a somewhat newer development nestling behind them.

"Those houses at the back weren't built then. It seemed as if the countryside started right there. Just green fields."

A stroll to the north, across the railway cutting, brings another striking contrast. Here we find elegant, wooded cul-de-sacs and, of course, the verdant, ruler-straight mall of Cyprus Avenue. Just yards away from the traffic roar of Upper Newtownards Road, this tree-lined haven would grace any city in the world.

Most of the houses stand in their own grounds, peeping out through the rich foliage, houses built for the merchants and ship-owners of the boom city. Now, like it or not, Cyprus Avenue takes its place with Abbey Road, Penny Lane and Waterloo (at sunset, that is) as one of Britain's rock'n'roll routes.

Looming across the River Lagan, dominating the tiny streets and as much a fixed point to the people of East Belfast as is the Canary Wharf tower to modern-day Londoners, are the biggest cranes in the world, the vast yellow gantries of the Harland and Wolff ship-yards. In Morrison's youth the yards were almost an automatic career choice for local young men, and even in these tough times for British shipbuilding they remain a significant player in the local economy. New confidence, following the 1994 ceasefire, was apparent in the development of a "retail park" on a derelict site nearby.

Most streets sport at least one Union Jack flying at first-floor level, a reminder of the religious and political allegiance of the area. In the "marching season" the banners, bunting and flags sprout in greater profusion, even strung across the street from roof to roof.

And so, within a few minutes of his childhood house, Morrison could find a world of urban contrasts. There was the street-corner life and gravel football of the immediate streets, there were the green city fields and, within easy reach, the calm, proud street where the prosperous quietly enjoyed their success, but where even a Hyndford Street scruff could stroll and breathe the silent air. This varied backdrop to his early life helped cultivate Morrison's imagination although the music that inspired him couldn't readily be found in his immediate environment.

The blues didn't come naturally to the British in the austere, ration-book 1950s. Mississippi farms and Chicago juke joints were a planet away from the grey, rainwashed streets of a nation slowly recovering from the wasted years of war. Most music fans of Van Morrison's generation learned about the great names of American blues and country music somewhat later, through a haphazard alliance of detective work and chance.

Domestic radio was of no significant help, of course. Unlike today, when all tastes are catered for by dedicated channels or at least by ghettoes of local programming, pop music was largely confined to jolly little aural youth clubs on the BBC Light Programme, like *Saturday Club* and *Easy Beat*.

Furthermore, employment agreements with the Musicians' Union restricted the number of records that could be played, and meant that most of the tunes were reproduced by an in-house band, largely limiting the choice to the Tin Pan Alley mainstream. Bob Miller and the Millermen, though versatile professionals to the marrow, were unlikely to tackle the latest Howlin' Wolf recording.

Help for the young fan was at hand, particularly on the mainland, from Radio Luxembourg, whose wavering, whooshing signal battled its way across the North Sea, bringing shows that were sponsored by the record companies themselves, mixed with request shows, American evangelism and gospel. Later their musical role would be augmented by the battle fleet fighting the pirate radio revolution, of which Radio Caroline North was the boat that was beaming most strongly towards Northern Ireland.

The length of time to be filled each week forced the disc jockeys, or rather those who provided them with their playlists, to explore the catalogues beyond the latest clutch of bankable hits. Along with the American Forces Network serving peacetime troops serving in Europe, this was the source of the music beyond the hit parade.

Having heard the new single by such exciting and mysterious artists as Chuck Berry or Bo Diddley, say, the enthusiast would place an order at the one hip record store in town, or put Dobell's Jazz Shop in the Charing Cross Road on the itinerary for the next London trip. And the label of the Chuck or Bo record on Pye International revealed that it originated in Chicago, recorded in the Chess studios. The record stores would attract like-minded fans, and the youthful collector who snapped up the latest single by Chuck or Bo could trace the Chess roster back to Muddy Waters, and from him to the Mississippi Delta, in conversation with older, wiser, customers.

When this generation purchased the first Rolling Stones album they discovered that their record collection had been mirrored in that of the scruffy London art-student band – blues from the Chess and Vee-Jay labels, the southern drawl of Slim Harpo, the proto-soul of Memphis.

Van Morrison, unusually if not uniquely, knew all this already. As a child he was steeped in the blues, in black gospel singing, in the agit-prop songs of Woody Guthrie and the hillbilly symphonies of Hank Williams.

If the previous generation, the children of the Great War and the 1920s, bought records at all they were likely to be the metronomic instrumentals of dance-band leader Victor Sylvester, the smooth crooning of Bing Crosby or maybe, daringly, the tuxedo-and-gingham country styles of Frankie Laine and Rosemary Clooney.

Not Belfast shipyard electrician George Morrison, however. He bought 78s by Muddy Waters, Hank Williams and – above all for his son's childhood musical education – by the black folk-and-blues artist and 12-string guitarist Huddie Ledbetter, "Leadbelly". While most of Van's generation were led back to Leadbelly via the hit records of skiffle king Lonnie Donegan, the Belfast boy had always been aware of him.

Like Liverpool, Belfast was hipper to the music than landlocked cities. It was linked to America by an umbilical cord of migration, and many citizens would have relatives tuned into black music stations in the New World. Exotic vinyl arrived on the boats in Belfast Dock, bound for the markets and such shops as Dougie Knight's.

Knight, who runs a record store on Botanic Avenue, south of the city centre, became hooked on the blues in the late 1940s. In those days he was selling and maintaining bicycles, but having heard such artists as John Lee Hooker on a late-night French radio programme he began importing 78rpm records. As the 1950s progressed the records gradually squeezed out the bicycles, and he also rented out rehearsal rooms above the shop and began promoting visiting bluesmen at local venues.

Another shop in town was Atlantic Records, run by Solly Lipsitz. "Solly just couldn't understand the appeal of the blues," recalls Knight. "He said the songs had no beginning and no end. The way I explained it – and I said this to Van when he started coming into the shop and asking about the blues artists on the records I was importing – was to compare it to a sonata. The artist sets up a theme and then decorates it."

Lipsitz, however, supplied George Morrison with the basis of his collection, jazz records. Van Morrison recalls: "My father had records from the big band era. I forget exactly – maybe Woody Herman or something. He was one of those collectors. He used to go to this record shop Solly Lipsitz had in the High Street. He bought loads of jazz records. And then later on I heard Leadbelly. Then there was a bloke on television, Rory McEwan, a Scottish folk singer. He did a very good Leadbelly, played good 12-string. That was the first thing. And then I thought it was too good to be true – Donegan came out and he was playing Leadbelly. So all this was happening – everything was Leadbelly!"

Knight is not aware in retrospect if George Morrison was one of his regular customers, but it would seem very likely. While Morrison senior was building his remarkable collection Knight was establishing his local reputation as a source of blues material.

Just as the Beatles were later to hold the inside track on the new sounds from Detroit or New York, so Van Morrison's father could explore the fertile fields of American folk music far earlier, more easily, than most Britons. Of all non-blues singers, Morrison breathes the spirit and techniques of the music more than anyone else, and this must be due to his childhood conditioning in the sounds that most people of his age had to consciously seek out in later years.

The connection between Ulster and the North American continent goes back centuries, and many of Morrison's countrymen have woven their names into the story of the New World. In 1682 Francis Makemie, an Ulsterman, established the American Presbyterian Church. John Hughes made the same westward journey nearly 150 years later and became the first Roman Catholic archbishop of New York. Between these two pilgrimages, during the 18th century, a quarter of a million people are reckoned to have left Ulster for North America, a huge number from such a small and rural country.

One of them was a jobbing printer from Strabane in County Londonderry, John Dunlap, whose most celebrated commission was to print the Declaration of Independence, signed in 1776. Five of the signatories were also Ulstermen. Dunlap reproduced the Declaration in the newspaper he published, the *Pennsylvania Packet*, which was to become the USA's first daily paper.

Twelve years later, when the first Congress of the United States was established in New York, its secretary was Charles Thomson from the shores of Lough Neagh.

In recent years we have become accustomed to presidents of the USA joining the thousands of Americans who make the holiday pilgrimage to Ireland in search of their roots. But the connection spans America's history – those with an Ulster background include Andrew "Stonewall" Jackson, immortalised both in the song "The Battle of New Orleans" and in an exhibition centre in Carrickfergus; Ulysses Grant, a general in the Union army during the Civil War; and Woodrow Wilson. The Wilson farm, still in the family's care, is just east of Strabane and it was the future president's grandfather who emigrated to the USA, in his case to Philadelphia. Like John Dunlap, curiously, he was a Strabane printer who became an American newspaper editor.

From Davy Crockett, who "killed him a bear when he was only three", to Neil Armstrong, who made one small step for man and a giant leap for mankind, the USA's historical tapestry is studded with such Ulster names.

And, inevitably, the musical connections between Ireland in general and the developing culture of America are strong, and plain for all to hear. The jam session by traditional musicians in the back bar of an Irish pub and the Saturday-night dance music of an Appalachian hoedown are clearly blood relations. As the migrants left their home shore for a new life their instruments and songs travelled with them, to enrich the roots of American music to such a degree that, in its white, southern form, it is clearly Celtic both in essential spirit and structure.

The most significant event in depopulating the Irish countryside, with so many of the survivors taking their bruised hopes in search of this new life, was the potato famine during the second half of the 1840s. Each year, in varying degrees of severity, the staple food crop was destroyed by blight, and with malnutrition came such scourges as typhus and scurvy. During these short years the natural growth of the Irish population was not only halted but drastically reduced by an estimated two million – half of them dead and the other half running for their lives. "We must be better anywhere else but here," said one desperate emigrant. The famine not only dramatically accelerated the flow of emigration established in the previous century but created a pattern for succeeding generations. From the famine years through to the 1920s, the North American continent absorbed some half-a-million Irish. Their American-born descendants were all conscious of their "roots".

Music – the music of the people, of the fields, the parlours and the taverns rather than the concert halls – was at the root of their culture. It is not surprising, then, that the Irish have always been particularly receptive to the rural American development of Celtic tunes, from the mountain string bands that long predated the recording industry to the products of modern-day Nashville. From there, for some, it would have been a logical step to take an interest in the black equivalent; the Mississippi moan of Muddy Waters, for example, or the chain-gang legends of Leadbelly.

Thus, thanks to the shellac treasures collected by his father, the young Van Morrison had a master class in the blues. And though his father was unusual in the depth of his devotion to the music, the attraction of the continent across the ocean was quite natural: in many ways Belfast people felt culturally and emotionally closer to the American cities where their uncles and cousins lived than to the distant administration in London.

Belfast may have been the point of embarkation for America, but in the 19th century it was bucking the trend of declining population. As the number of people in the entire island shrunk by half, Belfast grew from small-town status in 1800, with a population of some 20,000, to a major city of 350,000 a hundred years later. Linen and then shipbuilding were the main industries, and during this period Belfast was one of the UK's major ports. Later, with the success of Short Brothers, aeronautics was added to Belfast's achievements, and the company pioneered both the flying boat and the vertical-take-off plane in the city.

On 31 August 1945, at 125 Hyndford Street, a row of modest ter-raced dwellings, Belfast was presented with a new citizen. The boy to be christened George Ivan Morrison was born in the house where his mother had grown up, just a stone's throw from his father's child-hood home in Lord Street. Morrison's parents, George and Violet, were of different personalities but shared a love of music. Violet was "the life and soul of the party", always ready to sing or dance, while the more reserved, introverted George steadily built his record col-lection of precious imports.

George Morrison was in touch with relatives living in Detroit and Toronto, and in the early 1950s, shortly after Van started school, he made a reconnaissance visit to the Motor City. But instead of sending for his family, as had been the intention, he eventually returned to his home town. Had the move come off Van would have grown up as an American boy in the land of his musical heroes, instead of as "the Belfast Cowboy" – the perceptive nickname given to him years later by the late Richard Manuel of The Band.

It may be that we would have been denied a unique voice, one that is steeped both in Irishness and Americana, had he been uprooted from the streets of Belfast. However many years he may have spent subsequently as a resident of the USA, he remains tri-umphantly (and with increasing pride, it would seem), an Irish artist, and this cross-cultural dynamism could only have been weakened by a childhood migration.

So there was no Detroit high school for the young Van Morrison, just a kid's cowboy outfit and some American clothes when his dad returned. Instead, in 1950, he began his schooling at the nearest pri-mary school, Elmgrove, just round the corner on the main road, and from there went to Orangefield School for Boys – non-sectarian, in spite of the Protestant implications of the word "orange".

The Morrisons were Protestants, though not in a fervent way. Their son attended Sunday School and George explored the very roots of the blues in American gospel singing, a form of music in which the spiritual musings and jazz-like vocal improvisations that were to characterise Van Morrison's are often present. In the 1950s, Violet, though not her husband, adopted the creed of the Jehovah's Witnesses. "For a while," says Morrison. "A brief encounter, that was all. I was taken to a couple of meetings."

It is against this background that their son has throughout his career explored spiritual, if not dogmatically religious, themes, and it is one of the distinctive features of his work within the broad field of rock music that such concerns are as dominant as the more familiar ones of sexual relationships and "the search for the soul of Saturday night". He inherited his spiritual curiosity.

Among sacred performers a particular favourite of George Morrison was the New Orleans-born performer Mahalia Jackson, gospel's equivalent to the pioneering jazz diva Bessie Smith, who indeed influenced Jackson's style. The basis of her fame was laid in the Greater Salem Baptist Church Choir of Chicago, the city to which the Jackson family had moved when Mahalia was in her teens.

Years before the gospel star's fame began to spread internationally, through such vehicles as her appearance in the 1958 film *Jazz on a Summer's Day*, a document of the Newport Jazz Festival that was a revelatory spectacle to European cinema-goers, her work was familiar to George Morrison through imports of such 1940s hits as "Move on Up a Little Higher".

If Jackson was sanctified then another Morrison hero, Leadbelly, was undoubtedly a sinner. Born in Louisiana around 1889 his violent youth led to a 30-year sentence for murder, for which he was pardoned, but he was soon back in jail for assault charged "with intent to murder". In the early 1930s the folklorists John and Alan Lomax began documenting American music for the Library of

Congress (a project that also produced the earliest Muddy Waters recordings a decade later). They discovered Leadbelly, and legend has it that the convict was able to sing his way out of jail.

Leadbelly, like his white equivalent, the hobo poet of the Depression Woody Guthrie, was a forceful rather than a subtle performer, whose musical technique hardly justified the tag "King of the 12-string Guitar". But in writing or collecting such songs as "The Midnight Special", "The Rock Island Line" (a hit both in the UK and in its country of origin for Lonnie Donegan) and "Goodnight Irene" (a 1950 hit in a polite version by white folkies the Weavers), Leadbelly laid down hugely significant contributions to the soundtrack of American folk culture.

Morrison once told an amusing story about his worship of Leadbelly that suggested that the old reprobate had an almost supernatural hold over him. "He was my guru. Somebody once sent me a huge poster of Leadbelly just beaming down with a 12-string guitar. I framed it and put it on the wall, and I've had it on the wall everywhere I've been. One day I was looking at it and was thinking 'I've got to get rid of this, it's doing me in.' So I took it down and was about to throw it out. At that moment I was fiddling around with the radio – I wanted to hear some music – and I tuned in to this station and 'Rock Island Line' by Leadbelly came on. So I just turned around, man, and very quickly put the picture back on the wall!"

There were several other musical influences too. "Sonny Terry, Muddy Waters, Josh White, Hank Williams, country and western, blues… I heard Leadbelly songs and I thought I'd like to play like that. So I learned some of the riffs on guitar. And Carter Family records. Between Leadbelly and the Carter Family, that's how I got into singing."

For Van Morrison to have taken this music in almost with his mother's milk, rather than to have discovered the music as most did, as students or weekend coffee-bar beatniks later in life, was a privilege indeed, and surely the foundation of his uniqueness. But he credits the immediate world outside his childhood home as being significant, as well. "I heard a lot of blues records, we always had that," he has recalled. "And I heard a few street players, street singers and dancers; and my parents played music. We lived in a pretty funky neighbourhood. I mean, it wasn't a white-collar district, let me put it that way. The people weren't involved in any other place but Belfast." On another occasion: "There was a guy down the street was into Hank Williams. There was a lot of music in the street. Country and western was big."

Morrison remained at school for a mere ten years, escaping as soon as he could, and throughout this time he and the educational system were merely nodding acquaintances. "There was no school for people like me," he would say, when looking back. "Most of what was fed me didn't help me that much later."

He is remembered as shy and bookish, though even as a child he was subconsciously storing the memories and experiences that would add an autobiographical element to his songs, making them in part a meditation on his life and the culture that shaped it. One example, recalled by Rod Demick, will suffice here. Demick is a Belfast musician who used to play with The Wheels, later rivals of Them on the local r'n'b scene, and whose most regular collaboration over the years has been with Morrison sidekick Herbie Armstrong. Morrison used to call Demick, just two years his junior, "the kid" – perhaps an indication that, if you are out on the rock'n'roll road from the age of 15, you are old and wise beyond your years.

"He was a little isolated, an only child," remembers Demick. "Never a great communicator, even when he was relaxed, talking to friends. Now, of course, all the communication is in the songs. That's all he needs to say. As a kid Van used to play in the street behind the Ambassador Cinema. There was a pub there, and they stacked the bottles out the back. The bottletops were bright colours, I remember, like green and yellow. You could sneak in and steal some empty bottles, then run round to the front of the pub and get the money back for the empties in the off-sales. You'd buy those cigarettes one at a time, joysticks, about nine inches long, smoke a bit and dib them out."

In the song "Madame George", recorded in the late 1960s, this little cameo of Belfast street life becomes: "Outside they're making all the stops, kids out in the street collecting bottletops, gone for cigarettes and matches in the shops."

When Carl Perkins first heard Elvis Presley on the radio, he says, "I heard this cat playing the way I'd been playing all along. So I thought there must be a future in the music." A similar revelation came to Van Morrison when Lonnie Donegan, who had taken his stage name from the blues singer Lonnie Johnson, emerged from the British traditional jazz scene with a downhome type of folk music that was tagged skiffle. The song that made Donegan a star in 1956, when Morrison was a ten-year-old, was the number he already knew by heart from his dad's original recording by Leadbelly, "Rock Island Line". It is this experience that puts Leadbelly at the forefront of those childhood heroes.

"What I connected with," he once said, "was that I had been hearing Leadbelly before that, so when Donegan came along I thought everybody knew about it. Consequently I think I was really lucky to grow up at that time and hear what I heard then."

And the great advantage of skiffle was that it was comparatively accessible, home-made music. Donegan was in fact a skilled jazz musician, a youthful veteran of the top British trad bands run by Chris Barber and Ken Colyer, but a passable skiffle noise could be made with a pawnshop guitar, a washboard for percussion and a bass that had been fashioned from tea chest, broomstick and length of string.

And so, as Van entered his teens in the late 1950s, George Morrison took his son downtown to buy his first guitar. Like so many future stars of his generation, he cut his musical teeth during the skiffle boom. "The skiffle thing was starting to happen. I formed a skiffle group…"

TWO

A Musical Apprenticeship

Youthful skiffle groups were usually made up of school friends or kids from the neighbourhood, and Van's was no different. It was launched in the rack of roads around Hyndford Street, and, true to the low-budget nature of the music, the band got rhythm from the combination of washboard and tea-chest bass, with Van on his Smithfield Market guitar.

Unlike many such ventures, however, this loose congregation of young hopefuls progressed beyond bedroom practice sessions to public performance, and for a time played for local children at Saturday-morning cinema shows. These institutions of the 1950s, long since buried by "kids' TV", were a familiar feature throughout the British Isles, affording parents a couple of precious free hours at the end of the week.

The format was fairly standard – cartoons, cliff-hanger serials like *Flash Gordon*, knockabout comedy from the likes of the Three Stooges, a worthy mini-feature from such sources as the Children's Film Foundation, almost invariably involving a gang of children capturing jewel thieves, and being rewarded with a blow-out feast by the grateful constabulary – and a live act.

Most kids had to make do with a semi-pro magician or a ventriloquist, but the patrons of the Strand Cinema on Holywood Road were, for a while, treated to the prototype Van Morrison sound. The cinema is still in existence, although it is multi-screened nowadays, and it was here that the young Van Morrison would first receive payment for making his music.

In these pre-teenage days, band members and the names of groups were constantly shifting. Sometimes Van would take one of the many guitar-strumming roles in Deanie Sands and the Javelins, fronted by a girl called Evelyn Boucher (aka Deanie Sands). Of the early Morrison outfits remembered by contemporaries from the neighbourhood whose musical paths would later cross with his, the Javelins was the first to lodge in the memory.

There were other names, though, as Morrison remembers: "The Thunderbirds, the Four Jacks... depending on which way the wind was blowing. If the club thought it was a good name then we kept it. Changed about six times, but it was the Thunderbirds originally."

George Jones, born a couple of streets away from Morrison, was a Javelin, and the two formed a partnership that lasted throughout the pre-Them years. When the appeal of the road palled, Jones was one of those who returned home and made a successful life on familiar ground. To this day he is one of the most celebrated figures on the Belfast entertainment scene.

In the late 1970s he went into local broadcasting, and since 1991 he has fronted BBC Radio Ulster's afternoon show, along the way picking up a prestigious Sony award as best local radio presenter. His showband Club Sound celebrated their 25th anniversary in 1995, with Jones playing the roles of front man, comedian and bass player.

Jones, a couple of years older than Morrison, began his musical career with an acoustic Guyatone guitar bought on hire purchase by his sister, and formed his first teenage band in 1957. "We were originally the Thunderbolts," recalls Jones, slightly at odds with Morrison's recollections, "but that was before Van found us out. He came our way in 1958, and by that time we were the Javelins. We were learning our stuff from groups like Cliff Richard and the Shadows, and the British chart stars like Mark Wynter. But then along came Van raving about Jerry Lee Lewis, Ray Charles, Chuck Berry. So he turned us towards the great American originals.

"Kids met through music who might otherwise not have got to know one another. That's how it was with Van. He struck me as a talented lad from the very earliest days, but he was very shy, left to his own devices at home a lot while his parents were at work. But his father had all these blues records. They were his friends. With the common denominator of music he could get on with people."

In every neighbourhood, in every town and city throughout the British Isles, such bands as the Javelins existed with shoestring equipment and a shifting personnel. Javelin member Billy McAllen recalls: "The Javelins was me, George Jones, Van and Roy Kane. Deanie Sands was a girl called Evelyn Boucher who had had polio when she was a child and had callipers on her legs. She had a great voice and we used to mess about rehearsing after school." Before long, like the Beatles and the Searchers, they would be headlining in German clubs, so there was clearly both talent and determination in this street-corner alliance.

The development confirming that they were no longer just a kids' skiffle group, big within their own acre, was prompted by Morrison. "We used to practise in the back of a furniture van, running the lead out for the one amp, with a plastic snare drum and a cymbal," says Jones. "With Van, you'd never know what he'd do next. One night he appeared with this weird-looking instrument case. It was a saxophone his father had bought for him. We asked him if he could play it and he said: 'One note!' And the note was F.

"At that time we were learning the Peter Gunn theme, so we changed it to the key of F and he came honking in with this one note. Suddenly we had a big sound! He persevered on sax – he wasn't singing much at that time, there were a couple of us to do that – and we progressed to become a showband." And so, in 1959, the group evolved once more and from the Javelins was born the Monarchs Showband. The showband is a uniquely Irish phenomenon, an all-round entertainment package that travels the barn-like bars and village halls of the country. In a sparsely populated island, largely rural and often poor, the brass and sequins of a showband on a Saturday night were in former times seen as a necessary antidote to a drab week. Jones puts his own gloss on the popularity of the institution: "Throughout the length and breadth of Ireland there are many villages, particularly in the South, built around the Catholic church. There'd be huge problems with poverty and unemployment in the old days, but the priests would run dances in the village halls. So learning to play a musical instrument was a better alternative for many young people than just sitting around without any work.

"The bands served the national passion for dancing. The term 'showband' came originally from an outfit called the Clipper Carltons. They'd stop the music and put on a bit of a show – comedy and so on. And that's how the tradition started. There'd be cover versions of popular hits, country music, dancing, comedy – a big band, with brass, putting on a show."

This wasn't, of course, the ideal musical road for Van Morrison, with his head full of Muddy Waters and Chuck Berry. But, at the time, it was the Irish road. "Yeah, we did the circuit," says Jones, "and it bugged Van, because he was a rock'n'roller. But we stuck it out as best we could."

In the meantime Van Morrison's almost anonymous school career had come to an end, at the earliest moment that the system allowed. By now there could be no doubt in his own mind that the only possible world for him to move into was that of music, but careers masters and parents – even parents like the Morrisons, with their love of the art – could never consider this a fit pursuit.

In Belfast the school-leaving ideal was to go into one of the city's proud industries as an apprentice. The aerospace factory of Short Brothers or the shipyards of Harland & Wolff were prized places of employment. Van's mother secured him an engineering apprenticeship, but he gave it up after a few weeks. A job on the floor of a meat-processing factory didn't strike him as being the first rung of a worthwhile career ladder either. Since Morrison needed a little spending cash but at the same time required the freedom and the lack of commitment towards a career structure to pursue his musical ambitions, the world of the cash-in-hand freelance beckoned. And so, with his chum Sammy Woodburn, Van took to the streets in the role he later immortalised in song, cleaning windows.

As Morrison recalled it 30 years later, it was more than two boys and a bucket. "I had a window-cleaning business in East Belfast. For a couple of years. When I started touring my cousin was doing it for a while and then he couldn't do it so I had to give it up. I wanted to keep it going but he had something else to do. I actually bought a window-cleaning business – I was president of a window-cleaning business and I had people working for me!"

But he was at heart a professional musician. "Hospital stage productions, dances, local halls. Brookborough Hall, Saturday nights. Sandown Road, Belfast. Then there was a place in Chamberlain Street, The Hut. Dances, really. Johnny Kidd and the Pirates material. Shadows, Cliff Richard, Jerry Lee Lewis. Mainly Jerry Lee. 'Whole Lotta Shakin'', that was a big one. You couldn't really play blues then. I think we did one number. It was very esoteric to do blues at that point."

Once he was on stage, with the help of a few bevvies, Morrison was already belying his shy, introverted self. He was a 15-year-old, white Belfast bluesman, in spite of the lack of acceptance of straight blues material that was to make the Maritime Club unique in later years. He was learning his trade in the halls, student unions and dives, and his trade was that of putting on a show. He was the most dynamic performer anyone had seen. "He would gyrate around the stage," says Jones, "and leap down into the audience. He lost all his inhibitions while he was performing. He was also developing some of the things that became characteristic of his music later on – busking the words, developing a call and response thing like Ray Charles, and repeating a phrase over and over."

Morrison spoke of these early days in an interview with *Musician* magazine in April 1987. "All I wanted to do was start playing. It was all very ear-oriented stuff, it was oriented along the lines of 'I'm a personality, and I'm going to put myself across and wear these clothes.' When I started playing, I went down to the union and said, 'I'm a professional musician, give me a card.' So they gave me a card, and I began to play in various bands and get work. And that was it. But it was for the music itself, never the show, although that did enter into it. And that's really what my entrance point was, and that hasn't changed. But I think it's difficult to find a way of doing music that doesn't have all these peripheral attachments to it."

The Monarchs and rival band the Federals, who included another of Morrison's friends Geordie Sproule, once combined personnel to play a rock'n'roll set at Queen's University. "It was a Sunday-afternoon session," says Jones. "There were a couple of visiting English bands there, and some of the Monarchs and Federals got together under a jokey name – the Half Cuts, I think it was. There was Van and myself, Geordie and Billy McAllen. We wrecked the place – blew the other groups off the stage."

In general, the flow of musicians between the various youthful outfits reflected that of Morrison's early skiffle groups. As Johnny Rogan has noted, our hero also performed with the band's rivals the Great Eight and the Olympics for a short time, before returning to the Monarchs' fold.

Increasingly, their saxophonist Van Morrison was casting off his inhibitions just as he had with the Javelins, and was starting to play a central role in putting the "show" into "showband", developing his reputation for acrobatic improvisations – standing on his head, leaping on to the guitarist's shoulders – that helped to build the Monarchs' name locally.

In 1961 some Scots musicians came over to Belfast. Jones again: "There was Bill Carson, who played bass. He did a couple of gigs with us and then moved on to the west of Ireland, with another showband. The singer was George Hetherington, and Lawrie McQueen played the drums." By this time the band were a long way from skiffle, and had evolved into the type of showband that Irish promotors insisted on, though the band's heart was in r'n'b. "It was getting a little frustrating, particularly for Van. The Scots guys told us we should try our luck over there, because they were getting into this thing that was becoming known as r'n'b.

"We headed for Scotland with stars in our eyes. This was late 1961, early '62. We packed in our jobs, told our parents we were off. But by the time we got there the promised six-week tour had become a long weekend! We were a six-piece, with Harry Mack and Van on saxes. Soon we were starving, picking up work where we could. This went on for a few months.

"I remember one time, north of Inverness I think it was, when we had no money and our food was down to four eggs. We picked up these two girls, Thai or Korean. They filled a pot with water from the burn and made an eastern egg soup to feed us all.

"We reckoned that if we could get to London we'd make it. We decided that it was shit or bust. We played our last Scottish gig at the Beach Ballroom in Aberdeen. We convinced ourselves that they'd be waiting for us with open arms down in the Big Smoke. So we scraped together the petrol money and got down there, midsummer 1962. Sleeping in the van in car parks, six of us, you can imagine what it was like! We were living on drinking chocolate and always being moved on.

"The next bit was like a fairy story. We were walking around Leicester Square and we bumped into a guy we'd backed in Scotland, Don Charles. He'd had a small hit with "Walk with Me My Angel", or "The Hermit of Misty Mountain" – those were his two records – and so he was a minor star at the time. He took us to a Wimpy Bar and fed us, got our suits cleaned at the dry cleaners, and took us to Hyde Park to be photographed hanging from the trees. Then he introduced us to his agent, Ruby Bard, who was also looking after people like Kenny Ball and the Temperance Seven.

"She took us on board. We got an audition for dates in Germany, and turned up with ten zillion other bands. But we passed, and in August we were on a train for Heidelberg, the first English-speaking band to play in the southern sector of the country. We had no idea of the language, the money, anything, but we were the International Monarchs!"

Van Morrison's recollections of the time confirm those of Jones: "We did US bases in England. Clubs in Germany. Every night for four months. It was definitely gruelling but that's the way it was done. In those days you had to go to Germany. They had auditions, ran through the bands, said ten were going and ten weren't. That's just the way it was."

"We played from eight in the evening until four in the morning, six days a week," remembers Jones. "Plus a matinee! We just lived for the music and a few beers afterwards. Of course, Van was in his element, because he got to meet coloured guys for the first time. There weren't really any in Belfast, but most of his musical heroes were black, and there were black GIs in Germany. This was the life as far as he was concerned – they talked to him in a language he knew. Hip. Playing Ray Charles and all. Telling us all about Bobby 'Blue' Bland and these other guys."

On both the showband scene in Ireland and the club scene in Germany, the musical versatility that has been a subsequent feature of Morrison's solo career was called for. "You couldn't get a gig if you just played one instrument or sang," he says. "You had to play at least three instruments. So I was playing drums, guitar, sax. I was singing. There were other people in the band singing, because you played for so long. In Germany we played seven sets a night seven nights a week, nine on Saturday and Sunday. So you had to rotate. You had several singers, several guitar players, whatever. I played a lot more sax in those days. I suppose when I started getting into writing songs more, that faded into the background. The thing with horns is that you have to blow every day to keep your chops together, which I find hard to do."

Morrison made diary notes about the German experience. "Heidelberg. Tram lines. The Odeon Keller, lots of good beer. My one and only movie scene. The Bahnhof. Mark Twain Village. The hotel brawl. Bratwurst. American cigarettes. Soldiers. And the music fills the room as I'm writing. Miles Davis music. Big Ricky. Cognac. My surprise birthday party. Seven sets a night. Seven nights a week. Matinees Saturday and Sunday. The eagle flies on Friday. An apprenticeship they call it, paying dues. That's what it's called. It's all a busman's or woman's holiday…"

The movie scene he refers to is presumably the walk-on role as a jazz musician that Morrison played in a German feature called *Glide*.

"Then we had to go to Frankfurt," continues George Jones. "Suddenly our repertoire went up in smoke. Because all they wanted was the Beatles, the Swinging Blue Jeans, Johnny Kidd and the Pirates, the English bands that had been playing in town. The irony was that they were playing the same stuff as us – American r'n'b and so on – but the audiences expected us to play the songs in the English versions they knew, in their arrangements.

"We were approached by a guy called Ronald Kovacs, who was a big wheel at CBS in Germany. He talked us into recording this song called 'Boozoo Hully Gully', and he wanted me to sing it. We got about £50 each."

As Morrison recalls: "It was a really bad song but we gave it a dynamite instrumental track. It was the first record I played on, but not my first as singer. I just played sax."

George Jones again: "Then we reckoned it was time to leave the work camps, which is what we called the clubs over there, and go back to see our friends and family. But the CBS guy took me out to lunch and told me he could make me a star. He drove a Porsche, so it was all quite persuasive! We were a bit naïve about gay people in those days, but I passed on the offer anyway.

"We were getting a little older and most of us felt it was time to start earning a decent living. Van drifted off to London, while I got a 'proper job' as a bass player – big money, £30 a week. We'd brought this American guy back with us, a pianist called Jimmy Storey. He really wanted to see Belfast. We arrived at Dover, picked up the van, drove to Liverpool and took the ferry to Belfast. Jimmy was a little bemused, after all that had been going on in Germany, when my father turned up in his flat-top truck to collect us!"

The Monarchs ended because they had gone full circle, playing other people's music – in this case the Mersey style of r'n'b that was enforced on them during their later days in Germany. "We could have gone on to better things," reckons Jones, "but there was also the fact that we were just kids, a long way from home in a strange country that didn't speak our language. It was a lonely feeling. If I'd had the guts I'd have stayed on, taking the chance on the record company offer. But Van was frustrated, that was obvious. There were sparks and suggestions occasionally, but musically he was stuck in the same place. He wasn't writing songs yet – that was to come later. So the Monarchs came to an end."

In spite of their absence, the Monarchs' record "Boozoo Hully Gully" was a decent-sized hit on the German charts. But that period of their lives was deemed to be over in late 1963, and there was no vote for driving back to the ferry.

In the early years of the Troubles, the band's pianist Wesley Black was later to be murdered by terrorists in what George Jones describes as "a tragic case of mistaken identity. Wesley had broken away from the band and was bouncing in and out of religion. This seemed to affect his nerves and he was spending time in hospital. He was separated from his wife – I'm not sure if they'd divorced. She lived in a volatile area of Belfast.

"On the night before he died Wesley went to his sister's in West Belfast and asked to spend the night there. This was totally unheard of. He made enquiries about his wife's insurance. Then he went and asked if he could take his little girl out. He brought her back and wished his wife well for the future. Then he bought himself some fish and chips. Terrorists came running out of a garden and he shouted at them. They shot him. He was lying on the ground and when someone turned him over he started bleeding and died.

"So he'd had some kind of premonition. He had very few relatives and so Roy Kane, Billy McAllen and I from the old band helped to carry the coffin. The way I'll remember Wesley is as the very best rock'n'roll pianist to come out of Ireland."

But the remaining Monarchs – Jones and Morrison, Roy Kane and Billy McAllen, Harry Mack – are still around, and in spring 1995 Jones was talking about a long-mooted reunion of the troops, with the Belfast Cowboy returning home to play once more with the Monarchs, but without the drinking chocolate and the four-egg soup. Sadly it didn't come off. "My fault," admits Jones. "Van was up for it, I think, but I was too busy to get it together."

McAllen and ex-Federal Geordie Sproule briefly joined Morrison – along with guitarist Herbie Armstrong – in another showband called the Manhattans on Van's return to Belfast. They travelled regularly to England for gigs in expatriate Irish ballrooms.

By this time, 1964, the English club scene was alive with the very music that had been closest to Morrison's heart all along – rhythm and blues. The Rolling Stones had become established in promoter Giorgio Gomelsky's Crawdaddy Club in Richmond, Surrey, having come together at the Soho venue the Marquee under the fatherly eye of British r'n'b pioneer Alexis Korner. They were moving on now, to become a Decca-label chart band with their brattish but respectful London revival of Chicago blues.

The Marquee was also where the Yardbirds, another "purist" r'n'b band, cut their teeth. Meanwhile Georgie Fame and the Blue Flames were playing their jazzy version of the music down the street at the all-night Flamingo. In 1964 South London band Tony McPhee's Groundhogs briefly became John Lee's Groundhogs, backing their hero – and Morrison's – John Lee Hooker, when they replaced John Mayall's band on a tour that included a Flamingo date.

The Pretty Things, fronted by long-haired Phil May, were continuing the scruffy, raucous, art-student image pioneered by the Rolling Stones. Pretty Thing Dick Taylor had earlier been the Stones' bass player before returning to art college, so the similarity of image was far from coincidental.

In Manchester the aforementioned John Mayall was playing with his Bluesbreakers, soon to include ex-Yardbird Eric Clapton. Clapton had started out in London band the Roosters with Tom McGuinness, later of Manfred Mann, and at the same time Ronnie Wood was crafting his Chuck Berry licks in the Birds.

In Birmingham Spencer Davis discovered teenage prodigy Stevie Winwood. At the Club a Go Go in Newcastle-upon-Tyne Alan Price's band became the Animals. And wherever he played on the Irish showband circuit Van Morrison was shown evidence that youthful, white, small-combo blues was possible. As Herbie Armstrong recalls, it was a gig at jazzman Ken Colyer's club in Soho by the Downliners Sect that really opened Morrison's eyes to the potential. "That's the sort of group I want to have," he said. The Sect were clubland heroes, cheap and sometimes nasty – their 1965 EP *Sect Sing Sick Songs* is a cherishable collectors' item.

Morrison recalls the Sect: "Went to this 51 Club. There was this group called the Downliners Sect, you know. I thought this is great.

I have to do something like this in Belfast. So that was the whole idea behind it. A sort of Club 51 situation." The Downliners Sect arose in 1964, at the time of Morrison's time in Britain, at the club on Eel Pie Island in the River Thames in south-west London. Although they never had a big hit – the nearest was their 1964 revival of the Coasters' lascivious classic "Little Egypt" – at £30 a night they were a solid attraction on the beat club and art college circuit. Having flirted with country music and, later, flower power in their attempt at a bigger breakthrough they called it a day, but not before they had sown the seeds of Them in Morrison's mind. Fortunately he did not adopt the gimmick of the Sect's guitarist and autoharp exponent Johnny Sutton, who always wore a Sherlock Holmes-style deerstalker hat!

George Jones remembers, "Van re-appeared in Belfast, saying we had to grow our hair long like the Rolling Stones, the Yardbirds, all the London bands. He reckoned you had to walk around looking way out. We said we weren't interested, we had a living to learn. But he went round talking to everyone, and eventually hit upon a band who were rehearsing, who were called the Gamblers. They decided to go with Van and do what he wanted – grow their hair, the whole bit."

Harry Bird remembers that a distinct division was developing between the established showband tradition and the "new wave". "There was quite a bit of rivalry between the showbands and the smaller groups," he says. "The showbands regarded themselves as the elite, playing the bigger gigs, dressing better, using more expensive equipment. The smaller bands seemed to resent that but there was no reason to, especially as a band like ours would take one of the up-and-coming groups with us to play the first hour. Sometimes during our break as well – we'd be booked from, say, nine at night until two in the morning. These would be three- or four-piece local bands, playing around the smaller clubs. But in a ballroom with us they could play to 1000 people."

It is clear that Bird's allegiance remains with the smart-suited, professional showbands rather than with the long-haired upstarts. Indeed, he tells the tale with wry amusement of being one of the few, perhaps the only, man to sack Van Morrison. "We were going to play in Donegal so we had to leave around midday. The roads then weren't up to much and it was a fair old drive. We called round to pick Van up. The singer, a fellow called Marty Welch, went up to get him but his mother said that Van wasn't going out today – he was busy writing poetry. So Marty came back down to the motor and said that Van wasn't coming. 'What do you mean? We're playing in Donegal – he's got to come with us.' So I went to talk to his mother and asked if he was sick. She said: 'Oh no, he's just locked himself up in his room and he's writing poetry.' We didn't think too much of this! As I recall it, the singer and I went on up the stairs, pushed down the door and got him out of bed. Got him dressed, got out his band suit, his saxophone, stuck him in the van. On the way home, about four or five in the morning, we let him out of the van and I had to tell him that we weren't going to need him again. Poetry!"

Brian Rossi was a crucial figure in Belfast rock'n'roll at the time. He assembled an 11-piece showband to play a residency at the local Mecca ballroom, the Plaza, and he christened the band the Golden Eagles. Morrison had first seen him in the late 1950s, playing piano in a rock'n'roll quartet, and Rossi was a local hero to Morrison's generation: he has described Rossi as "the first person I saw who was rock'n'roll." Rossi was to die of pneumonia in Blackpool, in 1984.

Rod Demick recalls: "We'd had Ruby Murray and Ronnie Carroll – they were the stars who put Belfast on the map. And then there was Brian Rossi. Before he came back to town to run the Plaza he'd been working in theatres in England. When he was assistant manager at the State in Kilburn, where all the American rockers played, he'd swing down on a rope on to the stage when people like Gene Vincent were playing!"

Herbie Armstrong, back in Belfast with Morrison from working with the Manhattans in England, was offered work by Rossi, and Morrison was also employed as part-time singer, filling in on both harmonica and saxophone as well. This brief period of local employment only ended with the formation of Them and the Wheels.

"They also had lunchtime record sessions at the Plaza," says Demick. "Rossi ran those as well. It was a chance to hear all the latest r'n'b records, like Booker T's 'Green Onions', and girls from the nearby factories and offices could pop in for a coke. But they put on bands as well. Eventually both Them and the Wheels worked there. In fact, that's where I was asked to join the Wheels, I remember. I heard that Herbie was looking for me – bad news in Belfast! But he offered me a gig, £20 a week. I was earning 30 bob as an apprentice draper at the time."

But in the meantime, while Armstrong was still playing in the top band in town, Rossi's Golden Eagles, Morrison was getting restless.

THREE

Angry Young Them

The Gamblers would provide Van with a chance to try his luck in a band once again. The outfit had been formed in 1962 by another youthful and restless veteran of the showband scene, Billy Harrison. "The band was started simply to play the music of the day," says Harrison. "American rock'n'roll mainly – what became known as r'n'b. When they started out, though, people like Chuck Berry were just called rock'n'rollers. At the start we were a three-piece. Myself on guitar, Alan Henderson on bass, Ronnie Millings on drums. A while later we asked Eric Wrixon to join us on keyboards. He was still at school at the time."

Wrixon was just 15, some four years younger than Harrison and Henderson, while Millings was already approaching his mid-twenties, and was married with young children. His family responsibilities were later to prove incompatible with the underpaid, on-the-road life of the rock'n'roll drummer.

In spite of the control showbands exerted over the local entertainment scene there was, as Wrixon recalls, "quite a lot of work about. Though the professional set-up, the industry, was dominated by the showbands there were enough spin-offs to keep the smaller semi-pro groups busy enough."

This was the scene that Van Morrison drifted back into after the dissolution of the Monarchs, his time with the Manhattans and other more temporary gigs. "Van had come home to Belfast after playing with my cousin Billy McAllen in the Monarchs," says Wrixon. "At that time everyone on the music scene in town knew everybody else, so of course we were aware of each other, the Gamblers and Van. Nobody ever needed to be at a loose end, you could always keep playing. So it was one of those situations where neither of us sought the other out. Somebody bumped into somebody else, and we got together with Van."

Harrison, who is wholeheartedly credited as the founder and prime mover of the band by Wrixon and others, is keen to dispel any misunderstanding that the Gamblers, and hence Them, was ever Van Morrison's group. Since the latter is the only one who took the road to superstar status, that assumption is sometimes made. "Van came in last," says Harrison. "I was very fond of American rock-'n'roll so I was trying to get away from the Cliff Richard and the Shadows stuff, to be more like, say, Johnny and the Hurricanes. I knew Van from the showbands, and Eric knew he'd left the Monarchs, so we just got together. But Van came in as an extra member, when the band was already together. I get a bit pissed off when I hear that he started it all."

The band took over one of the rooms that were situated above Dougie Knight's shop. "He was in Great Victoria Street at the time," says Wrixon. "Above the record shop were two floors, four or five rooms, that he let out for rehearsals. The Matadors showband had one, I remember, and we used another." As Knight himself recalls, the Gamblers had one of the attic rooms, "with a jazz showband drummer stuck under the sloping roof of the other." Knight was impressed enough by the band to recommend them to a local representative of the Philips record company, who perceptively regarded them as "the biggest load of rubbish he'd ever heard". Later, of course, they were to be signed to Decca by Dick Rowe, who had earlier passed a similar opinion on the Beatles.

Morrison, thanks to his father's record collection and his inherited, intuitive feel for the blues, provided a hotline to the kind of music the band wanted to play. "I grew up with all this stuff because my father bought all those records," says Morrison. "So I grew up listening to it from when I was two or three." As Alan Henderson remembers it: "We were into the rhythm and blues scene with the Gamblers, but we didn't have the information that we needed. That came when we met up with Van, because he had such a fantastic knowledge of the music which he'd learned from hearing the records his father played."

Once the Morrison influence had been absorbed into the band along with Harrison's pioneering drive, the next stage was a change of name. "Renaming the band," says Wrixon, "marked a fairly significant change in attitude. The Gamblers had decided that perhaps half of what we were playing was a compromise, rehashing Eddie Cochran songs and so on, while the other half we enjoyed. Van brought in this new material, very r'n'b orientated, and this was in line with the half of our set that we enjoyed.

"He would bring along Bobby Bland numbers, Ray Charles and so on. And so we changed direction. I thought of the name. It's hard to say why exactly – the 1950s horror film was probably part of it. It just seemed to sound modern to have a band name without a 'the' in the front. But it's not one of the crucial moments of my career! We just became Them."

A third decisive factor, along with Morrison's recruitment and the name change, happened at exactly the right time. Jerry, Jerry and Jimmy – the three Js – immortalised in Morrison's nostalgic anecdote "The Story of Them" and remembered by all involved only by their Christian names and collective nickname, started running the Friday night gig at the Maritime Hotel. Jerry McKenna and Jimmy Conlon worked in Belfast for what was then called Post Office Telecom, but they had ambitions to get into music promotion. They joined forces with schoolfriend Jerry McCurvey as 3Js Enterprises.

Their first venture was at the Ulster Hall, presenting folk singers Robin Hall and Jimmie MacGregor. They then booked an upstairs room at a pub in the Old Lodge Road and advertised that they were auditioning for musicians. "Violins, spoons, accordions," remembers McCurvey. "The most important person to turn up was Van Morrison. We realised this was exactly what we wanted." Morrison introduced the fledgling promoters to the band, at a meeting held at Dougie Knight's rehearsal room.

The band was clearly different to the clean-cut image presented by the showbands, and the three Js met resistance as they trudged around the bigger, more traditional dancehalls trying to secure some bookings. It was the chemistry of the band and the Maritime that really clicked. "There wasn't much r'n'b in Ireland," says Morrison. "Blues... something [Bluesville] in Dublin. And us." He recalls: "There were quite a few jazz things happening; there was a folk club. But there was really nothing for blues. So the whole idea behind the Maritime was to present blues. So we started doing cover versions of Jimmy Reed songs, Slim Harpo, Bo Diddley, Muddy Waters... we opened the door for people here [in Ireland], people like Taste."

"It used to be a traditional jazz night," says Harrison, recalling their debut at the Maritime, "but their term was coming to an end. We were playing at a couple of other places but Them hadn't really got off the ground by then. The three Js asked us, said they were going to promote the Maritime as an r'n'b venue. So we said we'd give it a go and it really took off."

The Maritime Hotel, as it was generally known, was officially the British Sailors' Society Seamen's Residential Club, built in 1945 on a site in College Square North that had, since the turn of the century, housed a Royal Irish Constabulary station. And since the late 1950s its ballroom had been available for renting by outside promotors. John Wilson, drummer with Rory Gallagher's band Taste, who were later to establish their name at the Maritime, recalls the straightforward ethos of the upstairs ballroom: "Here is a room, you fill it full of kids and play as loud as you want."

Eric Wrixon's recollections confirm Billy Harrison's sequence of events – Morrison joins the Gamblers, the Gamblers become Them and then they get together with the three Js. Other accounts have suggested a different sequence, that Morrison was aware of the opportunity at the Maritime and came looking for a backing band.

"It was the three Js who really made it happen," says Wrixon. "Them and Billy Harrison. Without those two factors there would have been no band. Or if there had been it would be impossible to know what would have happened. Certainly the three Js turned it from being just a bunch of young guys who wanted to play into a specific project. They found the premises, found us and started taking out advertisements. That was unheard of for a semi-pro band."

The Maritime slotted into its place in the city's burgeoning music scene. In 1973 it was sub-let to the Post Office as a sports club, before being sold in 1985. Sadly, as with the Cavern in Liverpool, its role in the history of rock music was not recognised by the bulldozers and it was demolished in 1991. In its place there is now a massive, windowless brick wall.

"It was like all such community premises," explains Wrixon. "There'd be a room with a stage, either upstairs or at the back, for meetings and social functions. But it was just one of so many gigs. Six or seven of them in and around Belfast were very much pro-fessional gigs, in other words they were run by people whose busi-ness it was. Sammy Houston's Jazz Club, the Plaza with Brian Rossi, a guy called Sammy Clark, various ballrooms.

"But there was also an array of more casual, occasional gigs. Parish halls, community events, charities. Then there was the Royal Belfast Academical Institution, which could hold 700 – a big Saturday gig. At this time, as far as I can remember, they were all unlicensed, so they had to be successful on the basis of the band, not just as a way of promoting drink sales, which became the func-tion of rock bands in many venues."

The manner in which the three Js chose to make their new Maritime venture stand out from the rest of the pack, prior to the first Them gig on 17 April 1964, was to take out some teaser advertisments in the *Belfast Evening Telegraph*. "Who are, what are, Them?" "When? and Where? will you see Them?" "Rhythm and Blues and Them. When?" And finally, "Rhythm & Blues Club, Tonight 8.30. Introducing Them, Ireland's Specialists in Rhythm and Blues. Maritime Hotel, College Square North."

Harrison recalls how quickly the word spread. "On that first Friday we got about 60 people, and maybe half of those were left over from the trad jazz audience. The next week it built to around 100, and the traddies had disappeared. The third week it was mayhem, packed to the doors and beyond. The doors would open at 7.30 but soon they were queueing straight from work, at six o'clock. I reckon we must have broken the fire regulations every week after that."

"The band built a huge reputation in a very short space of time, maybe two months," says Wrixon. "The circumstances, the place, the time were right. There was a need for a social event… Them gigs became the event, something people could nail their colours to."

This reputation was among the comparatively sophisticated audience of young people in a university city. Out in the sticks, things were different. "The band became very big around Belfast," confirms Harrison, "though the money was usually a joke. We played out of town to a mixed reception – we had a police escort out of one town! Everything was very strait-laced, regular. Matching band uniforms, standard showband stuff.' John Trew, of Belfast's *City Week* magazine, recalls the contrasting receptions to Them. "The image was fine when they played to like-minded people in the Maritime. But when they were booked into some places in the country, the punters were astounded by the presence of guys who were long-haired, smoked and drank on stage and wore dirty jeans. They certainly didn't present themselves in the manner of the Royal or Capitol [showbands]."

Just as Morrison, during his brief career deputising as saxophone player in Harry Bird's Regent showband, had startled both his conventionally minded employer and the up-country farmers, so did Them outrage an audience unfamiliar with the new dress code pioneered by the Rolling Stones and other London clubland heroes.

Writer Vincent Power recalls one ballroom blitz in the north-west – possibly the same incident referred to cagily by Harrison, who wouldn't give chapter and verse. "They were pelted with pennies and anything that dancers could lay their hands on. The group was taken off by the proprietor after the first few numbers. He refused to pay Morrison and the others because they had not finished a full programme. However, the group stayed on until they were paid."

As with every band ambitious to move beyond the local scene, the next stage had to be a demonstration disc. Enter Peter Lloyd. "He had a little recording studio off Cromac Square," recalls Harrison. "He was involved with bands as well because he built amplifiers – he made the best bass amp I ever heard. I can't remember exactly how it came about – we would have got to know him simply because he was on the scene. We made these tapes with Peter, and this opened the door at Decca, because he'd worked there as an engineer. So he had contacts, like Dick Rowe. He took the tapes and ran off half a dozen demo discs. The material was stuff from our repertoire like 'Stormy Monday', 'I Got My Mojo Working', 'Turn On Your Lovelight' and so on. But we didn't play them like the records at all. It was raw madness!"

In the mid-1970s Morrison recalled this raw madness, confirming that as far as he was concerned Them were at their best at the Maritime. "We did gigs outside there too but the Maritime was like a stomping ground sort of thing. We ran the place, the whole show. Even when it came to making records, we were out of our element. Because we were there in a studio within another vibe. The way we did the numbers at the Maritime was more spontaneous, more energy, more everything, because we were feeding off the crowd. And it was never really captured on tape because there were no live recordings, or none that I know of anyway."

Peter Lloyd's studio, reputedly the only professional-standard one in Northern Ireland at the time, charged three guineas an hour for demo discs. "Morrison was electric," recalls Lloyd, "particularly on stage at the Maritime. And in the studio, once he'd launched into it he could have been anywhere. He seemed to forget. He became Them.' So the Lloyd demo, the closest the band has ever come to preserving the excitement of those early days, was their calling card. The track reckoned to capture the live spirit best was a long work-out on a highlight of their act, Bobby Bland's rousing "Turn On Your Lovelight", and the calling card found its way to Mervyn Solomon.

On the Belfast record scene the firm of Solomon and Peres was a major player. They were record distributors who also operated retail outlets and they, like Peter Lloyd, had links with Decca in London. "When Peter pressed up the demos," remembers Harrison, "Dick Rowe contacted the Solomons to check things out. It was Peter who got the ball rolling, and Mervyn came along to listen." Mervyn Solomon, son of company co-founder Morris Solomon, looked after the record shops, and came to hear of the band. "My first recollection," he says, "was of entering the Maritime and seeing Van sliding across the stage... the kids really ate out of his hands."

Since the Solomons were so central to the local record business it was, in the words of Eric Wrixon, "inevitable that Mervyn would soon come to see Them, to find out what all the fuss was about. And so he reported to his brother Phil in London. Phil had left the family firm and had built up a business in his wife's name, the Dorothy Solomon Organisation."

As later experience was to prove, Phil Solomon was not the obvious person to handle a raw young Belfast blues band – not, at least, for the total benefit of the musicians themselves. As Them's later lead guitarist Jim Armstrong puts it: "He was handling people like Tom Jones, Dorothy Squires. Los Bravos later on. I don't think he had any feel for what the band were trying to do."

Billy Harrison's recollections confirm this. "Dick Rowe came over with Mervyn and Phil Solomon one Friday night, to check out the reaction. I don't think they were interested in the music at all, but they were obviously aware that the Beatles had opened the door to this sort of music, getting away from the Shadows and so on." Mervyn had arranged that, as the cab containing his brother and Dick Rowe arrived at the Maritime and the pair entered the downstairs hall, girls would be screaming and passing out with excitement. The result was, as recalled by Mervyn, that Rowe said he wanted the band immediately.

Dick Rowe, a&r man for one of the biggest record companies in the country, remembered things differently: "I didn't want Them without Philip. It's the same with any group – without good management the chances are that they'll never finish the course. I'd been messed around a lot by groups with bad managers. It was crucial for us that they had good management and I loved Philip as a manager with any act I dealt with."

Rowe's testimony shows that, when music and business collide, there are two sides to every story. And, as far as business was concerned – hugely experienced business, it must be said – the very rawness that was at the heart of the band's passionate appeal to their audience was in itself grounds for caution, making it hard to see how the band could be corralled within a show-business structure without destroying its essential appeal. A&r men, then as now, are a conservative breed, servants of the corporation, seeking only to "shift units". They have never seen themselves – with one or two glorious exceptions, who probably wouldn't appreciate the compliment of being identified – as patrons of the arts, diverting corporate funds for the benefit of rock'n'roll.

Wrixon, however, identifies "three significant nodes on the route taken by Them. The three Js, Billy Harrison's ability to run a band – and the Solomon Organisation breaking it up. The three Js provided a platform, Billy Harrison was a workaholic, very practical, able to wheel and deal, to organise transport and equipment, able to make sure that people got on stage at least half sober. But Solomon's attitude was short term, with no investment. So he was a crucial part of the story, as to why the band fell apart."

On the other hand, most bands did fall apart sooner or later – often even sooner than Them did – and few left behind such an impressive recorded legacy, whatever reservations the group members may have individually about their output. Unfortunately, though, Them could never feel sure that their management was batting for the band against the rapacious music business, as could the Beatles with Brian Epstein and the Rolling Stones with Andrew Loog Oldham, young men together against the Establishment.

But this is in the future, a tortuous family tree away from that early, ambitious, hopeful five-piece ripping it up at the Maritime. "They approached us about contracts," continues Harrison, "and we went over to London in June 1964, to make demos at the Decca studios in Hampstead. We came back here, gigged, went back for more recording, did some gigs over there. But Phil Solomon didn't seem clear what he was dealing with. 'They're Irish, so put them in the Irish clubs!' We'd turn up at some of these places and walk away again, because it was obvious that they didn't want us. They were expecting a showband."

The first of the band's many personnel changes had just occurred, though it was certainly no sign of any inherent instability among them. As Eric Wrixon recalls: "I left for a while to finish my A levels. We'd already been to London to record 'Don't Start Crying Now', 'Gloria' and so on with Decca. And soon they were off over there again. The band was just pushed around all over the place.

Aberdeen to Exeter. I missed out on that." "So the change was forced upon us," says Harrison. "Eric was under-age and his parents wouldn't sign their permission. So Patrick John McAuley came in on keyboards."

The sessions in London, and the resulting records, have always been considered as something totally apart from the Maritime band by Morrison. "By that time the whole r'n'b thing in England was being hyped. So we'd have these people coming in from record companies. The strange thing is that most of the records we made had nothing to do with what we were playing live. They were purely manufactured, produced items. For the commercial market. In fact the whole point of the club was the opposite of that. That was the ironic thing. The most obscure pieces of music we could find on blues albums, that's what we were playing."

The next change soon followed. "We'd recorded 'Don't Stop Crying Now' in June 1964," continues Harrison. "It died the death – as the saying goes, it wasn't released, it escaped. And then we spent three months on the mainland and bugger all happened. We were skint. Ronnie [Millings] was married, he had kids, he just couldn't afford it. So he had to leave. He took his responsibilities seriously – he walked away because he had to earn money for his wife and kids. You've got to admire him for that."

As Wrixon recalls, his chums on the mainland were being paid £10 a week when Millings came back to Belfast. Pat McAuley switched from keyboards to drums. "It turned out," says Harrison, "that he was a better drummer than he was a keyboard player. Then we all came back to Ireland, tails between our legs, in autumn 1964. We'd already recorded 'Baby Please Don't Go' – and 'Here Comes the Night' for that matter – in September or October."

"Baby Please Don't Go" was released as the second Them single in November. It had begun the convoluted and unsatisfactory situation whereby the band would turn up at the Decca studios to find session men waiting for them. But, insists Harrison, they did not create a "different" Them.

"There were two session guys on that one," he says. "Bobby Graham on drums and Jimmy Page on guitar. That riff on 'Baby Please Don't Go' [often credited as a Page innovation] was my riff. I created it. We'd been playing the song like that all over Northern Ireland for a year and a half before it went on record. People will believe whatever they want to believe, but those session guys weren't needed. With other bands, maybe. Quite a lot didn't have the musical ability. But we'd been playing for two years by then. We knew the music – what we didn't have yet was the studio technique. In those days if you made a mistake you started all over again. So session men were often used simply to save money, to get it right first time. But in our case they just weren't necessary. They were on that first session, but after that, what the hell. As far as I'm concerned we'd proved ourselves."

As Morrison remembers it: "Jimmy Page was added on guitar. Playing a bass part on lead." The song "Baby Please Don't Go" goes way back into blues history. The most familiar name associated with its composition is Big Joe Williams, who recorded it for Columbia in 1947, with Sonny Boy Williamson on harmonica. In the same year Lightnin' Hopkins had a hit on Gold Star with the number. In spite of this coincidence Steve Turner suggests that the song dates back to the 1920s, and that it was written by Harvey Hull and Long Cleeve Reid. Like many time-hallowed blues classics, so often claimed by such artists as Hopkins and John Lee Hooker, there may well have been an original author, but it is inherent in the oral tradition of the blues, that a basic lyric will be built upon, edited and restructured to suit the individual artist. Whatever the source of the song, it was Hooker's version that Dougie Knight drew to the band's attention, on to which Harrison grafted and developed his spikey, acidic rock-abilly riff, one as distinctive as any in rock music.

So the sound on the record is presumably Jimmy Page, something Harrison neither confirms nor denies, but only if he learned the lick from Harrison in the first place. Similarly there are two versions of the drummer story: one has Ronnie Millings and Bobby Graham thrashing away in unison, the other has Graham replacing Millings. What need not be challenged, however, is that the record represents Them, and not some Monkee-like studio confection.

This, of course, was the record that broke the band on to a wider stage than the one at the Maritime. "Somehow," says Harrison, "Phil Solomon negotiated for it to be used as the signature tune of *Ready, Steady, Go*. The thing took off and on New Year's Eve it crept into the Top 40. We went back to the mainland to promote it in January 1965 and it eventually reached Number 7."

However, even though the band had now "made it", the personnel upheavals continued. "When Ronnie left and Pat McAuley switched to drums," says Wrixon, "I came back in. After that I split from the band and rejoined quite a few times, over the years. Jackie McAuley, Pat's brother, came in on keyboards but he didn't last, so I went back in again. 1965 was a very volatile period, just before what was still effectively the original band blew up completely."

The band's second recording session, which yielded hits in "Baby Please Don't Go" and "Here Comes the Night", had introduced them to the writer of the second of those songs, the producer Bert Berns. Phil Solomon was involved, with Dick Rowe, in what was at the time a very unusual decision: to bring a hip New York producer to London.

Since Solomon, or his wife Dorothy, also got "Baby Please Don't Go" on to television, as the identifying sound of the essential rock music show of the day, he clearly did have some positive input into the band's turbulent history. It was a negative decision, however, to make "Gloria", from the first session, the B-side of "Baby Please Don't Go". Although the place of the song in the history of rock, as a proto-punk garage classic, is only obvious with the help of hindsight, it was nevertheless clearly something special at the time to those with ears to hear. Those involved with Them didn't have the necessary ears. "The biggest mistake of all," agrees Harrison. "On its own it could have been a number one." Morrison recalls Dick Rowe's advice as producer on "Gloria". "Can you really shout? Make it aggressive."

Among Bert Berns' claims to fame at this time was the co-authorship (with Phil Medley) of "Twist and Shout", a hit for the Isley Brothers, and his name would have registered in the British music-business consciousness when the Beatles chose to cover the song. To Them, he came in as a breath of fresh air.

"Bert had been lined up to hear us," says Harrison. "He was a super guy, a brilliant producer, so different to what we'd been used to. In those days there was a set way of doing things. It was like when you appeared on television – there were chalk marks on the floor and you had to stay on them. No spontaneity. And it was like that in the studio. There seemed to be a code, a rule book. But Bert Berns was so free and easy. He'd come out of the control room, maybe pick up a drumstick and start bashing on a cymbal, geeing everyone up, getting things going. A helluva good producer."

"Here Comes the Night" was one of the results of the collaboration between the Belfast cowboys and the man from New York, but while the band were back in Britain promoting "Baby Please Don't Go", in the words of Billy Harrison, "some greedy prat at Decca gave the song to Lulu. It died the death so they released our version."

It seems that an arrangement between Decca and Solomon to finance Berns' visit to England would have included work with other artists. But for artists as different as Them and Lulu to have recorded the same song could have fatally weakened its chances of success with either. Fortunately, though, no harm was done, and Them scored an even bigger hit than with their previous single, peaking at Number 2. Morrison, incidentally, has recalled events slightly differently: that the song had already failed as a Lulu vehicle before Berns offered it to Them.

Solomon, meanwhile, was looking for a second Maritime band that could match the promise of Them, and the obvious choice was the one that had inherited Them's gig, the Mad Lads. They were summoned to London in turn, cut a couple of tracks with Berns, were whimsically renamed Moses K and the Prophets, and failed to follow Them into the charts.

The brief days when the Three Js and Them ruled the Maritime were over. "We never had the group under contract, which was naïvety on our part," says Jerry Conlon. "We then lost the hiring of the hall to another person, so that proved to be the end of that particular scene." The hall was inherited by dance instructor Eddie Kennedy, who brought in English bands and, from Dublin, Rory Gallagher with Taste. "Dublin was more pop and soul," Gallagher said in 1991, "and so we were attracted to Belfast." His 1974 instrumental "Maritime", with its heavy dancehall echo, pays tribute to his stint there with Taste. Kennedy renamed the hall Club Rado, but its place in rock history was established. "I happened because of that scene... r'n'b," says Morrison. "I earned my spurs at the Maritime and became part of the mainstream through that."

As well as work on the road and in the studio Them was by now inevitably involved in another essential arm of promotion, one that has always been anathema to Morrison – press interviews. They soon had an unenviable reputation for being rude, uncooperative and incoherent. Billy Harrison, calm and courteous though he may be these days, is unrepentant.

"As far as our attitude in interviews was concerned, well – a lot of people were airheads asking a lot of crap. The questions were idiocy, stupid shit like your favourite colour. It may not have been their fault entirely – they'd have had an agenda, questions they were expected to ask. But who gives a shit about my favourite colour? So maybe that created the image of being uncooperative when talking to the press.

"The other thing was that we didn't have the time for fucking interviews – we had a hit record out there, we were always travelling, into London and out again, and there just wasn't proper time. So it wasn't deliberate, it was just something that happened. Maybe they did have to write up something, make something out of nothing. But it wasn't so much a lack of cooperation as disgust at some of the questions, and pressure of time. Trying to get things together, whatever it was at the time – singles, EPs, albums, touring – it was all rush, rush, rush. We had to keep this pressure on because bands were coming and going all the time."

And the resulting stresses within the band ensured that by early summer 1965 there was another change of line-up, with Jackie McAuley out as keyboard player in favour of Peter Bardens. "There were fallings-out with Jackie," says Harrison tersely.

The recruitment of Bardens, though clearly happy to the extent that he returned to play with solo star Morrison in the 1970s, was a further stage, the most striking so far, in severing the band from its roots in the Belfast club scene. The identity of Them was becoming distinctly clouded. "We didn't know him," confirms Harrison. "We didn't really know anyone on the British scene because we just didn't have the time. We'd only meet someone if we were introduced to them in the Scotch of St James or one of those clubs. But somebody knew Peter, and so he came in with us."

In mid-summer the debut album, *Them*, recorded by the early five-piece line-up plus the occasional session man, was released amid growing tension. It managed to reflect the group's past in such blues classics as Jimmy Reed's "Bright Lights, Big City", a club favourite following its release on a Stateside EP shared with John Lee Hooker, and Them's present, notably in the group's archetypal song

"Gloria". The record also looked forward to Morrison's solo work in "Mystic Eyes", a fragment revealing both spiritual concerns and his technique of repeating a phrase, in the way that a jazz musician toys with a sequence of notes.

At a time when the band could have been surfing the crest of a wave, disillusion was rife. The end of a band still recognisable as being basically the Maritime model was fast approaching. They felt that they were adrift on a leaking raft, surrounded by sharks. "Everyone was making money out of the band except us, so they kept up this constant pressure on us," says Harrison. "It was the day of the robber barons, and everyone was being ripped off. All these guys who are entrepreneurs, they're not in business to make money for me, are they? Phil Solomon was there to make money for Phil Solomon. And Decca thought that they could make money out of us. It was as simple as that.

"We were out there playing because that's what we wanted to do. No business sense, playing for love. But it was always hand to mouth. Whatever you had at the end of the week was divvied up, and that was it. No advice, no fucking clue! In a proper structure we'd have been given correct advice, but it was all for the quick kill. Literally – if we kill off this artist there's another one around the corner."

There were also dissatisfactions, though these may have grown in hindsight, with the musical policy imposed on Them. As well as not wasting "Gloria" as a B-side, reckons Harrison, "we should have released Bert Berns' 'Half As Much' as a single. Everyone respected Bert, and he'd just given us a hit. But Phil Solomon didn't know what he was doing. We were also offered Bert's 'Hang On Sloopy', by the way. But it wasn't our cup of tea."

As the most efficient organiser in the band, it fell to Harrison to articulate the band's accumulating grievances. "Everyone reckoned we were getting ripped off, we agreed on that. And it was me who went to talk to Phil Solomon about it. Now, he operated on the principle of divide and rule, keeping control by keeping everybody fighting among themselves. So what he did was to go round and talk to everyone individually, and everyone backed down when they were confronted by him. There was a total lack of maturity involved – no-one had the balls to stand up to him.

"He said that the band would never work again. Bullshit. Two hit records, anyone would have taken us on. So this created a rift between me and the rest of the band. I was trying to look after everybody, signing the contracts, organising things. I even got people out of fights – I hauled Van out of the gents in a place in Putney once, just as he was winding up for a fight. So I was trying to look after it all, but after this confrontation with Solomon I just left. No sour grapes, just left.

"But I suppose that I couldn't help feeling that it fell apart without me to look after business. I heard horrendous stories about them turning up late for gigs and all that nonsense. It just doesn't work. You can't rub a promoter up the wrong way – he might be responsible for booking out the whole of the Midlands, or the north of England. And he's going to be thinking 'I can fill my halls with the Swinging Blue Jeans, so fuck you.' That's how Them would get blackballed. Lack of discipline."

After Harrison's departure, as Wrixon puts it: "There were line-ups photographed who didn't even exist. There was no band really at this time, just Van and Alan Henderson as the constant factor." But there was still a considerable amount of mileage left in the group, particularly when one of Belfast's best guitarists was recruited in an attempt to put together a "new" Them. Jim Armstrong came in during the 1965 upheavals.

"I was playing a residency in town at the time, quite jazzy, when Mervyn Solomon asked me if I'd like to play guitar with Them," says Armstrong. "I had two weeks' rehearsal. Van was getting into jazz chords, and he knew my work from sessions I'd done with the

Mad Lads in Dublin. I was working in a bank at the time. I got the call on a Thursday, spoke to the bank manager on Friday and started rehearsals on Monday.

"Them had gone through a lot of changes, and there'd been a lot of rowing between Van and Billy Harrison. Van wanted to get back to putting together a new Belfast band built around himself and Alan Henderson. At that time it was as if there were two bands, a studio band and a road band. In the studio they were using session drummers. It was a job to me – every week you'd go down to Solomon's office, get the wages for the previous week and the itinerary for the next. Christmas 1965 I was in hospital, and when I came out they'd changed drummers again!"

Just to confuse matters even further, Billy Harrison returned at this stage as Armstrong's deputy, temporarily replacing the man who had replaced him when he had walked away from the band, as he confirms: "It was just Van and Alan. Peter Bardens left at this stage, I left. They got in John Wilson on drums. Good player, went on to work in Taste with Rory Gallagher. But he was just a young sprog at the time. Jim Armstrong on guitar – great guitarist, but very much a music 'head', a precise, technical player. And Ray Elliot came in on sax and vibes, as a sort of substitute for the keyboards. Now there was more of a jazz influence in the band. Then Jim Armstrong's appendix burst, and Phil Solomon actually asked me to go back! I'd stayed on in London, doing sessions, demos. I'd become very friendly with the Pretty Things so I had played with them. Whenever Dick Taylor went walkabout they'd give me a call.

"When I rejoined Them I did England, Scandinavia, Paris. It was like coming back as an outsider, and I think I got on better on that basis. But I was beginning to get sick of the session scene by then. I'd got married, and I didn't know enough people in the business, so work was too erratic. As far as guitar sessions were concerned, Jimmy Page and Big Jim Sullivan had it stitched up between them, and it was hard to break in. So in 1966 I joined the GPO, on the electronics side. A regular £13 a week! The first weekend I joined I played the Isle of Wight festival with the Pretty Things, and back to the Post Office on the Monday."

Meanwhile, Jim Armstrong was out of hospital but he in turn was already getting disillusioned. "I felt that there were a lot of sharks about, and that I was getting ripped off. Also, Alan and Ray were getting heavily into the drink. I was handling the money at the time, and 35% off the top went straight to Solomon. He'd said when I joined, "Who's the man who left the bank? You should have stayed there." We'd be going out for three or four hundred but I found out that the venues were paying, say, seven or eight."

The new-look Them had recorded their second album, *Them Again*, produced by Tommy Scott, in December 1965 and then drummer John Wilson left to be replaced by David Harvey. In May 1966 the band left for a two-month tour of America, a make or break experience that proved to be the latter.

Armstrong remembers that "America in 1966 was a real eye-opener for a Belfast boy, flower power and all that. See America and die. The money was obviously there to be made, but yet again it wasn't us that made it.' Their most celebrated engagement would be a residency in Los Angeles. "We played at the Whisky a Go Go for 17 days," recalls Armstrong. "The first British band to play in a club like that. Ray, Alan, Van, myself, Dave Harvey on drums. Various bands were booked as support, like the Doors, Captain Beefheart, the Association."

Sadly, almost inevitably and this time fatally, the tour was clouded by another dispute about money. The band claimed that Solomon got it, Solomon claimed that it went direct to Morrison, and that an out-of-court settlement marked the end of Them as a working, charting band. The tour limped on to San Francisco, and this was to prove a crucial move for Morrison himself, because in

June, at the Fillmore Auditorium, he was introduced to Janet Planet, a local hippy and aspiring actress. Their subsequent relationship shaped the development of his work through the Bang period into Astral Weeks, providing him with a more settled domestic atmosphere in which to work.

The business of Them as a band that involved Van Morrison still had to be wound up, however. By this time, Jim Armstrong remembers, "Van really didn't want to know. He once took a swing at Ray Elliot on stage. And in his later career he has tended to put bands together and then disband them, some sort of self-destruct mechanism, I suppose. The Caledonia Soul Orchestra was an obvious example." And so Them drifted apart.

Except that the band refused to lie down and die. We may think of them as a short-lived, tempestuous band fronted by Van Morrison, and that is indeed how a chart-based rock history would record it. In fact they are still out there in spirit, and according to Eric Wrixon and Jim Armstrong they're playing better than ever.

Wrixon continues the story. "When Van left Jim Armstrong stayed on and Kenny McDowell from the Mad Lads took over on vocals. Alan Henderson reckoned that he owned the name and so they carried on. They made two albums in that set-up." Armstrong adds that the records were made in America, and "then in 1971 I came home for good. I got fed up with the management, with other people who were just sitting around getting stoned."

"Then," says Wrixon, "there was another version of the band with only Alan Henderson having any connection with the earlier Them, together with what you might call journeymen musicians. This continued into the 1970s, by which time I was playing with Thin Lizzy. I was in various other bands during the 1970s but I got out of music full-time in the 1980s because I was bringing up a son as a single parent. I worked for the Northern Ireland offshoot of the Department of Trade and Industry."

But just before this, in the late 1970s, there was a brief revival of Them recalled by Billy Harrison. "In 1975 I'd transferred back to Northern Ireland, and I'd sold all my gear. But then Eric, Alan and myself made an album in Germany as Them. I left yet again after a bit of a blow-up but within a year I was back in Germany for a solo album."

Once again Jim Armstrong took over from Harrison, and as well as Wrixon and Henderson the band now consisted of Billy Bell on drums and Mel Austin on vocals. "Around 1982 there was a split for a while and we ran two bands," says Wrixon, "followed by an amalgamation. After Van left Them all the post-Morrison versions, the Armstrong/McDowell one, Alan Henderson's, then the one with Mel Austin as singer, they all bombed out sooner or later and one problem was that the singer was inevitably compared to Van.

"So since 1991 we've been the Belfast Blues Band, and now there's no direct measurement any more, particularly as we don't have a specific singer. But the fact is that the three of us, myself, Jim Armstrong and Billy Bell, were in Them at one time or another. Or half a dozen times! So it does sometimes happen that we go over to the continent and the poster will say something like 'The Legend of Them', with the Belfast Blues Band credited in tiny type down by the printer's name.

"We are offered a lot of work that we don't take because it's '60s nostalgia work, the circuit that the Searchers and bands like that work on a lot. But we're not a '60s band. In fact you could say that this is the best version of Them ever. We're playing better. You see, in the old days it was a very enthusiastic, optimistic environment for a while, but some people on the scene had only been playing for a comparatively short time. Even back then Jim Armstrong was way ahead of the pack as a guitarist. Now the pack has had a chance to catch up and they can't. Jim is one of the best guitar players in Europe, no doubt about it."

Wrixon, though he has professional qualifications and a post-graduate degree to fall back on, is now a working musician once again. Armstrong combines music with a Belfast job as a civil servant, using accumulated leave and flexi-hours to play in the Belfast Blues Band. Since 1987, when he left British Telecom to set up on his own, Billy Harrison has run a marine electronics business in the sailing resort of Bangor, east of Belfast, and just plays for fun. He was the founder of Them, and so has the last word on the band.

"The tracks we recorded during the early days was what Them was really about. The second album, with Jim and Ray, showed different influences. It wasn't what the band had been known for, which isn't to say that a lot of it wasn't very good. The rawness was a characteristic early on, not planned, just natural. And before the arguments began there was a lot of camaraderie, you know. The pressures built up because of lack of time, lack of control. Everyone else seemed to be in control. 'I'm the manager.' 'I'm the producer.' 'I'm the a&r man.' At the end of the day all a band needs is a good engineer. If you've written the material, arranged it, rehearsed it, played it, you should know what it ought to sound like. And so we became dissatisfied. Van more than most, maybe, and of course he's subsequently proved that he could do it on his own."

FOUR

A Transitional Period

Back in Belfast during late 1966, with Them collapsing around him, Van Morrison was clearly dissatisfied, and after his long experience on the road and chaotic taste of America he had, for a while, outgrown his home town. He was looking for the next direction, laying down songs and fragments of songs on a domestic tape recorder. He was beginning to know what he wanted musically, but not how to make it happen.

"I wanted to get more into developing songs and arrangements. That didn't seem to be what was happening with that particular band. The band split up and the management wanted me to organise another band. So I did that but it was like going through the same thing. So by that point I'd left it anyway, in my head... I left it physically about six months later."

From a modern pespective, with hindsight, now that Morrison has been established for 25 years as an artist of world stature whose music is continually rejuvenated, it may be difficult to believe that at this stage of his career his name did not necessarily open doors, and that no-one was journeying out to East Belfast to beat on his parents' front door.

He was the former lead singer with a briefly successful rock band whose personnel changes had made them almost unrecognisable to their local constituency. The world at this time was becoming ever fuller of young men fitting this description, now settling down after their enjoyable moment of fame, returning to the family butcher's shop, becoming secure civil servants or moving backstage into the corporate structure of the business as record company executives. And, to make matters more problematic, Morrison had also become known in some quarters as "difficult", almost entirely on merit.

This was indeed a crucial period in Van Morrison's career, the point at which he could have sunk with little trace, to be remembered mainly on "gold" radio stations. While a version of Them continued touring without him, pursuing their further opportunities in America, Morrison remained on home territory, occasionally performing low-key gigs.

He had been working towards a brand new direction, a new approach away from showbands and beat groups, for a considerable time. Rod Demick recalls an evening in Van's flat in Ladbroke Grove, close to the end of the Them era. "We were drinking vodka and jamming, with Herbie and Van on guitars, me on harmonica. The phone rang at some stage late in the evening and it was his manager. We carried on playing and Van held out the phone towards us. Then he said into the mouthpiece, 'Hear that? That's the sort of thing I should be doing.' Loose, in other words. He had this tape recorder running and he was still playing when Herbie and I had crashed out. But I remember that at some stage I became aware that the end of the tape was flapping around and Van was still playing, still singing. Stream of consciousness, improvising, playing with phrases. When I heard *Astral Weeks* a couple of years later it all made sense, of course."

Both Demick and Armstrong confirm that, when Morrison was back home in the death throes of Them, one of the options was for him to join the rival Wheels. "Herbie had spoken to him about it," says Demick. "Offered him a singing job in the band. Van said: 'Yeah, but, I've got to wait for a phone call from America first.' Bert Berns called just in time!"

As Morrison recalls: "I was working in Belfast writing songs, with a tape recorder. I was in the process of getting a solo deal with Philips

Records which somehow didn't come to fruition because it was taking so long. Then I got this call from America to do a couple of singles there or something. So while I was trying to negotiate with Philips I went to New York to do a couple of singles and then I got myself involved in that situation, so by the time the Philips deal was ready I couldn't do it because I was already in over my head with this other company. So that's really the way it happened."

Among other Morrison pieces from Them days in raw form, Berns had heard a home-made demo tape of the song that was eventually to become "The Smile You Smile", just Morrison and a strummed acoustic guitar, which was eventually (1991) to be released on the collection *Bang Masters* under the title "I Love You (The Smile You Smile)". Under Berns' guiding hand it is a pleasant-enough love song, certainly not one of the great successes of the Bang interlude, but it does manage to express the desire to go "roaming in the gloaming", quoting the Scottish music-hall entertainer Sir Harry Lauder. Since even Bill Haley, when wearing an unlikely rock-'n'roll tartan for his bizarre "Rockin' thru the Rye", avoids the phrase, this is probably a rock-music first.

By this time Berns had left the parent company Atlantic, where he had worked as house producer and writer, because the label was now sufficiently impressed with his track record to set him up with his own imprint. The name Bang arose from the forenames of Berns himself and the Atlantic triumvirate of Ahmet and Nesuhi Ertegun together with their partner and producer Jerry Wexler (presumably the literally correct Banj was quickly rejected as something that sounded as if it came from a curry-house menu).

When Berns contacted Morrison the Bang label had already scored a Number 1 hit with "Hang on Sloopy" by the McCoys, one of the songs he'd previously packed for his trip to London. The band could never quite repeat this mid-1960s classic but nevertheless went only into a slow tailspin, giving the label seven more Hot 100 entries –

though each peaked lower in the charts than its predecessor. Even more successful, signing with the label at around the same time as Morrison's involvement, was Neil Diamond, who announced his arrival with a modest hit, "Solitary Man", immediately followed by "Cherry, Cherry", the first of many Top 20 entries for the label that Berns had founded.

When such money-spinners were added to Berns' solid reputation at Atlantic, where he had provided hits for such artists as Solomon Burke, it is understandable that his financial backers at the parent label were happy to allow him to bet on his hunch over the unknown-quantity Irishman. Morrison clearly had talent, and the Erteguns and Wexler were almost unique among big-shot record men at the time in that their driving force was a love of music. They had always assumed, and they were consistently proved correct while they compiled their outstanding catalogue of popular r'n'b, that if they followed their enthusiasms shrewdly, and behaved decently to their artists, then the company would prosper.

By this time Atlantic could well afford a gamble. So dominant was the label for two decades that it's hard to believe it wasn't some ready-made corporate logo. Instead, it was started in 1947 by two music freaks – Herb Abramson and Ahmet Ertegun – with a modest investment from Ertegun's dentist. Their jazz roster quickly became a who's who of the music – the Modern Jazz Quartet, Ornette Coleman, Charlie Mingus, John Coltrane among the top names. In r'n'b, which brought them early success, they had Ruth Brown, Ray Charles, Chuck Willis, the Clovers, Joe Turner, LaVern Baker, Clyde McPhatter and the Drifters. The Coasters, who were independently produced by Jerry Leiber and Mike Stoller, were leased to Atlantic, and during the 1960s they became the foremost soul label, both with their own signings and by distributing Stax: Otis Redding, Percy Sledge, Aretha Franklin, Solomon Burke, Sam and Dave et al. They were also to see the arrival of the white rock era, and signed Led Zeppelin, Yes, ELP and others. Their dominance of so many musical categories is unparalleled. And for a couple of years, inheriting the mantle of Leiber and Stoller, Bert Berns was the label's golden boy.

Just before travelling to the USA Morrison spent an evening at Dougie Knight's shop. Blues record sessions after hours had long been another manifestation of Knight's evangelistic delight in the music. "After everyone else had left there were four of us sitting on cushions on the floor, drinking beer and listening to records. Van decided he was going to walk home to get some fresh air, and a friend of his said he'd make sure he got home all right. His friend told us later that he'd just leaned Van up against his mother's front door and ran away. At one stage apparently Van decided he was going to swim across the Lagan, but he was persuaded not to."

Morrison spoke of this leap in the dark over to the USA, in 1987. "I was 21 years old and I didn't have an idea what I was doing. I was offered a contract with Philips here [in the UK] but the deal was dragging on, and while I was waiting for it to be sorted out I got an offer from this American company run by Bert Berns. So basically I didn't have a job, and I paid for myself to go over to New York. All the books say that Bert Berns paid for me to go over, but Bert Berns never paid for anything – ever. That's basically it. It was a job, and I needed the work and the money, and so I went to New York. And one thing led to another, and I just kept working for years, and one day I suddenly realised I was living there."

Clearly Morrison was feeling nervous enthusiasm at this time to get on with the next stage of his career, however uncertain it may have been. So Berns went ahead in arranging the Morrison sessions, using a familiar pool of musicians like guitarist Eric Gale, who had played on Solomon Burke records and other Atlantic dates. But Morrison found the experience difficult. Berns was no longer the man who had flown to London to work with Them, keen to impress, and was now too busy nurturing his own label to devote the care that this shy, disoriented artist needed in New York.

Morrison was taxed in his attempts to convey to the musicians, to whom of course this was just another job, what he was aiming at – particularly as he soon realised that he and Berns were tending to pull in different directions. Berns was an accomplished hit machine looking for hooks, while Morrison was moving towards a new form of pop music; contemplative, narrative and repetitive, a jazz man's bag. "I knew he was a good r'n'b producer but I suppose he saw me as more of a commercial entity," says Morrison. "It was a very contrived situation."

In 1970 Morrison summed up the lack of communication he felt during the sessions. "Bert wanted me to write a song with him that would be a hit, but I just didn't feel that kind of song. I mean, maybe that was his kind of song, but it wasn't my kind of song, so I just told him, I mean, if you want to do that kind of song, man, you should just go in and do it, get yourself a group and sing that song, but I've got my kind of song that's different. I've always been writing the kind of songs I do now, even with Them."

Among the pieces of work Berns suggested that Morrison should co-write was the song that became "Piece of My Heart". Berns had eventually taken his uncompleted song to another writer associate, Jerry Ragavoy, and it became a hit for Erma Franklin. It later became even more celebrated as a show-stopping classic of the Janis Joplin repertoire, after a blistering version on her debut album with Big Brother and the Holding Company, *Cheap Thrills*. It reached Number 12 when covered by Big Brother. Though the Ragavoy influence is audible, the song confirmed that Berns had an unusual white man's talent for recreating the bluesy essence of soul music.

This would have seemed an excellent get-together project for Morrison to work on with Berns, but he wasn't interested. He continues: "I'd write a song and bring it into the group and we'd sit there and bash it around and that's all it was – they weren't playing the song, they were just playing whatever it was. They'd say 'OK. We got drums so let's put drums on it,' and they weren't thinking about the song; all they were thinking about was putting drums on it, or putting an electric guitar on it, but it was my song and I had to watch it go down. So there was a point where I had to say, 'Wait a minute. Hold it. Stop!' Because I just couldn't see my songs go down like that all the time. It was wrong. There was much more involved in them than that."

This transcription of what Morrison was saying, clearly run by *Rolling Stone* with a minimum of the usual editing to clear out repetitions and rambling, gives a candid and dramatic peep into his state of mind. It also suggests that a backing musician, however sympathetic, might have struggled to get Morrison's gist. He is, of course, throwing out the baby ("TB Sheets" and the other successes of the sessions) with the bathwater. Not that "TB Sheets" was universally acclaimed. One critic called the song "Morrison's rambling, bluesy and often befuddling comments on a woman, her TB, her sheets and other things." And Greil Marcus, admittedly referring more to commercial reaction than to the quality of the work, said: "The signature track [of the album that Berns opportunistically released of these sessions, of which more later] was titled 'TB Sheets', which was exactly what it was about. Who wanted to listen to an endless song about tuberculosis when the air was filled with the sounds of the summer of love?"

Well, yes, if all Berns wanted was something to add to "Brown Eyed Girl" on AM radio, alongside the Lovin' Spoonful and the Beach Boys (and this was of course his main concern), then clearly this medical morality tale was not it. It did, however, become something of a cult classic on FM stations.

What Bert Berns had proposed was a concentrated period of recording in New York, looking specifically for singles – he wanted

enough for four releases. Morrison agreed and flew over to the USA
for the weekend of 28 and 29 March 1967, for two extended sessions
at A&R Studios.

The success of the first session was "Brown Eyed Girl", which,
when false starts and rejected alternatives are added together, only
clicked on the 22nd attempt. As Steve Turner has observed, the song
worked because it was the best result of the marriage between Berns'
pop sensibility and Morrison's r'n'b leanings to emerge from the
weekend. When the Berns tendency dominated, as in a song he co-
wrote that was also part of the first day's work, "Goodbye Baby
(Baby Goodbye)", the results are clearly more awkward. The song,
written some time earlier for Solomon Burke (it had reached
Number 51 in February 1964), is given a somewhat perfunctory performance. And, while "Ro Ro Rosey" has the soulful punch that
would probably have pleased the vocalist more, there is too little
Morrison in the treatment.

There is perhaps a tendency to think of Van Morrison's brief career
on the Bang label as an interlude, a period of transition between "beat
group" apprenticeship and the mature blossoming of *Astral Weeks*,
a time of frustration for the artist. A couple of factors lend weight
to this view, as well as Morrison's quoted dissatisfaction with the
experience. Firstly, he laid down early (therefore transitional) versions of "Beside You" and "Madame George", both of which were
to receive more celebrated expression on that album. Secondly, producer Berns certainly tried at times to fit Morrison into existing
moulds – the Al Kooper-style, Dylanesque organ of "He Ain't Give
You None", for example, or Morrison's punchy workout on "Ro Ro
Rosey", which could almost be a publisher's demo disc aimed at
New Orleans pop-soul star Lee Dorsey.

But this period did produce a kosher hit record in one of the defin-
itive sounds of the "summer of love", 1967. "Brown Eyed Girl"
showed that this individualistic talent could produce a jaunty, catchy

and disciplined chart single. Its sprightly guitar figure and uplifting mood adorns radio stations to this day. Furthermore, Morrison's voice, on the most successful tracks, has never before or since been as flexible and enthusiastic, and those tracks stand as some of his very finest work. This is in spite of the fact that, working in unfamiliar surroundings with musicians unknown to him, Morrison went through many takes of the songs. According to Morrison, there is no big deal in the fact that the song started life as "Brown Skinned Girl". "That was just a mistake. It was a kind of Jamaican song. Calypso. It just slipped my mind. I changed the title."

Morrison has referred to "Brown Eyed Girl" almost dismissively as "the Top 40 thing", and demonstrated on an acoustic guitar how he heard it when he wrote it. "The record came out different," he said. "I didn't change anything, it's just that what went on around me changed. I sang the same thing. This fellow Bert, he made it the way he wanted it, and I accepted the fact that he was producing it, so I just let him do it."

So, maybe Bert Berns couldn't win. Even when he gave Morrison a gift-wrapped hit, he could expect no thanks. And as for the consequences of success, what it meant to Morrison was that "I got to play in some wrong places. That's one thing, it put me in some of the worst joints I ever worked."

Some of these dreadful places would appear to be television studios, where the singer had to lip-synch, a silly requirement for such an improvisational artist. But was lip-synching really such an unbearable torture; paying the mortgage, reviving a career that could have died with Them and laying the foundation of his soon-to-be rock star status? This status, after all, was to bring with it as much artistic freedom as a tough industry allows. Morrison, the purist who had a clear apprehension of what he thought he should be doing musically, even if he couldn't articulate it, wasn't of a mind to recognise this, to be quietly grateful and keep on synching.

But, as admirers of much of his work on Bang, we don't have to concern ourselves as to whether he was in a benevolent mood or not. We can agree with him – it's in the records or it's nowhere, and can persist in tormenting him with our admiration even for work he dismisses. His opinion must have mellowed, indeed. He has returned to "Brown Eyed Girl", for example, at various times throughout his career, often in a form as tightly routined and pop-oriented as the hit version.

"TB Sheets" is in complete contrast. This is an overwhelming song, unlike anything before or since in rock music. And yet its rambling monologue, a chilling and desperate one-sided conversation, can only convey its power because Morrison and the session musicians are working within recognisable blues conventions, giving a half-familiar structure to the piece.

The riff that establishes the narrative and continues throughout is pure Slim Harpo, sensuous and southern, precisely laid down and then embellished with restraint, just sufficient to maintain interest in the cyclical musical structure of the piece without distracting from the power of Morrison's performance. Harpo wrote the number that became Them's first single, "Don't Stop Crying Now" (though he would hardly have recognised the song), and so his style was clearly embedded in Morrison's musical consciousness. Any crescendoes in the song are not musical, but in the lyrics, as the singer's mood ranges through admonishment, flipness, desperation, pity. The music simply provides discreet and sympathetic support.

Of course Harpo, a Louisiana singer and harmonica player best known for "I'm a King Bee", covered by the Rolling Stones, "Raining in My Heart" (a slow, mellow blues, not the Buddy Holly song) and the lascivious "Baby Scratch My Back", wrote nothing like this ten-minute death song. But he would have recognised the musical basis instantly, and would have approved of Morrison's spiky, atmospheric harmonica punctuations.

The lyrics would, however, ring a bell elsewhere within the blues field, as disease – specifically TB – is such a common theme. The vast Lightnin' Hopkins catalogue, for example, includes many such meditations, including "Death Bells" and "Pneumonia Blues", John Lee Hooker has sung of watching the gravediggers "pack dirt in my baby's face", and the theme of his song "Jackson, Tennessee" is "Don't you know, TB is killing me/Well I want my body buried way down in Jackson, Tennessee". Later, Hooker was to cover "TB Sheets" itself.

The pioneer country singer Jimmie Rodgers, whose songs were usually in the blues form, often sang of the disease that was to kill him and, perhaps most significantly, Morrison's childhood hero Leadbelly had his own version of "TB Blues". One of the verses touches on an aspect of terminal disease that Morrison confronts from the point of view of the reluctant sickroom visitor: "TB's all right to have if your friends didn't treat you so low down/Don't you ask them for no favor/They even stop a-comin' round."

The langourous, sensitively developed soundtrack is vital to the power of the song. Morrison has rarely been a cold craftsman when it comes to lyrics: his feelings are not easily transformed into honed words, his songs rarely chiselled into shape. Emotion is all, and it has rarely been better conveyed, in all its confusion.

In Ladbroke Grove his landlady and friend, Dee, had died of tuberculosis. In "TB Sheets", addressing a woman who is called Julie, the 22-year-old singer explores guilty feelings that most people are unlikely to have to confront until maturer years, feelings about bereavement, about living while witnessing death, of helplessness, of one's own relief at remaining alive, shamefaced, forlorn but disturbingly triumphant.

Soldiers fighting in the trenches of World War I, a squalid, dank and dirty duty where whimpering death was an odds-on bet, have spoken of the awful relief when the friend crouched next to them was the one to get the German bullet. Shock, of course, the desperate scramble to treat and then awkwardly comfort the dying comrade, but then a secret thanks that it had been someone else, even a best friend, and not themselves. Morrison explores similarly complex emotions in the song.

First of all, the singer chides the terminally ill invalid for crying. "It ain't natural," he says. The woman cries all night and the observer, trapped in the death room, is embarrassed and helpless.

Later in the song, the sun bouncing off a crack in the window pane "numbs my brain", a tiny detail of observation that the tubercular John Keats, the master at building a world from such specific sensual responses, would have approved of. And then there's the crushing claustrophobia of the sickroom – "Let me breathe," he demands of the woman whose breath is failing, bubbling in cheesy lungs. There is a street below, a street she'll never walk in again, and he is getting desperate to be down there, to rejoin the living, because "the cool room is a fool's room".

This cannot be callous – none of us would even tell the 100-a-day man, when the cigarettes are finally squeezing the life from his kippered chest, that it's his own fault, let alone chide the innocent victim of TB. In the cool room, the morgue, we are all reduced to fools, to chilling lumps of meat presided over by defensively-callous technicians, and we'll all be there sometime.

When he says that he can almost smell the TB sheets, Morrison conveys the whole situation in the particular image, the rich, sweaty stench of disease, again a Keatsian device. The only mystery is the word "almost", except that the two syllables would have been required to complete the line.

Even greater desperation now takes over. The singer has "gotta go", but is begged to stay. He escapes just as far as the kitchen for a drink of water before promising, perhaps untruthfully, that he'll send someone else round with a bottle of wine. A change of shift in the hospital ward, as it were. He's got things to do (like living?) and can only say "don't worry". He even makes turning on the radio seem like a favour, and in the awful fade-out admits that the situation "ain't funny". Never has the helpless guilt of still being alive been more powerfully conveyed than in this youthful masterpiece.

Morrison could later joke about this song. "I'm writing 'TB Sheets Part II' now," he said in 1972. "Keeping the same riff, the same groove." However, it's on record – though the story could be exaggerated – that after laying down this track he broke down in tears, unable to continue the session. During this interview Morrison confirmed that he changed the lyrics each time he performed it on stage, and yet it's hard to see it as a concert favourite. The listener can feel it grow in the making, as Morrison explores such complex feelings of loss and guilt. It is this naked process of discovery that ensures that the impact of this extraordinary piece of work will never dim.

After this the other great achievement of these sessions, the swirling, supple blues of "He Ain't Give You None", is comparatively straightforward. In spite of Berns' deliberately Dylanesque production, though, it remains an outstanding Morrison song, and his voice has never sounded better. He's clearly in a good mood, playful and lively. He exhorts guitarist Eric Gale into a roller coaster of a guitar solo, and laughs his way into the fade: "You can leave now if you don't like what's happening, you know. There's a few things going…" At least, it sounds like joking, though I suppose it could possibly be yet another expression of frustration.

There are conscious echoes of Dylan in Morrison's lyric, too, chiding a girl for preferring another man, over a rolling, loose-limbed backing. The singer claims that he is more generous with his jelly roll than his rival is. This comes as a surprise to anyone who had assumed that the jelly roll must always belong to the lady in the case, as in Charlie Lincoln's sensitive Georgia blues "If It Looks Like Jelly, Shakes Like Jelly, It Must Be Gel-a-Tine". Mr Lincoln observes:

"Mabel's cooking is a treat/Her jelly roll cannot be beat," in a raggy song that is simply one culinary double entendre after another. Now we learn that Van Morrison's got one. Maybe that's why people were edging out of the studio towards the end of the song.

On some releases of the Bang material "He Ain't Give You None" is introduced by a few bars of an aborted take, followed by some comments from Morrison suggesting that the self-defensive image of himself as Bert Berns' puppet must be qualified – though, admittedly, his reservations have usually been about the contrast between what he thought he was hearing in the studio and the mixed-down, tarted-up version in the shops. "I think it should be freer," he says. "We should have a freer thing going. At the moment we have a choked thing, you know?

Too right. But eventually the band relax and the results are masterful. This could not be said of the majority of the Bang material, though it should be pointed out that Morrison has not been a party to its regular recycling, and has even claimed that he regarded the March sessions as uncompleted.

Of the other material recorded during the weekend "Spanish Rose" sounds awkward, pitched too high to allow the range and flexibility of Morrison's voice to work to good effect, while "Midnight Special" is a respectful revival of the old chestnut with Morrison contributing a biting harmonica. His white-gospel intentions seem somewhat diluted, however, by Berns' opting for an off-the-shelf standard rock backing with the bass way up in the mix.

However, "Who Drove the Red Sports Car" means that the two-day session was a 50-per-cent success, along with "Brown Eyed Girl", "He Ain't Give You None" and "TB Sheets". Morrison refers to it in the lead-in to the song as a piece of his life, probably bitterly and feeling alienated, and it is a beautifully understated, slippery blues. Four good-to-great tracks in a weekend? And this was at the time that Brian Wilson was discovering that there is no time limit to how long you can spend producing one song, if you are allowed the indulgence. So this was productive labour.

Morrison may have been less than enamoured with the way his recording career seemed to be heading, but the USA itself held obvious attractions. There was the creative buzz of New York itself to enjoy, and he had been reunited with his "ballerina" from the West Coast, Janet Planet, and her son Peter. They moved up to Cambridge in Massachusetts while "Brown Eyed Girl" began its own move up the charts. In July 1967 the song broke into the Top 10. A road band was swiftly assembled to capitalise on this success, consisting of guitarist Charlie Brown, bass player Eric Oxendine and drummer Bob Grenier. Morrison was launched to the media at a party that took place aboard a hired boat cruising the Hudson River. There then followed that hated experience of playing in "the wrong places" and lip-synched television appearances.

Berns had meanwhile packaged the eight songs recorded in March as Morrison's debut album, without Morrison's approval or even, it seems, knowledge. The cover sported psychedelic graphics (that's putting it politely) and the record was given the inappropriate but very 1967 title *Blowin' Your Mind!* The exclamation mark somehow emphasised the tawdriness of the presentation. And if the artwork wasn't enough, Berns' remarkable sleeve note completed the picture: "Van Morrison… turbulent… today… inside… a multicoloured window through which one views at times himself and his counterself. Van Morrison… erratic and painful… whose music expresses the real now!! the right now of his own road his ancient highway." And this was the man who had made all those chunky Solomon Burke hits? Presumably the artist cringed, even though in 1995 he was singing of an "Ancient Highway"!

It is hard to imagine anything that would be more finely calculated to compound Morrison's growing disaffection with the label than this opportunistic album release. "It wasn't really an album, it was four singles. They put them together to put the album out. The blind leading the blind." Yet it was clearly not a death wish on Berns' part because he proposed further sessions at the A&R Studios, adding a creative carrot by promising Morrison more control. Berns was clearly a man of considerable personal charm (added to which, until the success of "Brown Eyed Girl", there was hardly a plethora of alternatives for Morrison to choose from – he was still simply the ex-singer from a briefly successful Irish beat group), because in spite of his unhappy time on Bang Morrison has consistently attested to his liking for Berns himself.

Of the first batch of material Morrison recalls: "It was one day. I walked into the studio about four in the afternoon and by 12 o'clock at night it was done. Then I went back to Belfast and they just mixed it after that." During November 1967 Morrison returned to the studio and cut the remainder of his Bang sides. These included two fruits of his earlier head-down sojourn in Belfast and his recent time in Cambridge, the prototype versions of the *Astral Weeks* tracks "Madame George" and "Beside You".

Reactions to these early versions will, of course, always be entirely subjective. Some critics have preferred, for example, the Bang take of "Beside You" to the one that appears on *Astral Weeks*. It shows a singer who is straining to work out a song on the hoof, while the band tries gamely to anticipate what is required. It displays improvised spontaneity, always a far more attractive quality than studio-polished sterility.

On the other hand, "Madame George", with its, to some, inappropriate (and somewhat false-sounding!) reactions from a club audience, can be understandably rejected as sounding phoney. Yet the contrast between the audience and this weird slice of Belfast street life is a charming musical collision, and the track is as strong in its curious way as the better-known Warner Brothers version. Morrison begins it by advising, "Put yer fur boots on."

One sons bears a Berns hallmark. His early claim to fame, indeed his calling card at Atlantic, was as co-writer of "Twist and Shout". The Atlantic version, produced by Jerry Wexler and Phil Spector, was by a duo called the Top Notes, and sunk without trace. In Charlie Gillett's history of Atlantic, *Making Tracks*, Wexler recalls Berns' verdict on their efforts in the control room. "Man," he said bravely to the man he was hoping would give him a job, "you fucked it up."

But the song was a summer 1962 hit for the Isley Brothers on the Wand label, soon to be covered in raw, archetypal Merseybeat style by the Beatles. So it made Berns' name and established a style for him. It follows the repeated, irresistible three-chord climb (usually C-F-G) of numerous Tex-Mex songs, most successfully Richie Valens' "La Bamba". The rhythm was imported to New York, and to Atlantic Records, by Berns' predecessors Jerry Leiber and Mike Stoller, who had come to the fore thanks to their work with the Coasters and with "Jailhouse Rock"-period Elvis Presley. They were the hottest writing and producing duo of the day.

The Spanish tinge turned modest hitmakers the Drifters into top-tenners, with such 1959–60 hits as "There Goes My Baby" and "Dance with Me", and above all with the Number 1 hit "Save the Last Dance for Me". It is no coincidence, then, that when Leiber and Stoller moved on to set up their own Red Bird label, the house job at Atlantic went to Berns.

So, some years later, it would seem that Berns needed no further urging to weld these rhythms on to the Morrison Bang sessions. He had taken his cue during the March date from the title "Spanish Rose" to wheel out this treatment, and now he used it on "Chick-a-Boom". This was chosen as the flip-side of the follow-up single to "Brown Eyed Girl", "Ro Ro Rosey", but it is given a somewhat half-hearted "La Bamba" styling. As if Berns is admitting that the formula didn't really work, he discreetly moves Morrison's voice way back in the mix.

The ponderous, Band-style tempo of "It's All Right" is lifted by the backing vocals. These were dubbed on by the trio known as the Sweet Inspirations – Whitney's mother Cissy Houston, Cissy's niece Dee Dee Warwick and Myrna Smith. They had worked with many of the Atlantic greats such as Aretha Franklin and Wilson Pickett and were to be be hired by Elvis Presley in 1970 soon after he returned to stage work, staying with his stage show until his death. The lyric, though, is a semi-coherent musing on freedom of choice which suggests that it is still more "work in progress".

The re-worked "The Smile You Smile" also comes from these sessions, along with yet another "roaming in the gloaming" song, the walking-pace meditation "Joe Harper Saturday Morning".

The other two tracks are the most successful of all the November cuts, one looking back to Morrison's earlier career, the other forward to his jazzier future. "Send Your Mind" is a fast-riffing rocker in extended 12-bar form that evokes fond memories of early Them, while "The Back Room" is performed in an easy-swinging blues tempo and is structured like a Ray Charles number, with call-and-response choruses alternating with fast-talking, top-of-the-head verses. It is an effective, loose improvisation with sympathetic, listening support from the session musicians.

But Morrison was not satisfied. "Sabotaged" was his view of the production work, and so it must have been clear by now that, however much he may still have liked Bert Berns personally, they could not see eye to eye over what a Van Morrison record should sound like. He has said that he regarded the *Astral Weeks* versions of the two songs already recorded for Bang as his opportunity to show how they should have been done. Of course, he's also on occasions been less than effusive about the production of *Astral Weeks*…

The last straw, surely, was when Berns went ahead and cobbled together a second album, equally ill-advisedly though no doubt by now realising that his professional relationship with Morrison was moving inexorably to its close. He compounded the insult by cheekily calling the album *The Best of Van Morrison*, using November material and five of the March tracks, the inevitable "Brown Eyed Girl" together with "Spanish Rose", "Goodbye Baby", "Ro Ro Rosey" and "He Ain't Give You None". In the artist's bitterly expressed dismissal it was "the worst of..." and proved that the Bang experiment was over. "That was a total non-production by Bert Berns. He was good when he wanted to be and lazy when he wanted to be. The second album was really terrible, I thought, production-wise."

It would have been over, anyway, within a month. Morrison's only, now loosened, tie to the company was Bert Berns himself, who collapsed and died of a heart attack, seemingly without any prior warning signs, in December 1967 at the age of 48. Rock history will include "Brown Eyed Girl" among his major achievements and may gloss over Morrison's otherwise somewhat glum time on the Bang label. However, a generous handful of the material recorded under Berns' aegis, including the peerless "TB Sheets", is a worthwhile part of the Morrison musical picture.

Morrison and Janet returned to Cambridge, probably without any clear-cut plans for the next stage of the singer's career, and they quietly got married. Morrison was still under contract to Bang, and Bert Berns' widow Eileen had inherited her husband's interest in the label. But, after his disappointments in the New York recording studio, Morrison was casting around elsewhere.

One of the employees of Warner Brothers Records in the USA was an expatriate English record man, Andy Wickham, later of the company's Nashville office. He knew Morrison from the old Them days on Decca, and he recommended him to the company's vice president Joe Smith. Morrison's response to the deal that was eventually to be struck between Bang and Warner Brothers suggests that his resentment at what he regarded as insensitive treatment by Berns must have run very deep. Either that, or it's a striking example of churlishness. Presumably the release of the two Bang albums still rankled with him.

Since the success of "Brown Eyed Girl" the raw and unsaleable commodity that Berns had gambled on was now of more commercial interest, and it would have been known that with Berns' death he was at least semi-available. Smith, on behalf of Warner's, expressed interest. Eileen Berns and her advisers, knowing that it would benefit them little to handcuff a disgruntled and possibly one-hit-wonder artist, agreed to release Morrison in return for the publishing rights to an album's worth of new songs. He gave them an album in length, but of little worth.

As a reluctant contractual commitment, something not unknown in the music business, this album breaks new ground – contrasting, for instance, with Marvin Gaye's bitter divorce settlement *Here, My Dear*, a bilious epic.

The fragments vary in length from 48 seconds to 1.28 minutes. The latter, "Ring Worm", explores the theme, "I can see by the look on your face that you've got ring worm… you're very lucky to have ring worm 'cos you might have had something else." This rocka-boogie morsel sets the tone for the session.

Most of the strumming repeats the "La Bamba" sequence beloved of Berns, cruises through half-hearted blues chords, or riffs the (typically) C-Am-F-G sequence of "Young Love" and a thousand other rock-ballad hits. In "Twist and Shake" he exhorts "twist and shake, baby", while in "Shake and Roll" the advice is to "shake and roll, baby." In "Stomp and Scream" and "Scream and Holler" – yes, you've guessed it. "Jump and Thump" shows a tasteful stylistic development – "Jump and thump, move your hump" – while the credited title "Drivin' Wheel" would seem to be a mishearing of the old jump-blues exhortation "jive and wail".

The odd moment of stoned surrealism, as in "You Say France and I'll Whistle" ("no, you whistle and I'll say France"), is buried in general insult. In "Freaky If You've Got This Far" (this far on the tape, presumably) he promises: "We'll put you in a jar and sell you as a freak," while in "Up Your Mind" he observes, "I think you've got about one living cell in your brain."

More revealing, though musically no less bearable, are the ones perhaps reflecting on how he perceived his professional situation at the time. "I'm waiting for my royalty cheque to come and it still hasn't come yet. It's about a year overdue," is the theme of "The Big Royalty Check". During the piece labelled as "Blow in Your Nose" he says: "We're putting an album together and we're releasing it next week. It's got a psychedelic jacket and it's called Blowin' Your Nose." Presumably this was the intended title, as if he actually cared, and suggests that he wasn't about to forgive Bert Berns for the *Blowin' Your Mind!* album even after the man's tragically early death. The next fragment is called "Nose In Your Blow" – "You're going insane, baby. Have another sandwich." In several of these songs he mentions getting in Herbie Lovelle on drums, and putting more and more guitars on, a comment on his perceived lack of control over the production of his material. And in "Dum Dum George" he observes: "This here's the story about Dum Dum George... He wanted to record me and I said, 'George, you're dumb'." It sounds as if George was better off out of it.

"Want a Danish" steals a half-remembered gag from a classic Lenny Bruce routine: "You want bread up front? Have a sandwich." And Morrison concludes his offering to Mrs Berns with "The Wobble" ("do the wobble, baby") and "Wobble and Ball" ("do the wobble, do the ball.")

In 1994 Charly Records, keeping a straight face, packaged all this into a two-CD set with the familiar Bang material and called it *Payin' Dues*. When put out in Portugal as *The Lost Tapes*, however, the sleeve-note writer was perhaps stretching the joke a little too far. "Now you can hear all the Bert Berns recordings for the first time on these two

CDs, *The Lost Tapes Volume 1 and 2*, eighteen well- and lesser-known songs, digitally remastered from the original master tapes, plus thirty-one previously unreleased outtakes. On the outtakes, one gets a behind-the-scenes glimpse of the artist in the recording studio: trying out unfinished new ideas, fiddling around – sometimes in frustration, sometimes just for fun (often with songs written by others). Altogether, *The Lost Tapes* provides a unique document of the young Van Morrison (age twenty-one) on the brink of a successful solo career. Though Morrison may have been dissatisfied under Berns' direction this *Lost Tapes* collection paints us a portrait of a significant phase in the musical development of Van Morrison. Enjoy it!' Well, there is indeed much to enjoy from Morrison's brief and turbulent relationship with Bang. But this, even when presented as "unfinished new ideas", is not among it. File under "completists only".

The new company boss Eileen Burns not only suddenly found herself a widow but also the mother of two tiny children, one of them born just a few days before her husband's untimely death. So she decided to cut her losses, and Morrison – as he had no doubt anticipated – was a free man.

FIVE

Stellar Heights

"I didn't really want to be in the rock'n'roll scene," says Morrison of this transitional stage in his career. "So I thought I'd have to do an album that was just singing, and songs that were about something. So I did get out of the rock'n'roll scene to some extent. Then the critics started saying that it [*Astral Weeks*] was a rock album! It's obvious to anyone with two ears there's no rock'n'roll on that album at all. So this was a bit strange. They were good reviews and all but they were saying it was a rock album, and the whole point was not to make a rock album. A bit puzzling!"

The move from the small independent to the multinational major record company didn't happen overnight, of course. Morrison has said that Warner Brothers' interest in his work, and the interest of Joe Smith in particular, dated back beyond the Bang days. But there were legal niceties to be unstitched and the "contractual obligation" strumming to deliver. In the meantime, with his future in limbo and his past a matter of some dispute, he was broke. And, he says, he was still broke when *Astral Weeks*, the first rich fruit of his new contract, was released.

Morrison took the only step he was qualified to do, and early in 1968 he formed a group. It was just a trio and the spare instrumentation, a long way from the standard r'n'b band line-up, shows the direction in which he was consciously moving at the time, a direction to be triumphantly confirmed in the recording studio. He joined up with another Cambridge resident, flautist John Payne, and bass player Tom Kilbania. They worked on a modest scale, small clubs and colleges on the east coast, while Morrison created and refined the material that would surface on *Astral Weeks*.

The music was not universally popular with the audiences. It was neither rock'n'roll nor folk, it was not obviously the work of the man best known for his catchy, light-as-air summer smash "Brown Eyed Girl", it was too slippery to pin down and categorise. Morrison found much respect, however, among practising musicians, confirmation if ever he needed it that this was a fruitful path to follow. As he once put it: "People like Jimi Hendrix would come up and sit right in front and listen all night. It seemed the musicians dug it but the general public didn't know what we were into." Another ally was Boston disc-jockey Peter Wolf, working locally as singer with a club band, the Hallucinations, eventually to reach a far wider audience as the blues-based J Geils Band. Wolf gave Morrison name-checks and pointed him towards work in the Boston area.

Interestingly, it was the Morrison of "Brown Eyed Girl" and of the proto-punk "Gloria", his reputation as a commercial singles artist that seemed so awkward to him,which attracted Smith and Warner Brothers. They were not thinking of buying into an artist who produced long, slow, jazzy meditations. "You must remember," Joe Smith reflected in the mid-1970s, "that single records were much more of a factor in establishing artists at that time than they are now. Van had a history of being around the pop single feeling and charts and that was of great interest to us."

What they were to get, of course, was a collection of songs that achieved only modest initial sales and yielded no hit records for Morrison, though that rock'n'roll magpie Johnny Rivers was to make the 1970 album charts with an LP boasting "Slim Slow Slider" as its title track. Rivers' biggest single success of that year was Morrison's "Into the Mystic"; just one entry in one of the most eclectic hit lists in pop history – Rivers could sell cover versions of anything from the Kingston Trio's polite anti-war observation "Where Have

All the Flowers Gone" to New Orleans r'n'b like "Sea Cruise" and "Rockin' Pneumonia and the Boogie-Woogie Flu". Warner Brothers, aiming at quick chart turnover from Morrison, finished up instead with one of the most reliable and long-lived "catalogue" items ever recorded: *Astral Weeks* continues to be discovered anew by every record-buying generation, when they develop beyond the latest evanescent hype.

Anyone researching Van Morrison's life cannot help but note that, in spite of his unhappy experiences under the management of Tin Pan Alley man Phil Solomon and – whatever Morrison's underlying respect for the man may have been – with Bert Berns as well, he was now in the process of embroiling himself in another complex management and production set-up that would inevitably, and presumably deliberately, act as a buffer between himself and his admirers at Warner Brothers.

He signed a deal with independent production company, Schwaid-Merenstein, which was made up of two music-business entrepreneurs: Bob Schwaid and Lewis Merenstein. Indeed, the deal was more complex than this, in that the contract was actually with Inherit Productions, a Schwaid-Merenstein offshoot, who in turn bound Morrison to a two-album deal with Warner Brothers. Schwaid looked after business, Merenstein, a studio engineer, was to act as producer.

The most inspired bit of business performed by Schwaid was in his choice of musicians to play on the *Astral Weeks* sessions. Whether or not there were budgetary restrictions imposed by Warner Brothers, seeing this as a small-scale project with no room for indulgence in untried musicians, there can be no doubt that Schwaid's jazz leanings and the chamber-music feel of the songs Morrison was coming up with pointed in the same direction. The result was that Schwaid hired four of the finest jazz sessionmen available in New York, between them defining the sound that made the album so striking at the time, so long-lived in its appeal.

This longevity was recently confirmed when the British rock monthly *Mojo* polled its contributors, asking for lists of their all-time favourite albums, and published the results in the August 1995 edition. Perhaps showing their age, or probably the age of their fantasies, the writers picked a Top 20 list of albums entirely from the second half of the 1960s and the first half of the 1970s. It wasn't until Numbers 22 and 23 that anything remotely more modern intruded, with *Never Mind the Bollocks* by the Sex Pistols and *London Calling* by the Clash. Second only to Brian Wilson's 1966 masterpiece for the Beach Boys, *Pet Sounds*, and therefore securing the all-time silver medal, was *Astral Weeks*.

"At the time," says Schwaid, "I thought it was an avant-garde marriage of jazz and rock. Really it was a combination of Van's approach to what he thought to be jazz with folk, blues, gospel and rock levels. At the time none of us thought that it fitted into any category." Schwaid knew bass player Richard Davis, the key to the *Astral Weeks* sound and a scintillating, road-seasoned technical virtuoso of the instrument. He had worked with Eric Dolphy, Elvin Jones and Miles Davis, and supported the small-combo work of such pianist bandleaders as Ahmad Jamal, Hank Jones, Jaki Byard and Don Shirley. Davis had also played with Connie Kay, the drummer who had succeeded founder member Kenny Clarke in the Modern Jazz Quartet, the band that had found the most successful formula for broadening the appeal of jazz without compromising its essential disciplines. Schwaid booked Kay for the second *Astral Weeks* session, though he didn't play on the earlier cuts, and his work was complemented by that of percussionist Warren Smith Jr, who could also offer vibraphone.

The stellar quartet was completed by guitarist Jay Berliner, who was completely unaware of Van Morrison's previous work and in fact didn't get round to listening to *Astral Weeks* for another ten years. "In those days I was so busy that I had no idea what I was playing on," he says. "On the first session I wasn't booked until 9pm and so didn't play on 'Cyprus Avenue' and 'Madame George', which had been recorded earlier in the evening. I played a lot of classical guitar on those sessions and it was very unusual to play classical guitar in that context. What stood out in my mind was the fact that he allowed us to stretch out. We were used to playing to charts, but Van just played us the songs on his guitar and then told us to go ahead and play exactly what we felt."

Although there was no place for Morrison's club bass-player Tom Kilbania, John Payne was eventually asked to contribute his distinctive flute and soprano sax improvisations to the project, while the rinkydink harpsichord figures on "Cyprus Avenue", along with the addition of strings and other instruments, were dubbed on later by arranger Larry Fallon. On the second of the two *Astral Weeks* sessions a further drummer, Ray Lucas, and pianist Paul Harris were also hired but, in the event, were deemed surplus to requirements. This suggests that no-one was sure that Connie Kay could make it.

Century Sound Studios on West 52nd Street, New York City, were booked for sessions on 25 September and 15 October 1968. The engineer was studio owner Brooks Arthur. Work began at 7.00 p.m. on the first evening and progress was clearly swift, efficient and improvisational if Berliner, arriving two hours later, missed out on both "Cyprus Avenue" and "Madame George". One thing that time was not wasted on was "getting to know you" pleasantries. Morrison, apart from routining each song – and in all cases the chord sequences are straightforward and repetitive, so this would have taken little time – remained somewhat aloof and lost in his own thoughts. He may well have felt the weight of the jazz pedigree that his management had provided him with, increasing his introversion even more than usual. It was also – after his showband apprenticeship, his r'n'b pop-star phase and the brief experience on Bang – a new beginning, a time to make his mark.

While he kept himself to himself, he was also clearly in charge of the project, as Bob Schwaid attests. "In all fairness to Van, he was the one who was directing the taping. Lew and I were in the control room but Van was the real producer."

In the years since the release of *Astral Weeks*, in a running order that was later settled on by Lewis Merenstein, Morrison has made various, often contradictory, statements about the sessions, hinting sometimes at out-takes that were actually intended for inclusion, of a misunderstanding of his initial concept, of the album not matching his intentions. "I was kind of restricted because it wasn't really understood what I wanted."

He has also claimed that the running order dictated by Merenstein compromised those intentions, though he has never made clear in what way. Admirers of the album, of course, have lived with it quite happily for more than a quarter of a century, finding their own logic in the order of the songs. It seemed to make some sort of sense at the time, and still does – it's all we've ever had, after all.

Merenstein grouped "Astral Weeks", "Beside You", "Sweet Thing" and "Cyprus Avenue" under the portentous title In the Beginning, while on the other side of the record, "Young Lovers Do", "Madame George", "Ballerina" and "Slim Slow Slider" are headed Afterwards. In the beginning of what? After what? The latter title evokes only images of that cliched post-coital cigarette, surely not the intention. And the theme of rebirth alluded to during the songs can look after itself. This is simply a remarkable, beautifully achieved set of eight songs, linked by a similarity of instrumentation and structure, reflecting the stage that a great songwriter had reached in 1968, and I suspect that the eight trump cards on show could have been shuffled and redealt in any order.

Of the tracks that made the final selection "Cyprus Avenue", "Madame George", "Beside You" and "Astral Weeks" came from the first evening, with John Payne joining in for "Astral Weeks".

There was an aborted session the next morning before the final one three weeks later, again more suitably scheduled for the evening, producing "Sweet Thing", "Ballerina", "The Way that Young Lovers Do" and "Slim Slow Slider".

Completing the package as released in November 1968 was the ghostly cover art, of a pensive Van Morrison superimposed on a delicate tracery of tree branches, and a back-cover poem to his "ballerina", linked to the song of that name by its concluding line, "Stepping lightly, just like a ballerina."

Though Jay Berliner wasn't present when the first evening's recording began, he emphatically was by the time they cut the last track of the evening, the song that begins the album, gives it its title and defines its mood. "Astral Weeks" finds Berliner locked with Richard Davis' urgent, inventive bass lines in a delicate shuffle rhythm, pinned down by the repetitive pulse of Morrison's strummed acoustic guitar.

As Morrison repeats the song's two chords over and over the other musicians – whose sounds would be augmented by Larry Fallon's shrewd overdubs later in October – build and build, taking their cue from Morrison's confident exploring voice and sparring with it, before ebbing away as the singer muses on his wish "to be born again". Gradually his words narrow down to the fundamental, "in another time, in another place, way up in heaven," while the other players remain alert, listening closely.

Fallon's first intervention is a telling one, introducing the line "Could you find me?" with a vibrant string chord, almost threatening, building a new element into a song the first two lines of which, the ones about slipstreams and mental viaducts, are far from promising. But with "Could you find me, would you kiss-a my eyes?" Morrison moves to safer ground, simpler and more affecting in his concerns, and it is a change urged in by Fallon's string-section afterthoughts. Further into the song John Payne celebrates his belated admission to the session with some slightly tentative but telling flute phrases, decorating the theme further. Morrison makes reference to his experience with the poster of his hero Leadbelly, described earlier: "A-talkin' to Huddie Leadbelly a-showing pictures on the wall."

Morrison later described *Astral Weeks* as "probably the most spiritually lyrical album I've ever done," and in the long wind-down at the end of the title song we begin to hear a very different Van Morrison to the one whohad so recently and coarsely spelt out Gloria's name for us.

The title song also sets a pattern that was to be repeated throughout Morrison's subsequent work, one to which we shall inevitably be returning, of expressing a thought or a question about spirituality in much the same way as he gives name-checks to poets. Just as the latter is usually, and of course intentionally, little or no more than a current reading list, so his spiritual musings are hardly ever taken beyond first principles. In the case of "Astral Weeks" he alludes to a process of rebirth, of reincarnation. Nothing more. "I remember reading something somebody said about you having to die to be born," is Morrison's recollection. The search for spiritual meaning has raised a particular topic. He states the topic. Then he moves on to the next song, just as in real life he adds another philosophical or religious text to his collection. Only those who look to this intellectual and spiritual magpie for answers, rather than questions, could be misled.

Still without drums, and with the musicians grappling with the meandering nature of the song, "Beside You" is nevertheless far more assured than the earlier version Morrison recorded for Bang. And it is in the nature of the song that a strident or too formalised a musical accompaniment would work totally against the mood of the piece. The overall mood is one of melancholy, of tenderness, of admiration for a loved one, and of separation from that person. "It's basically a love song," is Morrison's straightforward explanation. "It's just a song about being spiritually beside somebody."

In this case the spiritual element seems to be inspired simply by physical separation, by the yearning to be with the person, rather than in any supernatural exploration. But the feeling is so strong that it takes on mystical imagery, of flying clouds and magic shrouds.

The song is also notable for a number of observations, studded into the song, that would seem to come from memories of Morrison's Belfast childhood, as indeed does so much of the material on the album. Some of these remain powerful even though the inspiration is too private to be in any way available to a stranger. "That's why Broken Arrow waves his finger down the road so dark and narrow," is a mysterious example, perhaps recalling the street adventures of cowboys and Indians.

At the outset a mood of melancholy nostalgia is struck, in recalling that "Little Jimmy's gone way out of the back street, out of the window, to the fog and rain," and later Morrison sings of "Ev'ry scrapbook stuck with glue". These two strands, of physical yearning and of retreat into monochrome memories, are never artificially bound together but make an affecting whole, one which Morrison seemed still to be resolving in his own mind when he first recorded the song.

The mood lightens, the tempo quickens and Richard Davis' bass fairly skips along in the first song on the album to be recorded on the second evening, and therefore the first in which Connie Kay is on hand to add his talkative drums to the proceedings. "Sweet Thing" is the happier, celebratory flip-side to the mood of "Beside You", and now the singer wants for nothing.

The song begins with a line of unparalleled sprightliness: "And I shall stroll the merry way and jump the hedges first." But this is no lute-strumming swain in doublet and hose, it is still the moody Morrison, and this that gives what could otherwise be a lightweight diversion its necessary power. This is an album without any fillers, but it does need some optimism. "Sweet Thing" provides it.

If the singer's determination to "never ever grow so old again" seems to continue the theme of rebirth, it is more significantly a joyful resolution simply to make the most of life, to "dig it all and not to wonder, that's just fine". Not a resolution that the enquiring Morrison has ever managed to stick to for long, of course, but for a few valuable minutes the song strikes a bright, optimistic and uncomplicated note. "It's a romantic love ballad not about anybody in particular but about a feeling," is Morrison's verdict. It comes at an appropriate place in the *Astral Weeks* cycle, but of course we don't know where he himself would have chosen to put it on the record.

By this time we have experienced spiritual enquiry, melancholy yearning and uncomplicated joy, none of which prepares us for the album's most enduring masterpiece "Cyprus Avenue". The backbone of the song is provided by Morrison's responses to this stately, calm and calming street, an adolescent refuge away from the clatter of traffic and raucous street life. Into this he weaves the imagery of the songs that were obsessing him at this age, judicious stealings from the wordscape of blues, country and rock'n'roll.

Towards the end of the song its focus becomes clear, and earlier hints fall into place. What has so far been a pleasurable aloofness, not expressed as loneliness but as the feelings of an outsider, becomes centred on an object of desire, and he adopts imagery from the poetry of romance: "Yonder comes my lady, rainbow ribbons in her hair." The revelation that the lady, "so young and bold", is 14 years old is not, of course, the confession of a paedophile. At the time he is recalling, when he was "conquered in a car seat", so was Morrison.

As with all of his most striking work the basis of the song is a blues structure, and this underpinning is stated on his acoustic guitar. The lyric content may be private in its detail but the musicians respond magically to the mood, and the harpsichord figures added by Larry

Fallon contribute the final touch, a sharp, tinkling punctuation to the monologue.

Morrison, a boy from Hyndford Street just a world and 15 minutes away, is strolling in Cyprus Avenue as the girls come home from school, the girls whose fathers own these dignified, tree-guarded houses set back from the avenue behind carefully-tended gardens. His timing is not accidental, and will be familiar to many a young poet apparently lost in higher thoughts. He knows when the girls get back. For him the chosen place was Cyprus Avenue, but he evokes a worldwide memory of adolescence.

Since poetry to Morrison is in large part the poetry of the music he loves, he sometimes resorts in the song to borrowed words in reflecting this experience and in building a myth around it. It is said that when Nashville publisher Fred Rose was thinking of taking on a promising young writer called Hank Williams, he set him a test to write a song about a poor boy in the valley in love with a rich girl on the hill. In half an hour, the story continues, Williams returned with "A Mansion on the Hill". "As I sit here alone in my cabin I can see your mansion on the hill." The pay-off line might have particularly appealed to the young, romantic Van Morrison, the assurance that "I know you're living in sorrow in your loveless mansion on the hill." It certainly appealed to Fred Rose, who was so moved that he took a co-writer credit on Williams' song.

From Nashville to Belfast, and the mansion on the hill is suddenly situated on Cyprus Avenue. Then there's the desire to go "walk by the railroad with my cherry, cherry wine". The word "railroad", of course, evokes a world of boxcars and hoboes, of stockyards and fields of grain, with cheap wine as one's only true friend. In Morrison's case, the railroad was the suburban service cutting beneath the Beersbridge Road, separating the different social worlds of Hyndford Street and Cyprus Avenue. And this becomes, in his imagination, "where the lonesome engine drivers pine". To

Morrison's generation both rock'n'roll and railways were mysterious repositories of romance, and both were attractive career options.

The most audacious steal in the song is the almost word-for-word transplant from the Otis Blackwell classic "All Shook Up". In similar terms to those used by Elvis Presley, Morrison confesses that "my tongue gets tied every time I try to speak, and my insides shake just like a leaf on a tree." Incidentally, Presley's enthusiasm for "All Shook Up" was clearly similar to that of Fred Rose for "A Mansion on the Hill": his name was added to the songwriter credits! In Elvis' case, though, "Colonel" Tom Parker was the one who insisted that the creative honours be shared.

Such is the maturity of expression, both lyrical and instrumental, on the magnificent recording of "Cyprus Avenue" that it is does not instantly declare itself as a song about adolescent sexuality. As such, it is a world away from "teenybop" music, and speaks to us all.

If Joe Smith at Warner Brothers was thinking of Van Morrison as a singles artist then maybe the song that launches the second side of the album (or, as Merenstein had it, Afterwards) came closest to Smith's original concept of all those produced during the *Astral Weeks* sessions. Not close enough, though – no singles were released from the album. "The Way That Young Lovers Do" is the jazziest, the most up-tempo, the most straightforward and indeed the shortest cut of the eight, spiked up with vibraphone and brass, finger-snapping almost in Frank Sinatra style. A song for swinging lovers, indeed.

The song returns to an image that Morrison has already explored twice (in the album sequence of songs, that is). In "Sweet Thing" he intends to "walk and talk in gardens all wet with rain". In "Cyprus Avenue" his lady "came walkin' down, in the wind and the rain". And now "we strolled through fields all wet with rain". It is not the unpleasant associations of rain that Morrison evokes, the inconvenient dampness, the darkness and melancholy of "rotten weather", but the power of rain to cleanse, to refresh. And although the sense of "rebirth" in these songs can be overstressed, the cleansing power of rain takes its place with the imagery of renewal as one of the album's invigorating undercurrents. It is a metaphor he will frequently return to in later years.

"The Way That Young Lovers Do" is followed by the collection's second masterpiece, Morrison's mature revisit to one of the Bang songs, "Madame George", introduced by the strummed acoustic sequence that holds the whole song together. We are back briefly on Cyprus Avenue, but the location of this most visual of the *Astral Weeks* songs shifts through Fitzroy Street to, presumably, Hyndford Street before taking the train to Dublin.

And walking through it all is the mysterious, the "one and only", Madame George. Mysterious because this person shifts identity as does a character or a landscape in a dream – as indeed does this landscape. A dream reinvents itself each second, as does the song. It surely is a dream, but it is far from the pub bore's lengthy description of last night's nocturnal mind-movie. Instead, the story grips like a surrealist film by Dali and Bunuel. It has its own logic, even if that logic keeps changing.

Without subjecting the recording to digital analysis and voice-print techniques, it sounds as though Morrison always, or almost always, sings about "Madame Joy". Morrison once actually allowed a little insight to escape regarding this song, perhaps because he felt comfortably certain that any mystery surrounding it would remain intact.

"The title of the song confuses one, I must say that. The original title was 'Madame Joy' but the way I wrote it down was 'Madame George'. Don't ask me why I do this because I just don't know. The song is just a stream-of-consciousness thing, as is 'Cyprus Avenue'. Both those songs came right out. I didn't even think about what I was writing. There are some things that you write that just come out all at once, and there's other things that you think about and consider where you'll put each bit.

"'Madame George' just came right out. The song is basically about a spiritual feeling. It may have something to do with my great aunt, whose name was Joy. Apparently she was clairvoyant… that may have something to do with it. Aunt Joy lived around the area I mentioned in connection with Cyprus Avenue. She lived in a street just off Fitzroy Street which is quite near to Cyprus Avenue."

By 1986 Morrison was saying: "Madame George was about six or seven different people who probably couldn't find themselves in there if they tried."

It's hard to believe that to give a madame a man's name and then refer to "drag" in the song wasn't also in Morrison's mind. But this ghostly figure, making her stately progress through a Dickensian scene of street urchins, drug addicts and bobbies, is not just his aunt, not just a drag artist and certainly not Van's father George. She's just Madame George.

And so the two songs that "just came out all at once" were, in the case of "Cyprus Avenue", a precise and affecting memory of young sexuality and, in "Madame George", a surreal, miniature version of James Joyce's *Ulysses*, a dream-like stroll through East Belfast and on down to Sandy Row.

Connie Kay's drums are at their most valuable in giving form to "Ballerina", and the same is true of Larry Fallon's arrangements. So often such later additions as a string section are superfluous dressing, resulting from a fear back at the record company that the tapes are too naked to be commercial, that the punter needs plenty of dense noise thrown through the speaker. Such a cold-feet attitude has even muddied some straight blues releases. But the solemn string curtains on this song are as positive a contribution as Richard Davis' bass line, driving the show, cajoling the song into shape.

The inspiration for the song must be Morrison's 1966 visit to San Francisco during the death throes of his time with Them, if the assumption is that the ballerina is Janet Planet, whom he met there.

He has spoken of a "flash about an actress in an opera house appearing in a ballet", which seems to cover most theatrical bases apart from vaudeville, and he also teases that maybe it's about a hooker. Whatever, it's a romantic number and, as one of the longer cuts, a significant one as well.

The album finishes darkly, with the heavily edited blues number "Slim Slow Slider". This was an improvisation that involved Morrison, Davis and Payne, the latter on an eerily mixed soprano sax, a stumbling blues that Merenstein trimmed to 3'20" from a long, slow jam. Approximately ten minutes, according to Payne, was clipped from right at the end, after the vocals finish and his saxophone goes wild at the fade-out. "It sounds as if it's coming across a lake," he once said.

The song contains references to a junkie – "horse you ride is white as snow" – and probably to Morrison's Notting Hill lady Dee, dying of tuberculosis, the Julie of "TB Sheets". But the subject of the song is also "catchin' pebbles by some sandy beach," not a feature of London life, although the beach is placed squarely in Ladbroke Grove, Notting Hill. So this is an ad-lib collision of images rather than a structured piece.

It is "about a person who is caught up in a big city like London or maybe is on dope," Morrison explained to Ritchie Yorke. "I'm not sure. A lot of these songs are not really personal and that's why I have to try to interpret them. A lot of them are just speculation on a subject."

The only significant constant factors in *Astral Weeks* are the voice and acoustic guitar of Van Morrison, and Richard Davis' remarkable bass lines. Jay Berliner joined in during the first session, as did John Payne, and Connie Kay wasn't there at all. When Larry Fallon came to overdub his arrangements and extra instruments, he clearly viewed each song as a discrete piece, bringing in brass here, a harpsichord there, strings where they seemed appropriate.

And yet *Astral Weeks* has a sense of unity. Not unity of musical style, which ranges from the jaunty jazz of "The Way That Young Lovers Do" to the eerie blues of "Slim Slow Slider". Not unity of lyrics, which veer from straightforward love songs to dark surrealism. Not the unity that Lewis Merenstein decided to impose with his headings In the Beginning and Afterwards, nor indeed that heard by Morrison himself.

He has referred to the album as a "rock opera... long before its time. I wrote it as an opera, but it didn't really surface the way it could have." Well, maybe. Years later he disassociated himself from the concept of "rock opera", referring instead to an "operatic approach" to songwriting. Those of us who feel that no piece of work, not Pete Townshend's *Tommy*, nor Ray Davies' *Arthur*, has ever established that there is indeed something worthwhile called a "rock opera", might even feel grateful that the songs were shuffled, rather than being corralled into this modish straitjacket.

Late 1968 was a remarkable time for rock music. Jimi Hendrix reached a peak with *Electric Ladyland*, but in this pre-stadium era lucky Londoners could still be blasted by the Experience from a distance of ten feet. The Beatles released *The White Album* and the Rolling Stones *Beggars Banquet*, both albums radical departures from what those bands had come up with before. Meanwhile, Bob Dylan was redefining country music in Nashville while the old-fashioned disciplines of rockabilly, boogie and blues were being observed by John Fogerty's Creedence Clearwater Revival and Canned Heat. Into this rich variety came *Astral Weeks*, revolutionary, complete in itself.

You can't win with Morrison, of course. It had too much unity for him, and within two years he was being somewhat churlish about the contributions of his distinguished backing musicians. "Guys like Richard Davis and Jay Berliner have got a distinctive style and they're groovy for like two songs," he said in 1970. "But four or five other songs should have had a change in mood." Those changes in mood were always there, in Morrison's writing, but in 1970 he wasn't of a mind to hear them.

Astral Weeks was not immediately recognised as a high-water mark in rock music. Press reaction was subdued – the *New Musical Express* reviewer felt that Morrison sounded like José Feliciano's stand-in, for example – and it wasn't until after the "breakthrough" album *Moondance* that its predecessor began to garner a degree of respect, in retrospect. As Bob Schwaid says: "Initially it was a failure. I don't think we did 20,000 copies. It wasn't until years later that people started to come up to me and tell me that their lives had been changed by *Astral Weeks*."

"It was a success musically," says Morrison, "and at the same time I was starving. Practically not eating. So for the next album I realised I was going to have to do something like rock, or starve. Because the *Astral Weeks* thing sold a bit but I didn't get all the money. So I tried to forget about the artistic thing because it didn't make sense on a practical level. One has to live."

The deal with Warner Brothers gave Morrison another shot at fulfilling the record company's desire for a commercial success, but in the meantime his stock was at a pretty low ebb. What work he could find tended to be around New York and this didn't suit John Payne, who left the group and returned to Boston.

Morrison and Janet Planet soon left New York anyway, with Tom Kilbania, and early in 1969 they moved north to Woodstock in the Catskill Mountains, an area already home to The Band and Bob Dylan. Six months later, down the road apiece, the biggest rock festival in the world was to spread the fame of Woodstock and utterly compromise its appeal as an escapist, rural retreat from New York. And by the time of the festival Morrison's three-piece road band was also in the past tense. Without a band, without a hit, but happy with Janet Planet and with a contract to make another record, it was time for the next stage in Morrison's career.

"*Astral Weeks* was a breakthrough for me creatively," he says, "but then again I didn't have any particular rapport with those musicians outside of that. They were session jazz musicians who worked in another area. I couldn't say 'you're my band' sort of thing – do this. Because I didn't have the sort of rapport it takes to do that. But when I found these people I could use live and on the album that was a more ideal situation, and it worked."

SIX

Moondancing

The move north of New York to Oyaho Mountain was suggested by Graham Blackburn, John Payne's successor in Morrison's backing group. Morrison settled into a rented house with Janet, and worked on the songs for his next album.

In conventional rock career terms, the rural retreat might seem a little premature. But Morrison has never taken a conventional approach to such matters, as he has made clear. "I definitely don't fit into what's happening in the showbiz scene," he said. "They tend to think it's weird that I'm not coming in and telling everyone how great my records are and what my new suit's like... because everyone else is doing it. Hyping their records, hyping themselves. I really don't care what those people think, I'm concerned with getting to my audience."

Moondance makes a quite remarkable companion piece to *Astral Weeks*. Far from being "part two" or an obvious follow-up to that collection of songs, it shows a striking musical contrast, with the exception of one song, "Into the Mystic". The two albums are linked only by Morrison's vocal style. If it is *Astral Weeks* that has over the years acquired a patina of legend as one of the all-time landmarks in rock music, *Moondance* is in no way its inferior as a piece of work. Rarely if ever can successive albums by the same artist, released less than 18 months apart at that, have been less alike but equally strong.

Furthermore it was *Moondance* that re-established Morrison as a commercial musician, however modestly. He had been without an American hit since "Brown Eyed Girl", and the selected single from

Moondance, "Come Running", reached Number 39 in April 1970, lurking in the lower reaches of the charts for a couple of months, while the album itself made similar inroads into the long-playing list, eventually becoming the first Morrison record to go gold.

However, this was well in the future when Payne's departure was followed in July 1969 by that of Kilbania. And when Blackburn also decided to try his luck elsewhere Morrison found himself without any backing musicians. Being based in Woodstock, though, he was surrounded by suitable talent. As luck would have it a local band, the snappily titled Colwell-Winfield Blues Band, were also reaching the end of the road. They had left a small mark on musical history with a 1968 Verve album, *Cold Wind Blows*.

Saxophonists Jack Schroer and Collin Tilton (on the *Moondance* album Schroer was to play alto and soprano, Tilton tenor and flute), together with bass player John Klingberg, joined Morrison. "I met Jack Schroer in New York when I heard him play in a blues band, and I invited him to play on a gig with me the next night," recalls Morrison. They were augmented by another musician working in the area, guitarist John Platania, who had also recorded for the Bang label as part of a long-forgotten band called Silver Bicycle. While recruiting and shaping his new group Morrison completed and relentlessly rehearsed the material that was to become Moondance.

Jeff Labes, a keyboard player and session musician, together with drummer Garry Malabar (who also added vibraphone to the album) and conga-player Guy Masson completed the line-up. When they went into A&R Studios to record late in the year they were augmented by three backing vocalists on two of the tracks, "Crazy Love" and "Brand New Day" – Jackie Verdell, Emily Houston from the Sweet Inspirations and Judy Clay, who had charted as a member of two vocal partnerships. With Billy Vera she had scored on Atlantic either side of Christmas 1967 with "Storybook Children" and "Country Girl, City Man" before moving to Stax for one of the great soul duos of the era, "Private Number" (a UK top-tenner), in partnership with William Bell.

For the first time in his recording career Van Morrison appears on the album credits as producer ("for Inherit Productions – a division of Schwaid-Merenstein"), while Lew Merenstein is "kicked upstairs" as executive producer. Morrison also arranged the tracks, and so the album marks a significant stride forward in taking over control of his music. Lack of this control had, from Them onwards, been a source of frustration for him. Now, as he has put it: "No one knew what I was looking for except me, so I just did it."

It was undoubtedly of great assistance to him that he now had a growing group of seasoned musicians around him as the project developed. They built the songs under his direction, and this is in contrast to the inspired gamble of putting him in the studio with a bunch of strangers, such as the jazzmen who arrived "cold" to play on *Astral Weeks*. As a result *Moondance* shows greater density of texture and musical style. If *Astral Weeks* could be crudely characterised as a hybrid of jazz and folk, it is now the soul side of Morrison's music that comes to the fore, and the album vindicates his desire to produce it himself.

The writing is consciously optimistic, and though his relationship with Janet Planet was soon to falter this is not charted on *Moondance*, which is largely celebratory. One of the many contrasts with its predecessor is that *Moondance*, for the first time since the early Them recordings, sounds like a band album with Van Morrison at the front. The songs were carefully crafted and well worked over – during the preparation period, before Morrison's previous band went their separate ways, Graham Blackburn recalls that "it seemed as though every other week we were in the studio recording *Moondance*." But when Morrison finally went into A&R Studios with his new sidesmen, they worked out the arrangements for themselves, giving the songs their crisp, ensemble sound.

"I'd like to have done it live," Morrison said when looking back on those days from 1973. "I'd like to have got the same musicians again and recorded the album live. That would have been a killer. But the musicians weren't the sort of guys who work live gigs, they only work in the studio. I guess the reason that *Moondance* is more of a band album, Van Morrison with the band sort of thing, is because that was the type of band I dig. Two horns and a rhythm section – they're the type of bands that I like best."

In the late 1960s such bands as Chicago and Blood, Sweat and Tears had established a vogue for rock groups placing the accent on brass. This was standard in black soul music, whether it be a Stax revue, James Brown's meticulously drilled backing group or BB King's tuxedo blues. For a white singer to copy the soul format, however, was still a comparative novelty.

This gives the record its dominant feel, of "white soul". It starts impressively, with one of Morrison's most accessible and striking looks back at his childhood, where a specific memory of a brief experience combines with his spiritual, pantheistic response to his surroundings – exposure to the elements and the life-giving properties of cool water. So strong is the image and the memory to Morrison that he has spoken of it with rare coherence. "I suppose I was about 12 years old. We used to go to a place called Ballystockert to fish. We stopped in the village on the way up to this place and I went to this little stone house, and there was an old man there with dark, weather-beaten skin, and we asked him if he had any water. He gave us some water which he said he'd got from the stream. We drank some and everything seemed to stop for me. Time stood still. For five minutes everything was really quiet and I was in this other dimension. That's what the song is about."

Not only would William Wordsworth, sitting in Dove Cottage working on his epic *The Prelude*, recognise this sentiment, he would surely reach down the years to salute a kindred spirit. In the earliest, 1805–06, version (Wordsworth found it impossible to leave *The Prelude* alone, and the final revision was published soon after his death in 1850) he alludes to the same mysterious, pantheistic feeling at the very beginning of the poem:

> Enough that I am free; for months to come
> May dedicate myself to chosen tasks;
> May quit the tiresome sea and dwell on shore,
> If not a settler on the soil, at least
> To drink wild water, and to pluck green herbs,
> And gather fruits fresh from their native tree.
> Nay more, if I may trust myself, this hour
> Hath brought a gift that consecrates my joy;
> For I, methought, while the sweet breath of
> heaven
> Was blowing on my body, felt within
> A corresponding mild creative breeze,
> A vital breeze which travelled gently on
> O'er things which it had made, and is become
> A tempest, a redundant energy
> Vexing its own creation. 'Tis a power
> That does not come unrecognized, a storm,
> Which, breaking up a long-continued frost,
> Brings with it vernal promises, the hope
> Of active days, of dignity and thought,
> Of prowess in an honourable field,
> Pure passions, virtue, knowledge, and delight,
> The holy life of music and of verse.

This shared feeling, in Morrison's case a contemporary version of the romantic poet's manifesto, appears to be at the core of the Belfast bluesman's most striking work. He may at times clothe himself in the apparel of Christianity or Scientology, but he is a pantheist at heart, feeling that somehow the heart of the mystery resides in the hills, in the night sky – and in a cooling draught of water fresh from the stream, served in a stranger's cottage. He once put it more succinctly: "It's just about being stoned off nature."

From there to the title track, "Moondance", is quite a leap. We have left the stone(d) cottage and we are in a city night club, enjoying finger-snapping, sophisticated jazz, Morrison as Frank Sinatra. And yet, in his description of adult lust as opposed to childhood spirituality, Morrison is still drawn to natural imagery, to the "stars up above", "the cover of October skies", "the leaves on the trees" and "the sound of the breezes that blow". This is an important song in the development of Morrison's career, since it indicated to radio-station programmers a previously unsuspected versatility. Stations that would never have considered playing, say, "Slim Slow Slider" found that the smooth, jazzy sophistication of "Moondance" was more to their taste. "It started out as a saxophone solo, really. I used to play this sax number over and over, any time I picked up my horn. I didn't put words to it until later. I started to play it on guitar, and got some words."

Another change of style, to the southern soul of the Stax label, brings us to "Crazy Love". This belies its title (which might describe the priapic mood of "Moondance" more closely) in that it is a reflective meditation on love. It is so intimately recorded that the click of Morrison's tongue on the roof of his mouth is audible, as well as his breathing. Beautiful though the song is, a white singer plays with fire when paying such accurate homage to soul, since there is a rich "bottom" to such voices as those of Otis Redding, Percy Sledge or Aretha Franklin that white singers can either imitate or pastiche, but seemingly never achieve. One can only regret that Otis died too soon to hear and cover the song: surely Morrison himself would have relished the result.

"Caravan", pinned to a Band-like walking sequence of chords, is notable for John Platania's acoustic guitar line, threading its way around the lyric. This tribute to "merry gypsies" and their seemingly romantic way of life, combined with an actual strange experience of hearing a radio playing somewhere, even though at the time Morrison was living in Woodstock far from the nearest house, has an adhesive hook in the singer's instruction to "turn it up". There are too many "la la" choruses to make the song stand out as a work of depth, though it is undeniably catchy.

"Into the Mystic", though, finishes the first side (pre-CD) of the album in majestic style – and it is almost in the style of *Astral Weeks*, the one song to look back to past glories. Morrison has described how, just as "Madame Joy" became "Madame George" and "Brown Skinned Girl" became "Brown Eyed Girl", so his orginal idea for a title, "Into the Misty", changed almost of its own accord. Morrison also refers to the ambiguities of the lyric. "That song is kind of funny because when it came time to send the lyrics into Warner Brothers Music, I couldn't figure out just what to send them. Because really the song has two sets of lyrics. For example there's 'I was born before the wind' and 'I was borne before the wind'...and 'Also younger than the sun, Ere the bonny boat was one' and 'All so younger than the son, Ere the bonny boat was won.'"

It is a mysterious song, playing on seafaring imagery and alluding to a sailor's homecoming, but his central spiritual concern comes to the fore in the marvellous promise that "together we will fold into the mystic."

Morrison has often suggested distaste for the demands of Top 40 radio, but the executives at Warner Brothers must have pricked up their ears when they first heard "Come Running". Like "Brown Eyed Girl", it has the sprightly precision of a classic single, and though it peaked just inside the Top 40 it must have taken some pressure off the artist. Its strutting, smiling horn parts emphasise how lucky

Morrison was to bump into Schroer and Tilton at this stage of his career. "Happy-go-lucky" was Morrison's verdict.

But this is an ensemble record, and it is Jack Klingberg's pumping bass line, above all, that shapes the strange blues "These Dreams of You". The inspiration, it seems, was a dream about an assassination attempt on Ray Charles, who then "got up to do his best". The words are introspective and obscure, but the musical structure and assured playing give the piece its necessary coherence.

Morrison encountered the music of near neighbours The Band during the preparations for *Moondance*, never more obviously than on "Brand New Day", an optimistic, soulful anthem with clear echoes of Dylan and The Band's "I Shall Be Released", and with John Platania doing perfect Steve Cropper Stax guitar runs to resolve each lyric line. In fact, Morrison has acknowledged that, at a time when he was growing increasingly alienated from the music he heard on the radio, a track by The Band put him back on course. "Brand New Day" is the result.

In the middle verse Morrison complains that "I was lost and I was crossed/With my hands behind my back/I was long time hurt and thrown in the dirt.../ I been used, abused..." and so on. Well, you've got to look on the bright side. Morrison does, turning self-pity into hope: "My heart is still and I've got the will." Thus his theme of rebirth makes a further appearance.

"Everyone" is a charming, lightweight, if somewhat frantic curiosity. The use of clavinette, not an instrument familiar to any musical dictionary but sounding as if it is of the harpsichord family, combined with the country-dance feel of the melody and rhythm, evokes images of powdered wigs, hooped skirts and stately square dancing on the lawn. Optimism continues to be the theme. The singer and his lady will walk along the lane and the avenue "with our heads so high, smile at passers by". As anyone who has passed Van Morrison in the street will confirm, the song is a fantasy.

"Glad Tidings" concludes this remarkable album, though if the set has a weak link it is here, in a song offering yet more "la la's". Platania's guitar figures, reminiscent of "Brown Eyed Girl", give it some strength, and it is all but vindicated by one of those lines that Morrison can produce like a rabbit from a conjuror's hat. As a rhythmic hymn to happiness, "the lips that you kiss will say Christmas" is a stunning inspiration. ("I want to rock your gypsy soul", in "Into the Mystic" is another.)

Commercially, *Moondance* put Morrison back on course, following generally enthusiastic reviews. In the *San Francisco Chronicle* the veteran critic Ralph J Gleason was a convert. "He wails as the jazz musicians speak of wailing," Gleason explained, "as the gypsies, as the Gaels and the old folks in every culture speak of it…" Well, yes. Up to a point. It is a long time since the old folk in my culture sat around wailing like Van Morrison, steeped in the wisdom of ages, but the quality of *Moondance* excuses hyperbole.

Although Morrison could now be considered as an established artist, and was certainly being courted by big-time concert promoters, he preferred to continue playing small clubs as a way of avoiding greater entanglement in the business side of his career. The conveyor-belt nature of rock festivals, an increasingly popular phenomenon, was not to his taste, and his rural peace was about to be disturbed in the aftermath of the biggest festival of all, Woodstock. This had taken place at a farm near Bethel, 60 miles southwest of Woodstock, on an August weekend in 1969. Morrison's one performance at a festival during this period, at Randall's Island, was a disaster. He staged a sit-down protest when the audience didn't seem to be paying attention, before completing his set in ill humour.

The record company was naturally anxious to maintain the momentum of *Moondance*, however, and in early summer 1970 Morrison began recording the songs that were to make up his next album, *His Band and the Street Choir*.

"It was originally a concept to do an a capella album," he explained. "Street Choir was going to be an a capella group. I wanted these certain guys to form an a capella group so that I could cut a lot of songs with just maybe one guitar. But it didn't turn out. It all got weird." On the record, the choir was made up of Janet Planet, Ellen Schroer, Martha Velez, Andy Robinson and Larry Goldsmith, while on one track, "If I Ever Needed Someone", he turned to the trio who had sung on two *Moondance* tracks, Emily Houston, Judy Clay and Jackie Verdell.

Although the "street choir" concept changed from the original intentions, the album is significant in that what became known as the Caledonia Soul Orchestra, to many the finest group of all Morrison's collaborators, was assembled. From the *Moondance* group came Jack Schroer on alto and soprano saxophones, guitarist John Platania and bassist John Klingberg. The brass was augmented by Keith Johnson, formerly of the Paul Butterfield Blues Band, on trumpet, while keyboards were played by Alan Hand. On stage, Johnson could switch to organ when required. Completing the line-up was the peerless drummer Dahaud Elias Shaar (David Shaw).

After the revelations of *Astral Weeks* and *Moondance*, the third Warner Brothers album gives an impression of marking time. There are still rich rewards, and some delightful musicianship, but Morrison reveals nothing new. He couldn't win, maybe: "The record company was asking me for singles so I made some... then when I started giving them singles, they asked for albums..."

And he delivered, with three Hot 100 entries from the sessions. "Domino", in reaching Number 9 in November 1970, even pipped "Brown Eyed Girl" by a single rung. In February 1971 "Blue Money" reached 23, and in June "Call Me Up in Dreamland" crept as far as Number 95. Suddenly, Morrison was a consistent hit-maker.

All three songs are built around catchy choruses and instantly-memorable riffs, the basic requirements of Top 40 radio. There are other rewards on *His Band and the Street Choir*, too, though they are similarly less demanding than Morrison's admirers had come to expect – maybe this explains the comparatively muted critical reception for the album. He could not, apparently, appeal to format radio and the hip critics at the same time. It should be remembered, though, that at this time the latter were still somewhat sniffy towards the straightforward virtues of rock'n'roll and the 12-bar blues.

Too many rock writers had overlooked the bedrock of the music, or were simply ignorant of it, in a pretentious search for "art". On one occasion, for example, no space could be found in the recently founded London magazine *Time Out* for a review of the latest Al Green album on Hi, because it was not "serious" enough! At this distance, though, the cracking rockaboogie of "Give Me a Kiss" and the lissome, supple 12-bar riffing of "Sweet Jannie" are perfectly acceptable. The spurned Al Green fan, Ian Hoare, was later given space to praise *Tupelo Honey*, incidentally, so clearly Van Morrison was seen as "serious".

"Crazy Face" is an intriguing character sketch, as elusive as "Madame George", with some stunning work by Jack Schroer. Its tumbling melody makes it one of the album's most memorable tracks. The funk-rhythmed "I've Been Working" is somewhat perfunctory, but side one of the collection ends with a far more thoughtful application of Morrison's vocal skills in the optimistic, slow-building "I'll Be Your Lover, Too". There are further expressions of optimism, though significantly they now look forward to a future plateau of contentment rather than present celebration, in the Spanish-tinged "Virgo Clowns", the deep-soul pastiche "If I Ever Needed Someone" and the concluding track "Street Choir", a surviving indication of Morrison's early intentions for the album. Finally, there is another dabble at soul, "Gypsy Queen". The model is clearly Curtis Mayfield, whose earliest Top 20 hit with the Impressions was "Gypsy Woman", although the structure of the song recalls the smash hit that was written and produced by Mayfield's rival Smokey Robinson, for the Temptations – "My Girl".

Three years later Morrison dismissed *His Band and the Street Choir*: "I really don't think that album is anything much. There really isn't anything I'm saying there." What he was saying, if anything, was that he had a skill that he held in little regard – if he wanted to, he could turn out three hits in a year. But what he'd rather do was be a rural recluse for a while.

SEVEN

West from Woodstock

The music that Morrison continued to write in Woodstock, exploring his desire for peace, quiet and family life in the countryside, seems ironic given the changes that were taking place in his circumstances at the time. For a start he felt forced out of Woodstock by a combination of pressures.

This was an inevitable result of the festival that was tagged with the identity of his village, even though it took place many miles away. "Woodstock was getting to be such a heavy number," he said. "When I first went, people were moving there to get away from the scene – and then Woodstock itself started being the scene. They made a movie called *Woodstock* and it wasn't even in Woodstock. It was 60 miles away. Another myth, you know? Everybody and his uncle started showing up at the bus station…"

The second was that Morrison's wife Janet hankered after more familiar territory. As John Platania said: "He didn't want to leave but Janet wanted to move out west." And the third was that the lease on his Woodstock home was going to run out anyway, and the owner had indicated that he wanted to move back in. It all pointed to a move, and a move to the West Coast. Morrison was often there anyway, commuting across the continent to work with Robbie Robertson. The track "4% Pantomime", which was included on The Band's 1971 album *Cahoots*, was the only public result, however. Yet another factor was that relations with his then manager, Mary Martin, were deteriorating.

Among Morrison's farewells to the East Coast were a number of performances at the Fillmore East in New York, but they were sadly concluded with a rambling and slurred display by Morrison of the type to which he is occasionally prone to descend. Morrison totally lost the plot during a rendition of a rapturously received "Cyprus Avenue". After an embarrassing silence in mid-song he announced: "I'm extremely wasted and I'm pouring spaghetti bolognese over you." Not surprisingly, the audience grew progressively more restless at his antics, to which he responded: "Someone here's talking… You wanna shut up and watch us work, or what?"

With a nucleus of demonstration tracks recorded in Woodstock, and an idea of making a country-and-western album, Morrison and his family settled in Marin County, north of San Francisco, in April 1971. In the wake of such artists as the Byrds, Gram Parsons, Creedence Clearwater Revival and the Bob Dylan of *Nashville Skyline*, country music was at last being recognised by rock musicians as being at the root of their music as surely as was the blues. An awakened interest in country coincided with Morrison's current concerns – of finding rural peace and contentment – and it may be that the fact that the album didn't turn out this way was connected with the elusiveness of such happiness.

The Caledonia Soul Orchestra, which was arguably the finest backing group of Morrison's career, was to grow out of the pool of *Tupelo Honey* musicians, and Morrison confirms that he found them in a hurry. "When I went on the West Coast these people [the musicians he had been working with in Woodstock] weren't that available so I had to virtually put a completely new band together overnight to do this next record. So it was a very tough period. I didn't want to change my band but if I wanted to get into the studio I had to ring up and get somebody. That was the predicament I was in. I hooked up with that band for the live album [*It's Too Late to Stop Now*]. They were good."

The musicians assembled for sessions in San Francisco, to take place at Wally Heider's studio, were a careful mixture of new names and familiar collaborators. They included the Modern Jazz Quartet's drummer Connie Kay, who had contributed so tellingly to half of the *Astral Weeks* project, and Gary Malabar, the drummer who had played on *Moondance,,* as well as saxophone player Jack Schroer from Morrison's previous band. Guitarist Ronnie Montrose, who was later to front his own outfit Montrose, came in with bass player Bill Church, a third drummer Rick Shlosser, keyboard player Mark Jordan, trumpeter Luis Gasca, flautists "Boots" Houston and Bruce Royston, and pedal-steel player John McFee, of country-rock band Clover. On organ, and credited as co-producer alongside Morrison, was Ted Templeman, formerly of vocal group Harper's Bizarre. They had enjoyed a brief chart career on Warner Brothers in 1967, notably with their first hit, a version of Paul Simon's "The 59th Street Bridge Song (Feelin' Groovy)".

Templeman later worked as producer with Little Feat and the Doobie Brothers, and those relationships were no doubt happier than that with Morrison. "Ted Templeman I gave co-production credit," Morrison said. "In retrospect I don't know if it was such a good idea. Because he dumped on me later on. No reason. I gave him co-production credit for doing the things I didn't want to do. Making sure it was mixed. I'd send him the tapes back and tell him how I wanted it mixed. I could be anywhere, like on holiday, and I'd ring up and tell him I wanted it mixed like this. He'd go in with the engineer and mix it…" Templeman, however, was to survive in this role for the following album, *Saint Dominic's Preview* and was back again for 1974's live set *It's Too Late to Stop Now*. Never again, however. Given Morrison's condescending and insulting point of view, Templeman's considered verdict is understandable: "I'd never work with Van Morrison again as long as I live, even if he offered me $2 million in cash. I aged ten years producing three of his albums."

Most of the band that Morrison assembled were seasoned West Coast sessionmen. When the veteran rock'n'roll guitarist Link Wray revived his career in 1973, for example, recording his Polydor album *Be What You Want To* at the same studio, Shlosser and Schroer were on hand, and Mark Jordan played with Shlosser on the following album *The Link Wray Rumble*. Coincidentally, on the liner note to this album Pete Townshend wrote of his hero Wray, "He is sounding like a cross between Jagger and Van Morrison."

When he was not recording, Morrison was usually content to stay at home, attempting to make real the theme of starting afresh in the country, the thread running through the *Tupelo Honey* tracks. As for Janet Planet – well, Morrison observes in the song "Old, Old Woodstock" that "my woman's waiting by the kitchen door." She maintained her acting aspirations, and received occasional offers, but Morrison discouraged her, preferring a politically incorrect vision of domestic life.

It is impossible not to sense the frustration in comments that were made by Janet Planet at this time. "He doesn't like a lot of people around... Really he is a recluse... We never go out anywhere, we don't go to parties... We have an incredibly quiet life and going on the road is the only excitement we have..." But Morrison seemed unaware of her unease, boredom even. At exactly the same time, he was enthusing about the atmosphere on the West Coast: "The vibes here are very similar to the ones in Belfast when I was first working in bands there."

The theme of rural bliss was emphasised by the choice of cover photo for *Tupelo Honey*. Janet rides a white horse, with Morrison walking alongside holding the bridle, as they move through a sun-dappled woodland glade. "The picture was taken at a stable and I didn't live there," said Morrison. "We just went there and took the picture and split. A lot of people seem to think that album covers are your life or something." This is a strange and somewhat churlish observation. Whether or not the horse, or the sun-dappled glade for that matter, actually belonged to Morrison or not is of course

Left: Of all the artists in George Morrison's record collection, the one most frequently cited by his son as an influence is Huddie "Leadbelly" Ledbetter (1889-1949).

Above: Woody Guthrie (1912-1967), writer of such songs as "This Land Is Your Land", laid the basis for the American folk revival that inspired Morrison's generation.

Left: When Muddy Waters (1915-1983) moved north from Mississippi in 1943 he heralded the golden age of Chicago blues that inspired Them and other British r'n'b bands of the early 1960s.

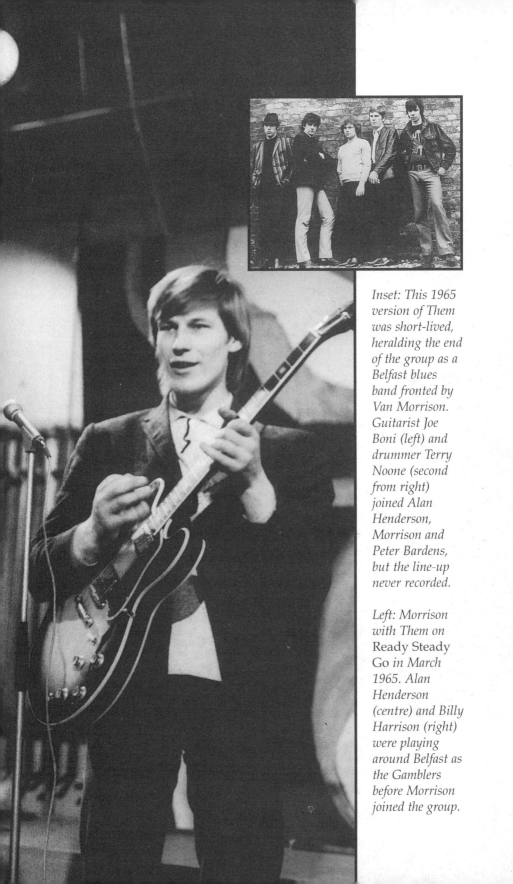

Inset: This 1965 version of Them was short-lived, heralding the end of the group as a Belfast blues band fronted by Van Morrison. Guitarist Joe Boni (left) and drummer Terry Noone (second from right) joined Alan Henderson, Morrison and Peter Bardens, but the line-up never recorded.

Left: Morrison with Them on Ready Steady Go in March 1965. Alan Henderson (centre) and Billy Harrison (right) were playing around Belfast as the Gamblers before Morrison joined the group.

Above: In the final days of Them, Morrison met Californian actress Janet Planet and they were married in 1968.

Opposite: Morrison found domestic contentment, if not dress sense, in Woodstock with Janet Planet.

Right: When Woodstock became too crowded, Morrison looked for peace and quiet in California.

Inset: In 1974 Morrison played Europe with the Caledonia Soul Orchestra, which was then at its peak.

Left: Later in 1974, during his first tour since disbanding the Caledonia Soul Orchestra, Morrison played the Knebworth Festival.

Left: Morrison's first professional jobs in music were as a saxophonist, and he has returned to the instrument throughout his career.

Opposite above: In November 1976 The Band called it a day with The Last Waltz, *a party captured on film by Martin Scorsese. Among those at the party were (from left) Dr John, Joni Mitchell, Neil Young, Rick Danko, Van Morrison, Bob Dylan and Robbie Robertson.*

Opposite below: Morrison getting deep into the music at London's Hammersmith Odeon in 1979.

Left: Morrison was an unexpected guest in 1982 at a Somerset village wedding reception, which led to his concert at St Mary's Church in Stogumber in 1990.

Left: In 1989, Morrison, in partnership with Cliff Richard, enjoyed his only British Number One with "Whenever God Shines His Light".

Right: A backstage party at the Hammersmith Odeon in 1989 saw Morrison in the company of perennial political candidate Screaming Lord Sutch, Queen's Brian May and John Lodge of the Moody Blues.

STOGUMBER FLOWER ROTA

December 31st)
January   7th) Mrs D. Lewis   January 14th) Dried Flower
                                         to   ) Arrangements *
                                    February 25th)

*For further information ple   otice in the magazine.

MONKSILVER FLO

January 7th - Mrs Barron
        14th - Mrs Yeo

NETTLEC

January 6th - Mrs K. Cook
        13th - Mrs N. Cope

B
JANUARY
Mon. 1st : 10.00 to 12 n
            in the Drak
Tue. 2nd : 2.30 pm Art
            Williton Br
Wed. 3rd : 11.00 am Ho
Mon. 8th : 12 noon S.L
             7.30 pm Wa
Tue. 9th : 8.30 am De
             7.30 pm M
            Society m
Thu. 11th : 7.30 pm At Home, Mill
Sun. 14th : Plough Sunday
Mon. 15th : 7.30 pm Stogumber PCC meets in the Drake Room
Tue. 16th : Monthly Meeting - Talk & Slides by Mr Baker
Wed. 17th : Van Morrison in Concert, Stogumber Church, SOLD OUT
Thu. 18th : 7.30 pm Poetry Reading at Kingswood Farm (Music
            Festival funds). All welcome.
Fri. 19th)
Sat. 20th) "Bishop in Mission"
Sun. 21st) See magazine entry under this heading
Sat. 20th : Bell Ringers Meeting and Tea
Mon. 22nd : 2.30 pm Rector to talk to TocH, Taunton Branch
             7.30 pm Men's Meeting Point at Rectory
             7.30 pm Village Hall Committee Meeting,
            Stogumber Village Hall
Tue. 23rd : 7.30 pm Women's Fellowship meets at the Rectory
Wed. 24th : Nettlecombe P.C.C. Meeting.

Opposite: The Stogumber church calendar for January 1990 included a slide lecture, the flower rota, bell ringing – and a performance by one of the world's most celebrated musicians.

Opposite inset: Van Morrison performing at St Mary's Church, Stogumber, Somerset.

Above: The collaboration with Georgie Fame gave new impetus to Morrison's career in the late 1980s.

Centre right: In March 1990 Morrison met up with one of his heroes at a television recording: Mose Allison was also the biggest influence on the style of Morrison's collaborator Georgie Fame.

Right: In the USA, London, Ireland, even Greece, Morrison's path has often crossed that of Bob Dylan.

Inset: Letting it all hang out: in the 1990s Morrison has swung from jazz through soul and r'n'b to the blues. And so it made perfect sense that in mid-1996 he should team up with the man who made that fusion possible, Ray Charles.

Right: The dark suit, the hat, the shades: Morrison performing at the Brit Awards in 1994.

Opposite above: Mutual respect: at many times in his career, Morrison has recorded and performed with John Lee Hooker, who cut his own version of "TB Sheets".

Morrison and fiancée Michelle Rocca at the 1995 Ivor Novello Awards.

On 1 December 1995, Morrison played an open-air concert at Belfast's City Hall as part of the welcome laid on by his home town to American President Bill Clinton.

irrelevant. Its deliberate choice as the image to package the album, with the artist's approval, is not: it is in keeping with his songs; it reinforces his chosen theme.

Morrison was later to reject the album, as well as the cover art, as a disappointment. It is far better than that, in spite of the proprietorial attitude towards his wife that the singer seems to feel is part of country life: "You are my sunshine, I am your guiding light," he sings. And yet this awkward line is buried in the beautiful love song "You're My Woman"; a melodic number that builds confidently, a six-minute slab of white soul.

"Wild Night" launches the collection in fast, catchy style, and the deliberately archaic, richly reverberating guitar riff that waltzes through "(Straight to Your Heart) Like a Cannonball" is instantly attractive. The reflective, affectionate sentiments of "Old, Old Woodstock" take on an added layer of meaning, given that Morrison was soon to leave town, but the theme is extended in the next song, with its self-explanatory title "Starting a New Life". The style of this song is reminiscent more of British country-rock than the American original – Ronnie Lane's Slim Chance, say, or McGuinness-Flint.

The soul mood of "You're My Woman" is continued in the ravishing title track, as mellifluously performed as that title demands. "She's as sweet as Tupelo honey," sings Morrison, as if auditioning for a job fronting the Temptations. The country waltz "I Wanna Roo You (Scottish Derivative)" returns to the theme that, impertinently no doubt, one feels must have gone some way towards explaining the impending failure of Morrison's marriage. "You in the kitchen… I'm in the parlour playing my old guitar." And dinner is on the table right on time, no doubt. The song does have charms, though, in particular in the way it evokes the contrast that John Keats described so erotically in "The Eve of St Agnes", between sensual warmth inside and freezing cold without.

"I want you to be around when that evening sun goes down," Morrison insists in the next song, "When That Evening Sun Goes Down". His interpretation of domestic bliss is continued in a song whose style owes something to Dylan's *Nashville Skyline* album. *Tupelo Honey* ends with a long, two-tempo work-out that Morrison has said was written with "Janis Joplin or something" in mind, "Moonshine Whiskey". There's a strange, perhaps deliberate, collision of urban and rural imagery in the declared intention to "promenade down funky Broadway 'til the cows come home," and there's a slow, ethereal waltz passage in mid-song, with John McFee's steel guitar evoking a smoky vision of a redneck bar in silent slow-motion.

"Wild Night" and "Tupelo Honey" were modest single hits and the album rose as high as 27 in the *Billboard* chart – enough to maintain the faith of Morrison's record company, who then saw the album establish itself as a steady "catalogue" seller, giving it welcome commercial life beyond the immediate period of its release. It spawned cover versions, too: Richie Havens picked up on the title track, Martha Reeves and the Vandellas recorded "Wild Night" and "I Wanna Roo You" was covered by Dusty Springfield, Jackie deShannon and Goldie Hawn. None, however, troubled the Hot 100.

Although the album has many rewards for the listener, the disjointed nature of the project meant that Morrison was dissatisfied with it. "I wasn't very happy with *Tupelo Honey*," he said. "It consisted of songs that were left over from before and that they'd finally gotten round to using. It wasn't really fresh. It was a whole bunch of songs that had been hanging around for a while. I was really trying to make a country-and-western album…"

In September 1971, as "Wild Night" was released as a single with an alternate take of "When That Evening Sun Goes Down" as the B-side, Morrison was back in Wally Heider's studio for two days recording with his hero John Lee Hooker, sessions that produced *Never Get Out of These Blues Alive* and *Going Down*. This was also the month when Morrison performed before an invited audience of 200 in Pacific High Studios, San Francisco, a gig that was taped for radio transmission and later widely bootlegged. Morrison, on top form, ranged back over his career, introduced material from the new album, broke into such old war-horses as "Que Sera, Sera" and "Buona Sera, Senorita", covered Dylan's "Just Like a Woman" and revived one or two rock'n'roll and soul classics. Rarely in live performance has he explored so many aspects of his versatility.

His taste for performing was being revived by impromptu appearances at a club five miles away from his home, The Lion's Share, initially with folk veteran Rambling Jack Elliott, and he developed a habit of being added, unannounced and at the last minute, to already-advertised concerts. Morrison has often struggled under the weight of expectation that his audiences tend to bring to his performances. By being allowed to avoid the audience's expectations, he worked his way back into concert shape.

"I've got a bad taste in my mouth for *Street Choir* and *Tupelo Honey*." Anyone who shared the artist's reservations about these albums knew, as soon as the next album was released in July 1972, that the dip on the creative graph – if there was indeed one – had only been temporary. *Saint Dominic's Preview* is included among his finest works, and in the wake of enthusiastic reviews proved to be his biggest seller at that point.

Those involved included Kay, playing on "Listen to the Lion" and probably feeling that not much had changed since the *Astral Weeks* date, Malabar, Schroer, Church, Shlosser, Jordan, Houston and McFee from the *Tupelo Honey* sessions, augmented by bassist Leroy Vinegar on the final cut "Almost Independence Day", sax player Jules Broussard, pianist Mark Naftalin and guitarist Doug Messenger, trombonist Pat O'Hara and Moog man Bernie Krause, who added a distinctive dub to "Almost Independence Day". Pianist Tom Salisbury also arranged the three tracks he was involved in, including the magnificent title song, while Ronnie Montrose and Janet Planet were among the backing vocalists.

Only "Gypsy", reminiscent in mood of "Caravan", seems less than prime Morrison. The exuberant scat phrase kicking off the first track, "Jackie Wilson Said (I'm in Heaven When You Smile)", hotly pursued by a confident, big band r'n'b arrangement, promises well. "That came with just voice and guitar first... I was just singing the sax riff." Jackie Wilson was one of the most technically ambitious of soul/r'n'b singers, who at the time of Morrison's tribute was just coming to the end of a remarkable 15-year run in the pop charts, and so Morrison's admiration for him makes perfect sense. In 1975 Wilson suffered a massive heart attack while on stage, and spent the last nine years of his life in a coma, but by the time of the tragedy his place at the very top of the commercial r'n'b heap was secure.

Another hero, this time unstated, is evoked by the piano-led blues "I Will Be There" – the spirit of Ray Charlesloooms large in the song. This is followed by the album's longest and most ambitious cut, "Listen to the Lion", a poem to the creative and intuitive spirit: "I shall search my very soul for the lion inside of me." Morrison's use of varying vocal dynamics, from meditative musing to the full-throated roar of the lion, is an uplifting experience. In the song Morrison journeys in search of a Caledonian heritage, buried somewhere deep in ancient Scotland.

The dynamic tension of the song, a sure sign of Morrison's confidence in his vocal technique, also illuminates "Saint Dominic's Preview", with its churchy piano/guitar/bass figures and its mysterious, evocative lyrics. "Redwood Tree" is a charming if somewhat folksy reminder of Morrison's interest in country music at the time, while the album ends with the second epic track, "Almost Independence Day". The structure evokes the *Astral Weeks* songs, pinned as it is to some repeated guitar chords – with Morrison opting for the richness of a 12-string to accompany his bluesy, improvised humming. Further distinction is given to the song by the background foghorn rumble of the Moog, supporting Morrison's romantic description of the lights on San Francisco bay.

Two interviews that were granted by Morrison in support of this album illustrate his extraordinary attitude towards the press. John Grissim Jr, writing in the influential journal that had always been supportive of Morrison, *Rolling Stone*, quoted Morrison's story of how the album's title track had been inspired. He had had an image of a church called Saint Dominic's, where a mass for peace in Northern Ireland was taking place. He then opened a newspaper and saw that such a mass was indeed to take place – at a Saint Dominic's church in San Francisco. "Totally blew me out," he said. Thus the song took shape.

By the time he came to be interviewed by John Tobler of *ZigZag* magazine, Morrison had decided that Grissim had misrepresented what he said. "He said I had a dream about a mass in church. I didn't have a dream..." And on he ranted. The only problem with this is that, in order to support his belief that he is always being misquoted by the press, Morrison himself had to misquote the *Rolling Stone* piece – it makes no reference to a dream! Grissim's account, with its quotes from Morrison, actually tallies with the one Morrison gave to Tobler "to put the record straight"!

Hard Nose the Highway, 1973's addition to the steadily growing Morrison catalogue, was recorded amid this continuing period of professional and personal changes. He escaped them to a degree by dabbling as a disc jockey for a while, on his local San Rafael station KTIM. Most importantly, Janet Planet had had enough of the reclusive life, and confirmed that her husband "was difficult to live with". She moved out, began divorce proceedings, sought custody of their daughter Shana and was looking for financial recompense for supporting him emotionally during the time that his career was being so successfully established.

On a professional level, Morrison was acquiring additions to his "Caledonia" empire, following the decision to manage himself and to employ an associate on a monthly wage. Stephen Pillster, who had managed Dan Hicks and His Hot Licks, was the man contracted to look after Morrison's day-to-day business. Most significantly, Morrison commissioned the construction of a 16-track studio, Caledonia Studios, at his home. This increased his control over his recorded music but inevitably made him even more of a recluse, relieved even of the need to commute to San Francisco when working on an album. As for the musicians around him, the Caledonia Soul Orchestra was taking permanent shape. "It was a combination [of musicians who had worked with him before and new ones]. I brought the piano player in. He actually moved there. Jeff Labes." Labes was a crucial element in the Soul Orchestra sound.

Partly in response to Morrison's personal upheavals, his parents moved from Belfast to California. He acquired a record shop for them in Fairfax, christened Caledonia Records, and George and Violet were installed as proprietors. The sign outside the shop, a little chunk of rock history, is now owned by a Scandinavian collector.

Hard Nose the Highway was released in July 1973. Overall it is somewhat disjointed and more of a holding operation than a confident stride forward. It is curious, for example, that the very first song not written by Morrison himself that he recorded during his solo career, Joe Raposo's "Bein' Green", was written for Kermit the Frog, puppet star of the children's TV series *Sesame Street*. In Kermit's adenoidal treatment it was quite an affecting, reflective piece of melancholic whimsy with vague environmental import. It may be an over-literal response, but Morrison isn't green, let alone is he a little felt frog. This makes it hard to appreciate the choice of this above all other songs as his first official "cover version". Morrison, on the other hand, was attracted to it as a "statement that you don't have to be flamboyant". Morrison had originally intended to use the song on the album that became *Saint Dominic's Preview*, and it had clearly been in his mind for some time.

The album ends pleasantly with Morrison's arrangement of the Scottish song usually known as "Wild Mountain Thyme", here called "Purple Heather", another sign of his search for Caledonian identity. One has reservations, however, about three other songs – all of them, with "Bein' Green" and "Purple Heather", making up the back end of the collection. "Wild Children", a song about Morrison's generation of baby boomers, begins encouragingly with a simple image that skilfully encapsulates a moment in British history, "…1945, when all the soldiers came marching home, love looks in their eye." But it then gets little further than listing Tennessee Williams, Marlon Brando, Rod Steiger and James Dean as 1950s icons.

"The Great Deception" seems to be some sort of social satire, not Morrison's strong suit. He rails against "plastic revolutionaries", a "world of lies" and rich rock'n'roll singers. He points out that Rembrandt was a great painter who sometimes couldn't afford brushes, an irony revealed in the sketchiest history of art. He hints at Hollywood shenanigans and castigates the hippies who would happily, he claims, steal your eyeballs. "Say son, kid, do you want your eyeballs back?" has none of the force of Dylan's contemptuous "here's your throat back, thanks for the loan," from "Ballad of a Thin Man". Indeed, Morrison has been uncharacteristically defensive about this song. "Just picking things up out of the air. You have to perform a song so it can sound like you're saying something when you're performing it. But it's entertainment. Making records, it's filling space. You mustn't take it all that seriously."

Finally, while considering the album's disappointments, the cosy "Autumn Song", with its falling leaves, coal on the fire and roasting chestnuts, is either a pastiche of the whole genre of seasonal easy-listening, in which case it lacks bite, or else it's an addition to the genre, in which case it's a minor example.

But, but… this is also the album that starts with the atmospheric "Snow in San Anselmo", the assured smooth soul of "Warm Love" and the tough waltz "Hard Nose the Highway", between them worth the price. The first, with the eerie contributions of the Oakland Symphony Chamber Chorus, is the antithesis of "Autumn Song". Far from mining a familiar seam of sleigh bells and church bells, it creates its atmosphere out of something that "hadn't happened in over 30 years" – snow doesn't come often to San Anselmo, and so is replete with rare mystery.

Though Morrison elects to enunciate the words of "Warm Love" with a controlled staccato technique, rather than with the smooth elisions that are associated with soft soul music, its guitar figures and mood evoke, as he puts it, "sort of a Motown feel, Curtis Mayfield". "Hard Nose the Highway" explores images of professionalism, something that has always been important to Morrison in his work. "Frank Sinatra sings against Nelson Riddle Strings/Then takes a vacation," is the epitome of no-nonsense skill, compared to laid-back Marin County or the hustling record business. The images are ill-defined and elusive, but they are powerful nonetheless. So, even a Morrison album with a number of disappointments has huge compensations.

The next two years, 1973–74, provided the biggest contrast of Morrison's career to date. With the magnificent Caledonia Soul Orchestra on song he came of age as a magnetic stage performer, culminating in the release of the double set *It's Too Late to Stop Now*, one of the most impressive of all attempts to squeeze the stage excitement of a rock performer on to vinyl. But eight months after its release came the next studio album, *Veedon Fleece*, sad evidence of the creative exhaustion that was to lead to a lengthy hiatus in Morrison's public career.

Early in 1973 Morrison embarked on a lengthy tour, initially in the USA. The Caledonia Soul Orchestra now consisted of Jeff Labes on keyboards, who also scored the string arrangements; longtime collaborator Jack Schroer on saxophones, providing the horn charts; bass player David Hayes and drummer Dahaud Shaar; guitarist John Platania and trumpeter Bill Atwood. The icing on the cake was a stunning string quintet – Nathan Rubin, Tim Kovatch, Tom Halpin, Nancy Ellis and Terry Adams.

John Platania recalls: "I would say that that tour represented the height of his confidence as a performer. Up until then it was often touch and go as to whether he'd go on stage." Morrison's new-found enthusiasm for stage work also gave him much-needed respite from his domestic troubles, with two-year-old daughter Shana at the centre of a custody battle. When promoting the resulting album a year later, Morrison was clearly as happy with the touring experience as were the critics and fans, and he had spent an entire year on and off the road – in America, Europe and back in America once more.

"I am getting more into performing," he said. "It's incredible. When I played Carnegie Hall in the fall something just happened. All of a sudden I felt like 'you're back into performing,' and it just happened like that… A lot of times in the past I've done gigs and it was rough to get through them. But now the combination seems to be right and it's been clicking a lot."

The European leg of the tour culminated in two nights at the Rainbow Theatre in Finsbury Park, North London, on 23 and 24 July. This magnificent art deco movie house was, all too briefly, the most humane of London's bigger venues and is a sad loss to the capital's rock scene: after many years of idleness it was bought in 1995 by a religious sect. Those lucky enough to attend all the big concerts in its 1970s heyday recall Van Morrison's visit above all. It should be remembered that, at this time, he was still something of a cult performer in mainland Britain, remembered as a rasping singer during the beat boom and as creator of the underground classic *Astral Weeks*. His subsequent chart successes had been limited to the USA. Two nights in London was rightly considered sufficient to cater for his potential audience.

His stage act did not, of course, consist of jokes, urbane monologues, anecdotal introductions or even a smile. The attraction consisted entirely of a great singer, on good form, fronting a dynamic band. When, towards the end, he started high-kicking in unison with the drum rimshots, it came as a huge and amusing surprise: he'd barely moved before that point.

The album was put together from tapes made at the starting point, Los Angeles' Troubadour, together with the Rainbow in London and the Santa Monica Civic. In the autumn, Morrison had travelled around Ireland in a hired car and the trip produced songs for *Veedon Fleece*. But, and this was inevitably a controversial decision, he did not play any gigs. This slight was not taken lightly, either north or south of the border, and the problem was compounded by one of Morrison's notorious interviews – rude, uncooperative and graceless – on Irish television.

However, what survives such local controversy (and Ireland continues to embrace its truculent, unreliable son) is the magnificent album. The bright, brassy r'n'b of "Ain't Nothing You Can Do" leads to "Warm Love", after which the strings are introduced for "Into the Mystic". The straightforward, fast-tempo r'n'b of "These Dreams of You" raises the temperature once more, and what follows is Morrison's at-this-point reflection of his career and his heroes. "Wild Children" is an improvement on the album version, with the ensemble's playing more important than the thin lyric, and the string quintet adds to "Listen to the Lion" while Morrison, having had time to grow into the song, plays around with its implications. The last four tracks are an intriguing summary of his career – the heritage trail begins with "Here Comes the Night", followed by the "Gloria" anthem, a dynamically varied workout on "Caravan" and a fresh look at "Cyprus Avenue". "Turn it on" shouts someone from the audience, and Morrison's reaction is for once good-natured: "It's turned on already!" With a heartfelt "It's too late to stop now!" – he stops. On top form.

By the time the record was released, however, Morrison had disbanded the Caledonia Soul Orchestra.

By late 1973 Morrison was back in California, working on the songs for *Veedon Fleece*, inspired by his Irish holiday. This coincided with the overdue announcement that he would be playing in Dublin in March 1974, as well as returning to mainland Britain. When he left for these dates only David Hayes and Dahaud Shaar survived from the Soul Orchestra: they were augmented by guitarist Ralph Walsh, replacing Platania, sax-player James Rothermel, in for the long-serving Schroer, and James Trumbo, replacing Jeff Labes. The new outfit traded under the name of the Caledonia Soul Express.

If the projected gigs in Dublin had been a conscious attempt to placate public opinion on the island, then the worst possible thing happened: Morrison contracted a virulent bout of flu as soon as he arrived in London to begin the tour. His record company and promotor Harvey Goldsmith were alarmed at how a "no show" would be interpreted. As far as Dublin was concerned the solution was probably the only possible compromise – Morrison fulfilled the commitment, but in a sadly debilitated condition. He still had no plans to play in his home town, then at the height of the "Troubles", but it is a sad irony that, at the very time when he was re-embracing his heritage, he was forced to put in below-par performances 100 miles to the south.

Back in California, true to form, Morrison dispensed with the services of both his assistant Pillster and the Express, contenting himself once more with low-key performances at The Lion's Share club. When he reappeared in Europe in the summer, for a tour that included the festivals at Montreux in Switzerland and Knebworth in England, he recruited keyboard player Pete Wingfield, Motown bass player Jerome Rimson and the drummer from Crosby, Stills, Nash and Young, Dallas Taylor. After Montreux Taylor left, to be replaced by Peter van Hooke. This band then played a substantial North American tour, and the smaller unit allowed Morrison to be more improvisational in his attitude to the set. As Wingfield recalled: "Sometimes Van would suddenly decide he didn't want to play the set we'd worked out, and he'd launch into a number he'd just written and which we'd never heard… Van controlled everything with hand signals."

Veedon Fleece was released in October 1974. Its fascination lies in Morrison's attempt to marry his sense of Irish identity, history, mythology and music with his growing interest in philosophy and "alternative" systems of thought, therapy and lifestyle. He sings of a complex hero, Linden Arden, of the streets of Arklow and country fairs, and of an imagined pilgrimage in search of the Veedon fleece, whatever that might be. Moving away from the r'n'b base of recent work, he now coloured his songs with the sounds of Irish traditional music.

That said, *Veedon Fleece* is an opaque piece of work. Morrison has always tended to think of his voice as part of the horn section, but now form was so dominant over content that, without the assistance of a lyric sheet, following his drift is difficult. His voice swoops into falsetto and sinks to a growl, as virtuoso a performance as ever, but too often the intention remains obscure. The melody line of the soulful waltz "Cul de Sac", for example, begins with a close echo of the classic cheating song by Chips Moman and Dan Penn, "The Dark End of the Street". A cul de sac may well have a dark end, but the reason for the aural reference remains mysterious.

Within such a personal piece of work, marking a distinct change of direction, Morrison was professional enough to bury an obvious choice for a single release; to keep the record company executives happy. "Bulbs" is a pleasant, catchy country ditty, a Dire Straits song before its time, and was indeed Warner Brothers' choice of A-side in all territories.

On completing the North American tour with his trio, Van Morrison went into temporary retirement. He was becoming more interested in exploring spirituality and philosophy, he had writer's block, and he was exhausted. "From 1964 right through to about 1974 it was nothing but work," he explained later. "I'd finish a record, come back from a tour and walk right back into the studio... I was working constantly. Just very intense. Two albums a year plus touring. I had to ring up Warner Brothers and say, "This doesn't work." It can't be two albums a year plus tours. I had to renegotiate my contract at that point. Overworked, overstretched... after *Veedon Fleece* I renegotiated the deal... It was a reaction to doing too much." One might even strengthen his case – he'd been touring, writing and recording sincehe left school at the age of 15. It is a case that may well fail to convince a coalminer or an ambulance driver, but as a creative artist Morrison was undoubtedly feeling in need of seeking nourishment elsewhere. He could no longer bury himself in family life, and so he turned to books, with insatiable curiosity.

He was later to announce "no guru, no method, no teacher". Instead, he looked at various systems, taking anything he wanted from each. The sense of youthful spirituality, of childish ecstasy, echoed back at him from the works of such poets as William Blake and John Donne. It would seem that the rich rewards of the Romantics were to come somewhat later. As for lifestyle philosophies, there were any number of systems to explore, "new age" or time-hallowed, notably Gestalt psychology. At the centre of this is the belief that the human psyche is more than the sum of its parts. From Christianity to Scientology, Morrison looked and learned.

Morrison still went into his studio, on one occasion with Joe Sample of the Crusaders. This led to rumours of a collaboration with the whole band. "There was never a Crusaders session. I don't know why they keep doing this to me. There was one of the Crusaders on the session, that's why. Joe Sample. The sessions didn't really work to my mind."

So after 18 months there was no "product" forthcoming and he agreed to a statement being issued, denying he had retired but confirming he had parked temporarily in a creative siding. He contributed some sax, guitar and harmonica to Bill Wyman's solo album *Stone Alone*. An album called *Mechanical Bliss/Naked in the Jungle* was strongly rumoured, but Morrison later dismissed the results: "We got a few tracks out of it, but it was more or less kind of a blow." The only official result surfaced in July 1977, when the uniquely comic "Mechanical Bliss" was issued as the B-side of "Joyous Sound".

In late spring 1976 he moved back to Britain. Harvey Goldsmith, promoter of his previous tour, was persuaded to become his manager, and Morrison took up residence at the studios owned by Virgin Records at The Manor, in Oxfordshire. The New Orleans legend Mac Rebennack, aka Dr John, who had played with Morrison two years earlier in Amsterdam (see *Amsterdam's Tapes* in the bootleg discography), was flown in as pianist and co-producer. Morrison, two years out of the studio except as proprietor or guest artist, was feeling his way, trying different things – including New Orleans jazz from British disciples the Chris Barber Band. None of Morrison's former musicians had survived his lay-off, and on the finished tracks he was backed by drummer Ollie Brown and bass-player Reggie McBride, guitarist Marlo Hendersen and brass players Jerry Jumonville, Joel Peskin and Mark Underwood. In addition, nine backing vocalists were credited.

By September Morrison was back on the West Coast, where overdubs were added to the results of the Oxfordshire summer. He appeared in the stellar cast at Winterland, in San Francisco, on Thanksgiving Day, when The Band performed *The Last Waltz*, their farewell performance, captured in one of the great rock movies by

Martin Scorsese. Other guests at the party included Joni Mitchell, Neil Diamond, Emmylou Harris, Neil Young, Muddy Waters, Ronnie Hawkins and Morrison's current collaborator Dr John. Morrison overcame an acute attack of stage fright to perform for the first time with Bob Dylan, on "I Shall Be Released", as well as singing his own "Caravan" and a piece of Irish whimsy, "Too Ra Loo Ra Loo Ral", with The Band's Richard Manuel.

Although it was not intended as such – indeed, Morrison was initially a somewhat reluctant participant – the publicity surrounding this nostalgic occasion rebounded favourably on him, since as far as the majority of record buyers were concerned he had simply disappeared from sight and sound.

Morrison returned to Britain in spring 1977 for the release of the Dr John project, his "comeback" album *A Period of Transition*. As with *Veedon Fleece* it had an obvious single, in this case the sprightly r'n'b workout "Joyous Sound", and the Dr John influence was clear, particularly in the swampy "It Fills You Up". There was one strikingly eerie song, a tribute to jazz greats called "The Eternal Kansas City", with its ethereal choir, and the album ended with a big number containing a characteristic Morrison hook – the chorus of "Cold Wind in August" ("shivers up and down my spine") moves through an exhilarating chord sequence.

And yet the album is a disappointment, once you accept that Morrison's unique gifts demand to be judged by the highest standards. Just as *Veedon Fleece* seemed to overstress one of his characteristics – voice as brass instrument – at the expense of coherence, so now another of them, the repetition of a phrase over and over again, leaves one wanting more. More what? Well, more words for a start. We are told repeatedly that "you've got to make it through the world, if you can", a reworking of an old gospel theme; we are advised that "it fills you up" and asked, time and time again, "excuse me, do you know the way to Kansas City?"

After the jaunty relief of "Joyous Sound" comes a song that had been knocking around for some time, "Flamingo's Fly", where everything seems to have been hurled into the mix in the search for a hook, followed by "Heavy Connection", where the repetition consists of "la, la, la, la, la la la". "Cold Wind in August", at least, concludes the set in style, but the comeback kid still seemed a little ring-rusty.

When the question of promoting the album arose, Morrison made the familiar unsatisfactory compromise – he did it, but with ill grace. There was a London press launch with a band consisting of Dr John, guitarist Mick Ronson, drummer Peter van Hooke and bass player Mo Foster, later joined from the audience by such luminaries as former Them keyboard player Peter Bardens and ex-Family singer Roger Chapman. It was a pleasant enough occasion but the record-company wine didn't entirely dispel the feeling that the star of the show wasn't comfortable. What was distinctly uncomfortable, however, was a notorious "non-interview" with Nicky Horne of Capital Radio, London's only commercial music station at the time and an important staging post on the promotional circuit. Morrison seemed determined to try and sabotage the programme, to humiliate Horne on air. The disc jockey's professionalism prevented him from descending to the level of the ill-mannered, graceless star.

EIGHT

On a New Wavelength

For the remainder of 1977 and into the following year, Morrison was recording his next album, *Wavelength*, once again at The Manor in Oxfordshire. The nucleus of the studio band consisted of Herbie Armstrong, from the Belfast days, on rhythm guitars, Bobby Tench on lead guitar, Peter Bardens and Peter van Hooke, surviving from recent collaborations, with Mickey Feat playing bass. Bassist Kuma deputised on two tracks, "Santa Fe/Beautiful Obsession" and "Take It Where You Find It", while the latter track, together with "Kingdom Hall" and "Venice USA", was decorated with contributions on organ, synthesiser and accordion by The Band's Garth Hudson. "Take It Where You Find It" also features Mitch Dalton on Spanish guitar, and Morrison himself roamed from saxophones to keyboards to guitars.

In late summer the band embarked on a long tour of the USA to coincide with the release of the album, which contained a surprise before buyers had even put the record on the turntable. The cover photograph, a sepia-washed monochrome portrait of Morrison taken from a session by Norman Seeff, showed a relaxed singer crisply attired in black T-shirt and white jeans, with carefully attended hairstyle and even the hint of a smile – a smile captured in all its rarity on other pictures from the photo shoot. Although Morrison had managed to look similarly cheerful for one of the 15 snaps used on the cover of *A Period of Transition*, the concern about image had clearly been minimal and the photographs look awkward. Now, however briefly, Morrison amused himself by promoting a rock-star look.

In the preparation for the album there had been various management upheavals. Harvey Goldsmith had contracted the former
manager of the Doors, Bill Siddons, to keep an eye on Morrison's
American interests, an experiment that soon resulted in Morrison
parting company with both of them in favour of the representation
offered by Bill Graham Management on the West Coast.

Whatever transition period had been marked by the previous
record now appeared to be over: *Wavelength* is a more satisfying set
overall and Morrison supported it by touring throughout the
autumn. At this distance, however, musical reservations may
apply to the early synthesiser experiments that noodle away
through the title track, an otherwise striking testament to the power
of music on the radio and therefore an obvious choice of single,
backed by the instantly attractive, easy swing of "Checkin' It Out".
Whereas "Wavelength" looks back to Morrison's earliest musical
curiosity in exploring the airwaves, "Checkin' It Out" advises us
to "get into it like a meditation", a nod to the singer's growing explorations of systems of thought and belief.

The album starts strongly with the exuberant "Kingdom Hall",
featuring Morrison at his big-brass best, no doubt with his mother's
association with the Jehovah's Witnesses in mind. Three weaker
numbers are dismissed early on: "Natalia" is enlivened by Tench's
guitar phrases but it soon resolves into one of Morrison's repetitive
choruses, "na, na, na... "; "Venice USA", with its relaxed Bo
Diddley beat, promises well by setting up a story – "Found myself
in a restaurant in Venice" – but it soon dissolves into "dum diddly
dum dum"; while on "Lifetimes", most unusually, Morrison's voice
seems somewhat strained.

No such reservations apply to "Santa Fe" – the first song on a
Morrison album to be credited as a collaboration – with Jackie
DeShannon. She had sung back-up on *Hard Nose the Highway,* and
Morrison had produced her around that time, but her reputation

had been established during the early 1960s with two hits that had been successfully covered by the Searchers, "Needles and Pins" and "When You Walk in the Room". As a singer she made the Top 10 twice, with Burt Bacharach's "What the World Needs Now Is Love" and her own "Put a Little Love in your Heart". With Morrison, her influence resulted in a straightforwardly affecting song with a country feel, the most "natural" track on the album and one of its highlights. It elides into Morrison's own intriguing "Beautiful Obsession", an inarticulate speech of the heart ending with the exhortation "Let the cowboy ride!"

"Hungry for Your Love" shows Morrison's talent, when he wishes to display it, for writing simple, unpretentious protestations of love, although once again those who feel that the case for the synthesiser had yet to be made might object to its somewhat flatulent intrusions. The album finishes stylishly with a "big" number, "Take It Where You Find It", in which Morrison sings of "lost dreams and found dreams in America", a fascinating line that seems to speak simultaneously of his own life and of the immigrant experience.

In an interview at the time, Morrison could have been excusing the fact that he sometimes lapsed into incoherence, or failed to live up to expectations of the lyrical content in his work. Referring specifically to the celebratory feel of "Kingdom Hall", he said: "When I started out I was in dance bands… and I wanted to get back to it… the words become irrelevant because you're in that space. And I feel that way about dancing, it goes beyond words."

In another interview at this time, Morrison gave amusing expression to his belief that he should no more be required to discuss his job than anyone else. "I mean, people who go to work from nine to five, how do they do it? They just get up in the morning and they go to work and they do it. Like, nobody stands with a microphone when they come out of the gate and asks, 'How did you do it today?' I mean, they just do it! It's life… 'How did you work the machine?

Was it different from yesterday? Do you do it better when you wear brown overalls than when you wear green overalls?'"

Later, he was to continue with the theme, revealing a somewhat patronising attitude to his audience. "Yeah… well… writing is just more or less a process where… it's hard to explain it in this context, and I'm not even sure that the people who read these magazines are even interested… I don't know if I'm ready to talk about it… What I'm trying to get at is that music to me is spontaneous, writing is spontaneous and it's all based on not trying to do it, y'know? It's all based on spontaneity, and that's my trip from beginning to end, whether it's writing a song or playing guitar, or a particular chord sequence, or blowing a horn, or whatever it is, it's based on improvisation and spontaneity, right? And that's what I keep on trying to get across in interviews, and it's very hard because the process is beyond words! You know what I'm saying? The process of doing it can't be put in words!"

If Morrison was a footballer, *Wavelength* would provide evidence that he was continuing to make a successful recovery from injury. And the next album, *Into the Music*, was to end the 1970s almost as strongly as the breakthrough album *Moondance* had launched him into them.

The tour promoting *Wavelength*, though, was not without awkwardness. It started well, with Morrison seemingly in buoyant mood, but sound-system problems in New York led to the cancellation of several dates, and the tour limped to a conclusion in Los Angeles. It was followed by a continuation into the UK and Ireland that included gigs in Belfast, Morrison performing there for the first time since his limbo period immediately after dissolving Them. He was filmed revisiting youthful haunts, and was well received in his native city, though throughout the tour he continued his one-man war against the press and all their works. His music was entering a new phase, but his manners were not.

The 1979 album *Into the Music* was largely written in Oxfordshire, where Morrison had recorded his previous two albums, and the spirit of the English countryside walks through many of the songs. He elected to record it, however, back on the West Coast. Herbie Armstrong and Peter van Hooke were still with him, keyboard player Mark Jordan and the Caledonia Soul Orchestra bass player David Hayes returned, and they were tellingly augmented by violinist Toni Marcus, brass players Pee Wee Ellis and Mark Isham, and back-up singer Katie Kissoon. In the 1960s alto saxophonist Ellis had been a member, and for a while leader, of James Brown's backing band the JBs, the most accomplished and influential outfit in the r'n'b/funk field. From 1979 onwards, much of Morrison's music benefited from that influence.

Although it has moments of faltering inspiration, *Into the Music* reflects many of Morrison's already established strengths and concerns, while also making a giant stride towards embracing the form of pantheistic, mystical Christianity that is one of the most rewarding qualities of his music. As such it is a key work in his career. Norman Seeff was again responsible for the cover portrait, this time rinsed in blue, and showing a thoughtful Morrison, presumably playing a guitar although only a hint of shoulder strap is visible, with eyes closed as he journeys "into the music". And it is music produced by "real" instruments, without the synthesised adornments featured in *Wavelength*.

Morrison has often expressed a certain amount of indifference, of contempt even, towards the demands of the charts. This deliberately, and probably wilfully, ignores the fact that his formative contracts on both Bang and Warner Brothers came about because of his perceived skill with the three-minute, radio-friendly single, and that his career has been invigorated and broadened, opportunities opened and bank accounts refreshed, by regular appearances in those vulgar hit listings.

"Bright Side of the Road", an uplifting opening track kicked off by Morrison's harmonica before the piano/brass arrangement boots in, was just such a hit. Apart from playing second guitar to Armstrong on this album, Morrison confines his instrumental contributions to the mouth organ. Although he has demonstrated considerable virtuosity during his recordings and concerts, notably on saxophone and guitar, less so on piano, it is on harmonica that he is a true virtuoso rather than a skilful artisan.

"Full Force Gale", founded on a simple, repeated chord pattern, as are so many of Morrison's strongest songs, is one of Morrison's most uplifting works – indeed, as he tells us, he is "lifted up again by the Lord". But the Lord is not lurking in ancient Hebrew texts, as was the one being discovered at this time by the "born again" Bob Dylan – he is there in the full force gale, he is the lord of nature. This exultant song, which is decorated by Ry Cooder's distinctive slide guitar, is a straightforward expression of Morrison's current spiritual staging post.

"Stepping Out Queen" is more obscure, though distinguished by a keening violin solo, and the difficulty partly arises from Morrison's diction. It seems that the surer the singer is of his message, the clearer is his enunciation, and that he is more prone to chew on his words when he is less confident in the song itself. This also seems true of a later track, "You Make Me Feel So Free", though the message of the title is clear enough, and once again there are musical compensations in David Hayes' bubbling bass pattern and Pee Wee Ellis' saxophone solo.

These songs, though, are separated by two stunning tracks, a panorama of English rather than Celtic heritage, which were inspired by Morrison's Oxfordshire sojourn. The guest performer on both is Robin Williamson, formerly multi-instrumentalist with the Incredible String Band, and, significantly, both a folk musicologist and a disciple of Scientology.

"Troubadours", which is ushered in by Mark Isham's piccolo trumpet, pins Morrison's art to a long tradition of strolling players, giving it historical dignity and social purpose. Before the printed word disseminated everything from the daily news and tittle tattle to the works of philosophy and religion, the troubadours were at the heart of the nation's culture, and Morrison associates himself with them. The jig-like ballad "Rolling Hills", English country music as distinct from that of Ireland or Tennessee, casts Morrison's relationship with God in a different perspective, and in suitably archaic language. "I will do no man no ill among the rolling hills," he avers. If the Wurzels, instead of peddling their hilarious, straw-in-the-hair but well observed version of rural culture, were a serious and spiritual group – Somerset's Chieftains, say – they might sound like this. "Angeliou" is another of Morrison's songs repetitively built around the name of a particular but fictitious woman, and the meditative nature of the piece gives it a mystery missing from, say, "Natalia". Morrison once commented cryptically, with reference to this song: "What is behind all this stuff is the message is not in actual lyrics. The message is getting very, very quiet. When you get really quiet you can actually hear yourself."

"And the Healing Has Begun" is a wonderful piece of work. Morrison's underlying guitar sequence recalls the form of *Astral Weeks* songs, now stressed by a viola figure, and the theme is one of reconciliation, of using past experience to heal rather than divide. In such a line as "we'll walk down the avenues again" we think both of Belfast's Cyprus Avenue and, given Morrison's current themes, of rural rides as well.

The album ends tantalisingly. In taking that most melodic and attractive of ballad standards, "It's All in the Game", as his starting point, Morrison wanders into a meditative piece using the same sequence, "You Know What They're Writing About". "They" must be the sages, or the craftsmen who fashion love ballads – they cannot be the despicable, ignorant, guttersnipe journalists, dedicating their lives to deriding and misquoting Van Morrison. From half-spoken musing to full-throated ecstatic roar, Morrison beckons us into his state of meditation until the improvisation dwindles peacefully away. It is a daring conceit, ending with the quiet Morrison refers to above.

In February 1980 Van Morrison took his current musicians to the south of France to record an album, *Common One*, that marked a sea change in his music. For the first time he failed to give his record company the sop of an obvious single, and having listened to the tapes Mercury accepted that no amount of editing could create one. Furthermore, Morrison moved temporarily beyond his home base in r'n'b, and instead wandered off into the mystic.

Although equipment was shifted wholesale down to Super Bear studios for a week and a half of intensive recording, Morrison still elected to dub and mix on the West Coast. His musicians now consisted of survivors Herbie Armstrong, Peter van Hooke, David Hayes, Pee Wee Ellis and Mark Isham, augmented by keyboard player John Allair and lead guitarist Mick Cox. Jeff Labes also returned to the fold, not as a player but as string-section and choir arranger, while Pee Wee Ellis was given a "musical director/ arranger" credit and engineer Henry Lewy received an extra name-check for production work. This gives the project an unusual air of teamwork, and yet the results must be considered as Morrison's alone.

On the album Morrison lays out his current philosophical agenda, tellingly characterised by Steve Turner, a writer particularly sensitive to Morrison's spiritual qualities, as "the whole New Age smorgasbord". Two of the tracks meander on for more than 15 minutes: one of them, "Summertime in England", simply demonstrates how easily Morrison's cultural baggage can tip over into pretentiousness, while the other, "When Heart is Open", is frankly impossible to listen to.

Ironically, the set opens with a striking, evocative and warming statement of Morrison's pantheism. "Haunts of Ancient Peace" is a key song in his apprehension that the heart of the mystery lies in landscape. He is still on the trail of the new Jerusalem, and as with the *Wavelength* songs on a similar theme it resides in the calm of the English countryside. As he sings the line "when I can't find my feet" the spittle forms around the f-words but the effect is intimate, spontaneous, rather than off-putting. "Be still" he commands quietly as the song comes to an end.

Unfortunately, it is downhill all the way after this, with one extraordinary exception, "Satisfied". In the midst of this frustrating album Morrison – of all people – demonstrates a self-mocking sense of humour. Having kidded us that he's still looking for the holy grail – "Let's go walking up that mountainside" – he abandons the search. "I'm satisfied with my world/'Cause I made it the way it is," he announces, and sits back smugly on his laurels, happily confessing that "Sometimes I think I know where it's at/Other times I'm completely in the dark." A weird song – could it have been recorded last, with Morrison getting in his retaliation first?

"Summertime in England" can only seem insulting to anyone to whom the great poets matter. Morrison, the uneducated reader, reduces them to nothing more than a check list, and it is here that we find the unforgiveable line, "Did you ever hear about Wordsworth and Coleridge?/They were smokin' up in Kendal/By the lakeside." They are joined by William Blake, naturally, by a T S Eliot who must feel strangely out of place, by WB Yeats and James Joyce, and by honorary poets Mahalia Jackson and Jesus. The intent is clear and commendably ambitious: an uplifting pilgrimage into Avalon, to the wellspring of our spirituality. The execution is dire and self-indulgent. And in this context the deliberately earthy intrusion of a lady's "red robe dangling all around your body" seems simply vulgar.

"Wild Honey" is a ponderous love song relieved only by the soaring quality of Morrison's voice, while on "Spirit" he volunteers for a shift manning the Samaritans' switchboard, advising those in the extremities of lonely despair to "Say, help me, angel". This leads to the seemingly endless "When Heart Is Open", the worst song Morrison has ever released. By the time he decides that he wants to go for a walk in the woods and issues the curt instruction to his "darling", "Hand me down my old great coat... hand me down my big boots," the only possible response is, "Fetch 'em yourself." There is a philosophical base to the song, some sort of meditative healing process, but it is larded over in indulgence, and it can thus only remain obscure.

At this time Morrison was still commuting between Oxfordshire and California, putting together the next set of songs. At first he was based in a hotel when in England, but then he came to hear of a house in the nearby village of Stadhampton. The then-owner, Hilary Sanderson, recalls: "He would call directly and ask if the house was free. Sometimes when we weren't going to be away he would come and stay in the house during the daytime and then go back to the hotel. We'd go out to work and he'd move in.

"It was a point at which he was becoming interested in Christianity. He always had a girl with him. Often a different girl. He was terribly shy at first and wouldn't communicate directly. He asked his girlfriend to do it. Unless it was a practical matter of how something worked in the house. He'd quite happily ask about that. My role seemed to be to sort out problems for him.

"He was always searching, inquisitive. I felt that he definitely wanted to go back to his Celtic roots. And he'd get into quite deep discussions about things like Stonehenge. Questions rather than answers. I remember I was always finding scraps of paper with writing on them. Sadly, I never kept them. Later he bought the house from us – I believe he kept it on for about four years." Subsequently,

Morrison made his English base in his old stamping grounds of Notting Hill and Holland Park, in West London.

The girlfriend who left the biggest mark on Morrison's music at this period was Ulla Munch, from Vanlose in Copenhagen. Her influence and that reawakened sense of his Celtic heritage both surfaced on *Beautiful Vision*, the album he was writing when he first came to Stadhampton. Longstanding admirers of his work, wondering if "When Heart Is Open" heralded a terminal decline, or at best that Morrison's thoughts were spiralling way beyond his ability to express them usefully in song, were rewarded with a relaxed, tidy, if largely unexciting, collection of songs.

Additions to Morrison's repertory company of musicians included guitarist Chris Michie, drummer Tom Donlinger and, buried discreetly in the mix, guest star Mark Knopfler. The choice of studio, as it had often been at this stage of his career, was The Record Plant in Sausalito, California, just north of the Golden Gate, even though Morrison was beginning to loosen his ties with the USA.

Overall, the songs combine Celtic imagery, a more straight-ahead version of Christianity than had been previously apparent, and two reflections of his current Danish connection – "Vanlose Stairway", a simple soul song reminiscent in feel to Lloyd Price's "Send Me Some Loving", and the peaceful closing instrumental "Scandinavia". Indeed, peacefulness is the dominant mood, most serenely demonstrated on "Across the Bridge Where Angels Dwell", where the simple unison singing, with Morrison blending in with the choir rather than dominating the vocals, gives the song a hymnal quality. The "bridge", the leap of faith, makes for a more rewarding experience for the listener than that offered a few years earlier by the newly Christian Bob Dylan, who could only shout that he'd seen the light and more fool us if we couldn't as well.

The outstanding song on *Beautiful Vision* is the one that least fits into the general pattern of the album, although maybe Morrison's refreshed Celtic pride prompted memories of old Belfast days – the sprightly "Cleaning Windows" seems totally autobiographical, a rare quality, with its memories of lemonade and Paris buns, packets of five Woodbines, "blowing saxophone on the weekend" and a youthful reading list founded in Zen – the leading English Buddhist Christmas Humphreys and the "beat" writer Jack Kerouac. If Morrison is indeed offering accurate autobiography, and he has indicated that this is so, then his philosophical curiosity predates the rise of Them. The song famously includes that proud blue-collar line "I'm a working man in my prime."

The release of the album was marked by a series of London concerts at the Dominion Theatre, a central venue similar in size to the Rainbow, scene of his triumph ten years earlier. The evenings were opened by an acoustic set by Herbie Armstrong, and once Morrison warmed up he proved to be on top form. Once a decade, it seemed, London was treated to this difficult artist as he should best be remembered. Morrison's live performance at around this stage of his career was to be officially captured on the 1984 album *Live at the Grand Opera House, Belfast*.

The peaceful mood of *Beautiful Vision* is carried over into 1983's *Inarticulate Speech of the Heart*, but the overall effect is dangerously close to being soporific rather than serene. The four lengthy instrumentals that stud the set recall the vogue for "ambient" music, which to the non-convert seems designed to be anodyne and inoffensive, acting as some sort of soothing aural wallpaper. However, "Connswater" and "Celtic Swing" do indeed capture much of the spirit of traditional Irish music. A more daring evocation of this spirit is found in the charming "Irish Heartbeat", in which the Irish folk element is coloured by a melody and a treatment often reminiscent of the southern soul singer Percy Sledge. This is a perfect fit – Sledge is the most country-influenced of the black soul artists, Morrison the most soul-influenced of white singers. Soul blends into a polite

form of r'n'b/funk on "The Street Only Knew Your Name", a welcome change of mood but seemingly out of keeping with Morrison's
current concerns: a different publisher credit hints that maybe it was
written some time earlier. The other significant number, largely
treated as a spoken poem, is "Rave On, John Donne". Although in
part yet another reading list, and full as it is of such tricky lyrical
phrases as "the industrial revolution" and "the atomic and nuclear
age", the song is nonetheless far more effective than the *Common
One* equivalents.

"Special thanks" on the album liner are directed towards L Ron
Hubbard, founder of the Church of Scientology, based in East
Grinstead near London. Subsequently Morrison has often denied
that he went too deeply into the cult, preferring to suggest that it
was simply one of the many systems of belief that he was constantly
exploring. Other witnesses would suggest that his interest was more
than superficial at the time, though within three years he was
claiming that he had "no guru, no method, no teacher".

Morrison seemed disenchanted with the mechanics of his profession, with the repetitive nature of recording and touring.
Regarding gigs, he said: "I've cut down to the minimum at the present time. It's a matter of moving on into other creative areas." And
on recording: "I used to enjoy it much more. I've been doing it quite
a while and it gets to be over-run. You say what you've got to say
and people want you to say it again." This is a telling statement –
in the course of such a long and productive career, Morrison could
rarely be accused of serving up the same dish under a different name.
There may be a Morrison "tune", instantly recognisable, and pat-
terns of subject matter and concerns reflected in his lyrics, but each
album is a distinct statement of his musical career at that point, and
could not be placed at any other stage. "Part of the problem with
performing," he said, "is this expectancy that you're going to do stuff
you did five years ago or ten years ago. You're not there any more.

You're going backwards. Performing is like going into the past. It doesn't exist. You're moving on."

Regarding his homeland he said: "I find inspiration in relation to Irish literature, poetry. That kind of inspiration. I don't really find musical inspiration here. I'm not looking for that here." He somewhat contradicted himself later in the same conversation: "I've been listening to Celtic folk music. Various – music from Brittany, England, Scotland, Wales, Ireland." The Breton musician Alan Stivell was on his listening list at the time, and Morrison put his lifelong interest in the blues into perspective: "The blues is 'their' music. You can play it but it doesn't belong to you." He also made a tantalising, as yet unrealised revelation. "I'm writing a book at the moment. It's not really an autobiography. Fact, fiction, philosophy, mysticism. The best way to explain it is that it's how it is, rather than how people think it is. My experience."

On 11 and 12 March 1983, coinciding with the release of *Inarticulate Speech of the Heart*, the mobile recording unit from The Manor was stationed outside Belfast's beautiful Grand Opera House, with the purpose of capturing material for Morrison's "once in a decade" live album. He has said that sometimes he wishes that he could just write the songs, and then pass on to someone else the trouble of actually recording and performing them. And the very nature of the songs of this period suggests that he is most at peace when exploring a new book, or tramping through the woods like Coleridge, opening himself to the muse.

However, it is in live performance, with which Morrison has maintained an awkward on-off relationship, that his songs can appear in peak condition. He has rarely felt that need, often exhibited by Bob Dylan, to try and kick life back into an old song by taking it to pieces and re-assembling it in a different way – when he gets bored with a song, or finds that its meaning has become blunted by familiarity, he is more likely simply to drop it from his repertoire until inspiration returns. While the songs are still fresh, but more seasoned than in their raw studio form, we can often hear his work as its best – as did London concertgoers at the Rainbow in 1973 and at the Dominion nine years later, for example.

Belfast was similarly treated in 1983. There's no "Gloria" or "Cyprus Avenue" surviving on to the published record of the gigs – as befits his resistance at the time to revisiting his back pages, everything apart from the introductory, scene-setting chords to "Into the Mystic" is drawn from *Into the Music, Common One, Beautiful Vision* and *Inarticulate Speech of the Heart*, a four-year work schedule. The band was made up of those musicians most familar with the songs in studio form: Pee Wee Ellis and Mark Isham on horns, John Allair on keyboards and David Hayes on bass, drummers Peter van Hooke, Chris Michie with his southern soul guitar licks and recent recruit Tom Donlinger, Vocalists Katie Kissoon, Bianca Thornton and Carol Kenyon completed the orchestra.

From the confident, punchy version of "Dweller on the Threshold" through his segue of "It's All in the Game" and "You Know What They're Writing About", "She Gives Me Religion" and a magical "Haunts of Ancient Peace", rudely interrupted by a deliberately manic saxophone solo, the reviving roar of "Full Force Gale", "Beautiful Vision" and "Vanlose Stairway", a rambling "John Donne" and the encores, "Northern Ground" and "Cleaning Windows", the record is a warming summary of early-1980s Morrison's musical and spiritual concerns.

By this time Morrison had ended his long relationship with Warner Brothers in the USA, and this led to a rumour, assisted by speculation in *Rolling Stone*, that he had been dropped by the label. Morrison firmly denied the rumour. "It isn't true," he said a year later. "I tried to find out through lawyers and things what was really happening and everyone told me that *Rolling Stone* had made this up. I heard about it second-hand. A friend told me, 'Have a look at

Rolling Stone.' Everyone I talked to who was mentioned in the article said they didn't say this. I don't know if that's true or not and I don't really care, because it was far from my mind at that point. I think they dropped a lot of people and I was the biggest name on there. In terms of popularity. I just figured that somebody had a bright idea and thought that I was in Timbuctoo or something sleeping under a hedge and thought that this would get past. And it didn't get past and Waronker [Sy Waronker, Warner Brothers executive] was extremely embarrassed. I think that's the story. Waronker said that he'd apologise publicly and do an interview in the *Los Angeles Times* to clean this up. He did the interview but he didn't clean it up. He said we were negotiating but... we weren't negotiating. The fact of the matter is I was on Polygram everywhere but the US and Warner Brothers had the rights for the US up to a certain point. Which was the *Inarticulate Speech* album. When they got that they didn't have any rights. So my next move was to give my US rights to Polygram because they'd been representing me for six years everywhere else. Just a natural follow-up. That's what happened from my end. From his end I don't know what was going on... "

Precisely a year after the Belfast set, in February 1985, Morrison's next studio album was released. The musicians were the nucleus of those from recent albums, with Bob Doll replacing Mark Isham on trumpets and Pauline Lazano on backing vocals with Bianca Thornton. On the cover photograph Morrison is indubitably smiling, peering through a wreath of autumn leaves, while on the inner photograph he fails to set any fashion trends by posing self-consciously in black cape and matador's hat.

A Sense of Wonder was the clearest yet indication of Morrison's interest in the work of William Blake. Blake (1757-1827) was a Londoner, a prolific poet and painter, whose most celebrated work was published in 1794, combining an earlier collection of lyrics with new ones, called *Songs of Innocence and of Experience, Shewing the Two*

Contrary States of the Human Soul. Those two states were the pastoral innocence of childhood, which was represented by the Lamb, and the world of adult corruption and destructive energy, symbolised by the Tyger. An awareness of this struggle is surely at the core of Morrison's spirituality.

A rich guitar riff introduces the first song on *A Sense of Wonder*, as strong a start as usual. "Tore Down a la Rimbaud" adopts a muscular approach to self-doubt, with the singer unclear of his message and his purpose, and suffering from writer's block as a result: "I wish my writing would come." "I'd been reading him [Rimbaud] when I got the original idea," says Morrison. "The idea is ten or 12 years old, and I just rewrote it. I wasn't writing anything at all and I really didn't understand why. Sometimes I get over a block by just sitting down at a typewriter and typing what I've just done. Got up, had breakfast. Sometimes I get out of it that way. Sometimes not." "Ancient of Days" seeks to find his purpose in the natural landscape, while peace is sought in the soothing instrumental "Evening Meditation". As with earlier such pieces on which Morrison elects to play piano, however, his somewhat rudimentary piano technique tends to introduce a hint of the Oriental to the Celtic mood.

"His Master's Eyes" takes us closer to Blake. It is an inspirational hymn which has a direct message: "My questions all were answered / When the light shone from the master... / from the master's eyes." But the song alone is served by the message, not the singer: as Morrison has indicated, if his questions ever were to be answered his career would be over. "It's not a specific master," he says. "It's the master within." On the next track he interrupts his devotions for a simple Ray Charles love song before, on "A Sense of Wonder", he sets off on a pilgrimage through childhood haunts, searching for Blakean innocence.

A springy Irish instrumental, "Boffyflow and Spike", provides a swift change of mood. These two characters are referred to in a whimsical sleeve note, presumably by Morrison, quietly reminiscent of the Irish humorous writer Flann O'Brien, who would have approved in particular of the idea of deep-freezing autumn leaves. A self-mocking Mose Allison lyric, "If Only You Knew", follows, unwittingly looking forward to Morrison's future collaboration with Georgie Fame, who founded his style largely on that of Allison. For the last two tracks, Blake moves back to centre stage. Adrian Mitchell and Mike Westbrook, who collaborated in the 1960s on a Blake musical *Tyger, Tyger*, arranged the Blake lyric "Let the Slave", and it is interesting to hear Morrison interpreting the words of the "master", whose ideas are continued in the final track, Morrison's own "A New Kind of Man".

The album was to have included an adaptation of a Yeats lyric, "Crazy Jane on God", which survived as far as the promotional copies before being removed. "We were told by the Yeats estate that they wouldn't give us permission to put this song on the album," explains Morrison. "So I thought about it for a couple of days and I thought, OK, fine. I thought I was doing them a favour. My songs are better than Yeats!" So much for literary heroes.

In May 1985 a gossip column in the *Daily Mirror* claimed that Morrison had begun to attend Alcoholics Anonymous meetings in Chelsea. During the summer he toured to promote the album, and worked on the musical score for Colin Gregg's film *Lamb*, adapted from a novel by Bernard McLaverty, about the healing relationship between an Irish priest and a ten-year-old boy. He then took some time off, and in December visited Belfast.

"I'm not doing anything special. I'm just off," he said. "I want to get my head showered as I've been very busy touring the UK, Europe, America and Australia. The pace has been too much this year so I'm taking a long holiday. In fact, I've no idea when I'll be back on the road." His enthusiasm for playing music wasn't in doubt, it was the paraphenalia of touring that, as ever, had got to him.

"There's nothing I'd like more than to have a blow with a few boys but you can't do that without touring. I like to play but I hate the road. And that's the price you have to pay. I can't think of any other way to play unless I owned a club, but I don't like that environment. I don't drink and I don't see myself as an impresario. Besides, I couldn't go into a club like Ronnie Scott's, because there would be a couple of thousand people in the street.

"And it's difficult to get a few boys together just for a rehearsal – I'm dealing with professional musicians. They just want a cheque. The people I'm dealing with are employees who get paid for what they do. If I could do a couple of gigs every six weeks that would be enough." Morrison also expressed disappointment at the record-company support given to *A Sense of Wonder* in Britain. "It was the best-kept secret of '85… it wasn't promoted here. Everywhere else in the world it was pushed and it sold very well. I don't want to even think of my next one yet."

He soon did, however, since *No Guru, No Method, No Teacher* was released in July 1986, having been recorded at two studios in Sausalito and at the Townhouse in London. Jeff Labes was back on keyboards and John Platania from the days of the Caledonia Soul Orchestra added some lead guitar dubs. Joining regulars David Hayes and Chris Michie were drummer Baba Trunde, saxophonist Richie Buckley, trumpeter Martin Drover and, responsible for some of the most distinctive sounds on the album, Kate St John on cor anglais and oboe.

The title deliberately distanced Morrison from Scientology and its works. "There have been many lies put out about me," commented the prickly performer somewhat superciliously, "and this finally states my position. I have never joined any organisation, nor plan to. I am not affiliated to any guru, I don't subscribe to any method and, for those people who don't know what a guru is, I don't have a teacher either."

The Blakean themes that infused the previous album continue in
the first cut, a waltz called "Got to Go Back", which introduces the
set's dominant concern of retreat into the healing innocence of childhood. In "Oh the Warm Feeling" he is "like a child within the
kingdom", and as he watches someone journeying "to the palace
of the Lord" in the third track, "Foreign Window", Morrison
explores images of Gothic romance. The revelation of truths that are
the privilege of innocence are conveyed in the lines: "They were
giving you religion/Breaking bread and drinking wine/And you
laid out on the green hills/Just like when you were a child."

The concerns of "A Town Called Paradise" are more cloudy, with
Morrison claiming that "copycats ripped off my words" (and his
songs and his melodies as well), but the idea of climbing a mountainside, then swinging through all points of the compass before
descending into a town called Paradise recalls not only Blake but
John Bunyan as well.

The key song, containing the line that gives the album its title, is
"In the Garden", and like so much of the imagery at the start of his
solo career it is a garden "wet with rain". Morrison saw this song
as a path to serene meditation. "I take you through the meditation
programme... a definite meditation process which is a form of tran-
scendental meditation. It's not TM, forget about that. It takes you
from the middle to the end [of the song]. You should have some
degree of tranquility by the time you get to the end. So when this
happens in the song I say, 'And I turned to you and I said no guru,
no method, no teacher, just you and me and nature, and the father
and the son and the holy ghost.' So really you have to do the whole
line to know what it means." In once again denying allegiance to
any guru he said: "You could call this a press release!"

The path towards peace and revelation through meditation was
clearly at the forefront of his mind while he was making the album.
"It only takes about ten minutes to do this process. So then you ask

yourself why make albums, why tour, when the whole thing I'm
saying only takes ten minutes, actually. If I can take the people
through a meditation process, which is what I'm really about, which
is what I'm saying… it's very difficult to do this… the bigger the
audience is then the harder it is to put across what you're doing.
When you've got intimacy you've got more of a chance of taking
people through this experientially. So this is really it. This is what
I'm doing in this song 'In the Garden'. I used to do this quite a bit.
For instance, when I did this in the '60s we'd get to a place where
there's a meditative part, say at the end of 'Cyprus Avenue' or something. The whole 'Cyprus Avenue' was just a build-up to bring it
to a point where we could go into meditation.

"Maybe this wasn't explained to people properly. What actually
happened was that when we got to this point some people got that
it was about meditation and they were willing to receive it, and other
people thought that this was a chance to say 'right on' or something.
It didn't really come across, you see. There was so much other stuff
going on. Politically, and drug-wise, and all this. People couldn't
really relate on that level… Rock'n'roll is not set up that way. It's
the opposite – set up to stimulate. It's got to be exciting. That's got
nothing to do with the meditation process, which is what I'm about
and what ultimately the songs and everything else are all about. At
some point I'll have to make the split from rock'n'roll. You don't have
to have an album out to do this, you don't have to be on the charts
or necessarily be famous." As the last decade has proved, with each
year bringing its new Van Morrison album, he has nevertheless felt
the need to stay on the treadmill.

After "In the Garden" the theme continues and the garden is still
there, and is still wet with rain, in another affecting expression of
the theme: "Tir Na Nog", the mythical Celtic land of eternal youth.
The following song, "Here Comes the Knight", with its jokey title,
follows a quest for love and truth, while "Thanks for the Information"

would appear to be a sneer at Morrison's critics. "Never give a sucker an even break when he's breaking through to a new level of consciousness", he says, and stuffs the lyric with clichés, presumably to contrast his pure, heartfelt poetry with the slack hackery of journalists. Obstacles, inevitably, are "in the way", there's a "combat zone", he sings "thanks for the memory", we have to "make it from day to day", remembering that "what you gain on the hobby horse you lose on the swing". He has tried "every trick in the book" and knows that "I should look before I leap". There's a "watering hole" and people start "coming out of the woodwork", to be informed that "a bird in the hand is worth two in the bush".

"One Irish Rover" finds the Celtic traveller in search of home while the excellent final cut, "Ivory Tower", totally breaks the mould – it's an r'n'b shaker just like those produced by the Morrison of old, though now he suffers from self-pity: "Don't you know the price that I have to pay/Just to do everything I have to do..."

He described that price tag at the time. "This is my job, and all that other bullshit [the record business] is not my responsibility. The whole thing of being famous is an illusion and I pay no attention to illusions. I was once in the business when I played rock and r'n'b, but now I'm as far removed as night is from day. I'm forced to do music part-time now; 95 per cent of my time is taken up with the business of getting the music out. The record company does nothing except distribution. I book the musicians and in most cases I pay for it. I book the sessions. I have to go through a major record company for distribution so I'm forced into this game. I'm not fond of playing games. Sometimes it feels as though I will never do another album and I've no idea of what may happen next. I enjoy playing the music. The rest is complete nonsense."

At this time, while facing yet another promotional tour, Morrison again expressed a degree of weariness with everything except the songs and the thoughts that they expressed. "I think there's a lot of illusions in this world. The man in the street knows that it's non-sense but it's perpetuated. Why? Because a lot of people are making a lot of money out of it. It's not happening for artistic reasons. The record business is not artistic. The film business is not artistic. They're money businesses."

And, pursuing the theme: "After this I'll be winding down... I'm not going to say this'll be my last tour. I'll just say hopefully I won't do it this way any more. I'm not going to quote, 'Van Morrison says this is his last tour.' That just leads to problems. But it's not working for me any more. Maybe people can come and see me under different circumstances. In different places that aren't rock'n'roll places. I certainly don't want to do this album-tour bit any more."

One thing he did do, however, was to make contact with the Wrekin Trust, an organisation founded "to awaken the vision of the spiritual nature of man and the universe". The result was a joint venture between Morrison and the Trust, a three-day event held at Loughborough University on 18-20 September 1987, called "The Secret Heart of Music". The poster described it as "An Exploration into the Power of Music to Change Consciousness", and the literature included a revealing summary of Morrison's art. "His struggle to reconcile the mythic, almost otherworldly vision of the Celts, and his own search for spiritual satisfaction, with the apparent hedonism of blues and soul music has produced many inspired and visionary performances." The conference combined seminars and performance, and among those invited to take part were Robin Williamson and the Chieftains' Derek Bell.

This event coincided with a new album, *Poetic Champions Compose*. Morrison did not return to Sausalito this time, and the sessions took place at the Townhouse in London and a new choice of studio, the Wool Hall at Beckington, near Bath. This relocation also indicated fresh musicians: pianist Neil Drinkwater, bass player Steve Pearce and drummer Roy Jones formed the nucleus of the band with the trumpeter Martin Drover, while for the first time the Dublin musical arranger and composer Fiachra Trench became involved, scoring the string and woodwind decorations.

"I started off making a jazz album," Morrison explained, "but after three numbers I thought I should put some words in." Just as well, one might feel – though "Spanish Steps" effectively continues the peaceful mood of the previous set, his instrumentals like "Celtic Excavation" were beginning to merge with one another, and the final cut "Allow Me" is little more than cocktail-hour tinkling.

Indeed the album is overall one of the less inspired in Morrison's vast catalogue. In confronting "The Mystery" the advice is little more than "open up your heart". "Queen of the Slipstream" is sought as an ally in the search for purity and innocence, and in "I Forgot That Love Existed" Morrison muses humbly on the difficulty of marrying the heart and the head. The traditional song "Sometimes I Feel Like a Motherless Child", with a title summarising the underlying theme of the record, is given a rather perfunctory treatment, while in "Alan Watts Blues" the singer yearns to leave the rat race – to those who are genuinely trapped in it, without Morrison's freedom to put his great coat and big boots on and go tramping in the woods, this will seem a little ironic.

Morrison is incapable of making a mediocre album, however, and two of the songs add to and develop his current concern with Christianity. "Give Me My Rapture" is a direct, striking request to the Lord, one of the key songs at this period of Morrison's spiritual quest – though if he was indeed satirising the hated journalistic profession on the previous album by cramming "Thanks for the Information" with cliches, it should be noted that this moving, devotional song does include a loving cup and a dark night of the soul. In "Did Ye Get Healed?", the other outstanding piece on the album, Morrison displays an almost voyeuristic curiosity about the faith of another, unnamed convert.

Irish Heartbeat

In March 1988 Morrison appeared on television with the Chieftains for a Saint Patrick's Day celebration. This developed from his collaboration with the band during autumn 1987 and again after Christmas, when they had been in the Windmill Lane Studios in Dublin recording a joint album, *Irish Heartbeat*.

The Chieftains' recording and performing career stretches back as far as Morrison's own, and in 1988 two of the original members remained – Paddy Moloney on uilleann pipes and tin whistle and Martin Fay on fiddle. The group emerged in 1963 from Dublin composer Sean O'Riada's folk ensemble Coeltiori Cualann, but they really came to the fore in the 1970s with a series of well-received albums and worldwide concerts, including an Edinburgh Festival appearance with Morrison. In 1979 they played in Phoenix Park, Dublin, to a crowd of 1.3 million that had assembled for a Papal mass – perhaps the world's biggest ever gig – and in that year the line-up that was to collaborate with Morrison nine years later was completed: together with Moloney and Fay were two former classical musicians, violinist Sean Keane and ex-BBC Symphony Orchestra harpist Derek Bell, vocalist Kevin Conneff and, joining them from the Bothy Band, flautist Matt Molloy.

At the end of April Morrison and the Chieftains began an *Irish Heartbeat* tour in Aberdeen that reached London's Riverside arts centre two weeks later. The reactions of Irish journalist Sean O'Hagan, covering the performance for the *New Musical Express*, were typical of the general mood. "Tonight genius has his legs bent, his arms spread and his face contorted in creative exorcism," enthused O'Hagan. "The music is pouring down over his shoulders and Van Morrison is way out there – beyond words and meaning... Something has happened to the most uncomfortable of live performers and I'd bet it hinges on his proximity to the sheer joyousness of the Chieftains' work in motion. He's smiling, laughing, cracking the odd off-mike joke and trading sarcasm with court jester Paddy Moloney...

"Morrison's set begins with a long Celtic instrumental, the man himself blowing some sinuous sax, that merged into 'Vanlose Stairway'. He sustains this celestial mood throughout, pursuing the gospel of poetic wholeness and metaphysical quest that has been a mainstay of his music for a long time now.

"'In the Garden' moves into the realms of trance, Morrison lost in music as the six-piece band – including the Chieftains' Derek Bell on keyboards – move with his every nuance...

"Enter the Chieftains and the collected ensemble tear into 'The Star of the County Down', Morrison's grin matched only by the beam of delight cemented on the bass player's face. 'She Moved through the Fair' literally takes the audience's breath away, Morrison repeating his dredged-up exorcism to invoke the heroine's violent death."

At the end of the performance, "'My Lagan Love' rushes headlong into a Pogueish 'Mairie's Wedding' and all and sundry are on their feet tearing the roof off the once sedate Riverside." Morrison sends the audience home with the instruction "Home for tea and Leadbelly!" O'Hagan's final verdict was "awesome".

In spite of the piecemeal recording of the album, fitted around other commitments, the spirit of enjoyment was already plain on *Irish Heartbeat*. With rousing vocal support by Mary Black, Maura O'Connell and June Boyce, co-producers Morrison and Moloney mix their arrangements of traditional Irish songs with Morrison originals. The core of the album is an ensemble version of the title song, first recorded by Morrison for *Inarticulate Speech of the Heart*. It now emerges as one of the most beautiful of all explorations of the yearning for roots, of the need to be with "your own ones", so direct in its evocation that it is movingly acessible to Celt and heathen alike. Morrison suggests that this form of nostalgia is something he shares with all Irish writers. "Going away and coming back are the recurring themes. They want to get back to when things felt better and it was all good crack, or else they're writing about the sadness of going back and not finding any answers."

In October Morrison and the Chieftains were back in London, now at the Royal Albert Hall, but the joyous muse that had so affected the reviewer at the Riverside was absent, and in the meantime Morrison had been demonstrating, in reluctantly publicising his liaison with the Chieftains, that his attitude towards journalists had not softened at all.

This collaboration occupied roughly a year of Morrison's career, and he then began work on the next collection of songs, *Avalon Sunset*, released in June 1989 with its striking cover image of a white swan on a sun-gilded river. Along with *Astral Weeks* and *Into the Music*, it continued Morrison's accidental habit of leaving each decade with a striking summary of his art at that point – indeed, it is perhaps his most completely satisfying album since 1979.

Recorded at several London studios as well as the Wool Hall, the album features familiar collaborators from Morrison's recent past together with guitarist Arty McGlynn and, significantly, the distinctive tone of Georgie Fame's Hammond organ on several tracks. But the partnership that gave Morrison his biggest UK hit since the days of Them was with Cliff Richard, duetting on "Whenever God Shines His Light".

This rich album covers all the themes that had been concerning Morrison in recent years. He is now in a direct relationship with the

Christian God, and "Whenever God... " includes such straightforward statements as "When I reach out for Him He is there", a line that could have sprung from any page of *Hymns Ancient and Modern*. In "When Will I Ever Learn to Live in God" Morrison evokes William Blake once more and describes his relationship with the Almighty in unusually humble terms – God, as in so many of Morrison's songs, is at work in the landscape.

The mystical strand in his work is now embodied in the mysterious land of Avalon, just to the south-west of Bath, where he had recently bought a house. The old abbey of Glastonbury stands on what was the Isle of Avalon, then surrounded by a vast reach of the Bristol Channel flooding between the hills of Mendip and Quantock, and stretching down to Ilchester in the south-east of Somerset. This sea was subsequently drained to form the Somerset Levels, on which the Battle of Sedgemoor was fought as the final desperate act of the Monmouth Rebellion.

A fascinating mixture of history and legend has clung to Glastonbury's Avalon, and was presumably significant in attracting Morrison to the region. It was here that Joseph of Arimathea arrived from the Holy Land to build his church, and here he buried the Holy Grail, here that Saint Patrick established a monastic order, here that King Arthur founded Camelot and was later buried with his Queen Guinevere. As a Celt, Morrison was no doubt exploring legends, in some cases misplaced a little too far to the east!

His explorations of earthly love on *Avalon Sunset* reflect its various manifestations – spiritual in "Contacting My Angel", romantic in "Have I Told You Lately" – surely the Morrison song most certain to become a popular-music "standard" – and sexual in "Daring Night". But even when the sweaty singer is mouthing excited clichés like "squeeze me, don't leave me", congress still takes place beneath the heavens, under the auspices of the lord of the dance.

The blues and the muse are respectively the vehicle and the subject of "I'd Love to Write Another Song", where jazzmen Henry Lowther, Cliff Hardie, Stan Sultzman and Alan Barnes join Georgie Fame in what is on one level a light, swinging approach to writer's block, but which also conveys the bleak implication that, to Morrison, the inability to write renders life meaningless.

He revisits childhood haunts once more in "Orangefield" and in the charming recitation "Coney Island", an evocative journey recalling simple, life-enhancing pleasures; birdwatching, sightseeing, enjoying innocent company and the "crack", buying the Sunday papers and "a couple of jars of mussels and some potted herrings in case we get famished before dinner". The destination is Coney Island, and the song ends with a wistful, child-like thought: "Wouldn't it be great if it was like this all the time."

The BBC Radio 4 travel programme *Going Places*, on 26 January 1996, chose to take Morrison's lyric to this song as a road map, deliberately ignoring the confusions of time in the words that indicate that this is a kaleidoscope of memory, even an unfulfilled wish, rather than actual description. As the presenter zigzags the County Down coast to the southeast of Belfast, from Downpatrick to St John's Point, to Strangford Lough and Shrigly, from the Lecale district to Ardglass, asking at every stage for directions to the mysterious Coney Island, he can only conclude that Morrison is a man with absolutely no sense of direction.

The more celebrated pleasure resort of Coney Island is a sausage of land protruding into the sea south of Brooklyn, for decades the New Yorkers' weekend playground, immortalised in an early Buster Keaton comedy and innumerable films since. A proud Ulster local claims in the programme that, to his certain knowledge, it took its name from the Down original.

The nostalgic search for peace in simplicity, described in "Coney Island", continues in the wistful "I'm Tired Joey Boy", in which Morrison admits "I would like to be cheerful again," perhaps a some-

what far-fetched wish. He longs to climb away from strife into a landscape where "silence will touch you and heartbreak will mend".

As if to stress that the breadth of the album's concerns is a deliberate rather than an intuitive agenda, the final song "These are the
Days" pulls them all together. In one moment ("there is no past…
there's only now") Morrison combines earthly love with that
inspired by a sun-warmed landscape, the yearning for simplicity
with the love of "the one magician [who] turned water into wine".

When Morrison started working regularly with Georgie Fame at
this time he seemed to regain an appetite for performing that had
by and large been lost. "I started touring very young," he said in
1990. "I was 15 when I went on the road and spent years living out
of a suitcase from about 15 to 22. I was living in hotels for years. That
was my tolerance level. I don't want to waste my life touring, because
I did that early on." He added: "It's one day at a time. Some days
are good, some are bad. That's life. I'm just taking it as it comes."

A few months later, however, he was saying: "Since hooking up
with Georgie Fame it's a whole new thing. Before this for six or seven
years I was really bored with performing."   But Dublin sax-
ophonsit Richie Buckley had noticed this new-found enthusiasm
much earlier, following well-received concerts at the Dublin
Stadium in 1989. "Georgie's very open and he probably takes the
pressure off him [Morrison] in a way as far as the limelight is concerned. The band improvises 60 per cent of the time and we'd rarely
go through a play list. Van is into another aspect of music."

In February 1990 Polydor decided that it was time to release a "best
of" compilation, although unlike the inactive period in the mid-1970s
that Warner Brothers filled in with two "Originals of Van Morrison"
(*His Band and the Street Choir* and *Tupelo Honey*), Morrison entered
the 1990s hard at work, delivering an album every year. There can
be no argument with the selection, covering everything from
"Gloria" to his recent collaboration with Cliff Richard, but Morrison

wasn't involved in it. "I didn't have anything to do with the selection at all... I just okayed it... I don't have time to do that sort of thing. I'm too busy doing other things." Of course many artists, however busy, given the opportunity to select their "best of" from 25 years' work, would have made the time, but Morrison is being consistent here – however proud he may be of his work, however happy to encore with "Here Comes the Night" if the mood takes him, he is indeed busy doing other things – writing the next album.

His next album, *Enlightenment*, was released in the autumn of 1990, and although the subject matter forms a link with *Avalon Sunset* there is a return on many tracks to his own form of r'n'b, the aspect of his music that had been overlooked of late. "Real Real Gone", the opener, is an example, with its check list not of poets but of soul heroes: Sam Cooke, Wilson Pickett, Solomon Burke, James Brown and Gene Chandler. The title suggests rockabilly, echoing Charlie Feathers' "Gone, Gone, Gone", but the theme is a deeper one, with Morrison admitting that he can't make it on his own, that he needs a relationship with someone else, and that protestations of emotional independence are illusory. The partnership with Georgie Fame must have brought back into contention the r'n'b side of Morrison's music.

The title track shows the singer similarly uncertain of himself, "still suffering" and admitting: "Enlightenment, don't know what it is." But in the next song, "So Quiet in Here", having achieved the state suggested by the title, he can say "This must be what paradise is like", and this generally unsociable man can wax lyrical about the joys of "a glass of wine with some friends". The sound of foghorns in the night, the knowledge that there are big ships out in the bay, increases the sense of cosiness, just as children in the pre-container, pre-diesel age of the railways were comforted in their beds by the distant clanging of the marshalling yards.

"Avalon of the Heart" continues the pilgrimage of the previous album, but accompanied now by soul-music decorations. The ancient mysteries of Avalon, once meditatively absorbed into the heart, offer "a brand new start". "See Me Through" again asks for help, and flirts with self-pity, and some of the lyrics suggest that alcoholism is the problem addressed by the song: "See me through the days of wine and roses/See me through one day at a time." "Youth of 1,000 Summers" is another of Morrison's Blakean songs, while "In the Days Before Rock'n'roll" is a nostalgic memory of 1950s radio, searching the airwaves for musical excitement. This is a collaboration with the Irish poet Paul Durcan, who declaims his lines in a distinctive, fragmented style. Durcan recalls "four very intense days of work" to produce the track. "There in that studio there were four people [Durcan, Morrison singing and playing piano, bass player Steve Pearce and drummer Dave Early] you can't separate out in that moment. We'd been locked up together for four days, everyone giving to everyone else. Everyone was playing to the other."

In Durcan's opinion: "Van Morrison was now at last where he wants to be: lost in the music – totally and utterly unreachable, except through music."

The last three songs continue the theme of renewal, of dependence and the loneliness of the search for emotional contentment. "Start All Over Again" is enlivened by Frank Ricotti's vibraphone, "She's a Baby" is a "missing you" song crammed with soft-soul references, in particular to Smokey Robinson's "Tracks of My Tears", while "Memories" gives the album a downbeat ending. The rest of 1990 was largely taken up, as usual after an album release, with touring, clouded by the death of Morrison's father George in Belfast.

In March 1991 two television programmes about Morrison were coincidentally screened in the UK. In the Channel 4 documentary series *Without Walls* he took part in a discussion called *Coney Island of the Mind*, an attempt to place his writing in the context of Irish poetry. It was preceded by a BBC2 *Arena* film, *One Irish Rover*, in which a camera crew tracked him around the world singing with such luminaries as Bob Dylan (in front of the Acropolis) and John Lee Hooker (by the Mississippi).

The review in *The Independent* summed up the resulting atmosphere. It "began with a shot of the Irish singer flanked by Bob Dylan and the Acropolis: all three of them legendary, all looking their age, and all a waste of time talking to with a microphone in your hand. Dylan appeared never to have heard the songs he was supposed to be accompanying, and his customary diffidence seemed to increase with his visible realisation that he was not the main attraction."

Another of the collaborations filmed for the show was with the Danish Radio Big Band, one of Morrison's explorations in setting his music in various contexts – r'n'b, Irish traditional, "ambient", and so on. The big band sessions have been bootlegged and were broadcast, but have yet to find their way on to an official release.

In February he was involved in a further unusual partnership – going into the Townhouse Studios with a sheaf of his recent songs and Tom Jones. The song that had in particular prompted Morrison to think of Jones was "Carrying a Torch", and the others were "Some Peace of Mind", "It Must Be You" and "I'm Not Feeling It Anymore", all of which Morrison was to put on his next album *Hymns to the Silence*. "Being in the studio with Van Morrison," said Tom Jones later, "was the best feeling I've had on a recording session since the early days." The studio's chief engineer Alan Douglas said that "it was the most hectic session I've worked on in a long time. But it was great – and they both seemed happy with it." Laying down the four tracks took little more than half of the 12 hours that had been booked, with Morrison acting as producer and backing guitarist, and when the two artists posed for photographs, the Irishman was smiling broadly.

In August Morrison was back at the Edinburgh Festival, performing with a nine-piece band that included Georgie Fame and Dutch saxophonist Candy Dulfer. Playing a set that drew on the r'n'b side of his work, he was topping the bill at one of two nights at Edinburgh Castle devoted to Celtic rock, along with his sometime partners the Chieftains, Scottish fiddler Aly Bain and folk-rockers Runrig. This was the first time that the traditional Edinburgh Tattoo venue had staged a rock concert, and Morrison was on top form. "The show unfurled like a sweet soul dream," said *The Guardian*, while *The Scotsman* enthused: "Morrison switched from sax to guitar to harp and moaned ecstatically, eyes closed and oblivious to the floodlit ramparts of the castle as they peeped in the back of the stage. As always his performance was restless, searching for some kind of peace of mind. His songs are hymns to his continued survival, his voice devotional and spiritual. For the audience, his finale, 'Moondance', was a prayer answered… "

The search for peace of mind continued in September, when Morrison's latest album *Hymns to the Silence* was released – the first studio double album of Morrison's long career. As one might expect, he does not spend more than 90 minutes exploring just one of his current concerns or musical styles: the collection is rich in range and offers many rewards.

The store-front church combination of Neil Drinkwater's piano and Georgie Fame's organ setting up the gospel feel of "See Me Through" is an example, leading to a snatch of "Just a Closer Walk with Thee", but the piece degenerates into one of Morrison's nostalgic rants, seeking peace in his childhood. The traditional hymn "Be Thou My Vision" and Morrison's own "By His Grace" are unpretentiously effective. Drinkwater is again to the fore in the rousing honky-tonk blues of "Ordinary Life", and once again his meshing with Fame, pinned together by Nicky Scott's walking bass, gives substance to the lightweight lyric of "All Saints Day". The straightforward love songs work well, in particular the one retrospectively designed for Tom Jones, the soulful "Carrying a Torch", the Dr John lyric "Quality Street" and the celebratory "It Must Be You". The direct, unalloyed narration of "On Hyndford Street", along with "Cleaning Windows" a rare example of straight autobiography, is one of Morrison's more effective recitations, spoken over the atmospheric drone of Derek Bell's synthesiser.

And yet, the album is marred by an assumption that the world is out to annoy the sensitive soul making this music. "Personal invasion can ruin a man," he complains in the opening broadside "Professional Jealousy", a whinge about being hard done by. "I'm Not Feeling It Anymore" claims that "I was givin' everybody what they wanted/And I lost my peace of mind." In "Some Peace of Mind" (why use a good cliché just the once?) being forced to "stand in line, baby, when I'm in a queue," just as if he was an ordinary mortal, reduces him to tears of frustration, and in "So Complicated" he finds the vulgar business side of earning a fat living from his music, when all he wants to do is "blow my horn", deeply depressing. In "Why Must I Always Explain?" his paranoia in describing everyone he has to deal with – audiences and jackal journalists alike – as "hypocrites and parasites and people that drain" is simply offensive, graceless and ungrateful, a low-water mark in his battle with an insensitive world.

At this point one begins to suspect that there is indeed a tragic core to his personality, as he seems so keen to imply: he cannot find the answers to the questions he poses because that would negate the need to write songs, and he cannot risk having no need to write songs because there is nothing else in his life worth doing. He gives no sign of an interest in sport, good food, travel, or any of that multitude of passions, even hobbies, that a rich man could turn into fruitful leisure, and so he is condemned to go on writing songs and, yes, complaining about it. Cliff Richard once put a different slant on this: he suggested that Morrison is "filled with self-loathing".

In December the Belfast Blues Appreciation Society unveiled the plaque at 125 Hyndford Street that annoyed the man it was intended to honour, and Morrison finished the year with performances in both Belfast and Dublin. In the summer of 1992 he did, however, accept an honour, when the University of Ulster bestowed on him an honorary doctorate of letters. He turned up in Coleraine, polite, grey-suited and scarlet-gowned, to receive the citation. There was no new album forthcoming in this year, however, prompting anthology releases from two official sources: Epic recycled the Bang material while in January 1993 Polydor released *The Best of Van Morrison Volume Two*, somewhat too hurriedly after the first collection to make much artistic sense. Hardcore fans, meanwhile, had been kept supplied with such bootlegs as *Soul Labyrinth*, recorded on 31 March 1991 in the Hague, and *Pagan Streams*, from the gig two days later in Utrecht: both found their way on to the market during 1992.

In March 1993 London's most civilised mid-sized venue, a former Irish ballroom in north London called the Town and Country Club, closed down at the end of the promotor's tenancy, and the final gig was performed by a top-form Morrison. In June he appeared at what was by now established as an annual festival of Irish folk and rock in London, the Fleadh in Finsbury Park. Morrison, as had been his pattern for the past year of touring, played a rhythm & blues set and joined honorary Irishman Bob Dylan for an off-the-cuff "Irish Rover". At this time, having worked at Dave Stewart's studio nearby, Dylan was rumoured to have bought property just north of the Park.

Morrison himself, meanwhile, was being spotted more and more around Dublin in the company of his new girlfriend, ex-Miss Ireland Michelle Rocca. This unlikely pair excited much press gossip both north and south of the border, of which a piece in the *Sunday Independent* on 19 September was typical.

"The lust-free liaison between Van Morrison and his escort Michelle Rocca continues to boggle the minds of close friends and confidants alike, not to mention my readers. A post-Curragh do at

Rathsallagh was last week's setting for the passionless peccadilloes. A lively and intriguing affair by all accounts. Keith Richards and Paul Brady made it lively, while the intrigue was added by the Platonic Pairing.

"Luckily, the couple did not frighten the horses and Van at his first race meeting backed three winners.

"'It's the best fun I've had since 1968,' declared Van, referring to the Woodstock festival during the so-called Summer of Love. Still in high spirits at the post-meet party at Rathsallagh, Van announced he was buying a horse for 'my fiancée.' To which Michelle reportedly replied: "Let's see how the horse pans out first and then we'll see about the fiancée'. She's a cool customer and no mistake. Still, her birthday was in the offing and there's nothing a Virgo likes better than a ticket to ride…

"…Confusing signals continue to emanate from this compelling couple. While protesting their platonicism to all who would listen, Van got a sharp slap on the wrist when he had the temerity to lift his shades to look at another pretty woman."

Dublin media chatterers were in agreement as to why Morrison might be attracted to the statuesque Rocca, but could only make scurrilous suggestions as to why she might have set her sights on the portly, balding, middle-aged but very successful musician.

The London Fleadh performance coincided with the release of Morrison's first album in almost two years, appropriately titled *Too Long in Exile*, leased to Polydor via Morrison's newly-established production company Exile. The gap between releases may have been longer than usual, but not Morrison's continuing commercial power: the album was swiftly installed in the Top 10.

None of the recording took place in Dublin: Morrison resorted to three familiar studios – the Wool Hall, the Townhouse in London and, for the first time in many years, the Plant in Sausalito, where he was reunited with John Lee Hooker.

Overall the album exhibited a far more expansive, less uptight Morrison than had been the case on *Hymns to the Silence*. His voice had gained in depth and resonance and this enabled him to sing a languorous 12-bar like "Big Time Operators", to which he also contributed a memorably spikey lead guitar, as a blues singer first and as a demonstrator of all the familiar Morrison mannerisms second. The narrative, of a New York record business run by phone-bugging thugs in long black limousines, is presumably not based on his personal experience – surely to have had his solo career launched with an album called *Blowin' Your Mind!* could not rankle this long?

This more resonant, less mannered vocal technique is apparent on an intriguing clutch of cover versions that stud the album – Doc Pomus' "Lonely Avenue", a 1956 r'n'b top-tenner for Ray Charles, Sonny Boy Williamson's salacious "Good Morning Little Schoolgirl", the folk-gospel standard "Lonesome Road", James Moody's torchy "Moody's Mood for Love" and Brook Benton's "I'll Take Care of You" – between them they cover the range of r'n'b styles. Added to this are two friendly collaborations with Hooker – a surprise reprise of "Gloria" and an all-purpose whinge, "Wasted Years" – the waste does not, of course, come from any weakness within the singer, but from brainwashing and "wrong advice". "Oh yeah, oh yeah Van," nods his veteran partner.

There are a couple of songs that remain in keeping with Morrison's recent themes, the Blakean "In the Forest" and a powerful meditation, "Till We Get the Healing Done", tracing an earthly journey that must continue until "you live in the glory of the One", until "we dwell in the house of the Lord". In contrast, however, to more explicitly Christian songs of late, the nature of the One, of the Lord, is diffuse. Yearning of a more earthy kind is apparent in the love song "Ball and Chain", in which the singer offers himself as an emotional slave. A sprightly instrumental, "Close Enough for Jazz", leads to the lyric "Before the World Was Made", expressing a desire to strip away layers of sophistication to reveal the innocence beneath. It was written by W B Yeats, so presumably the poet's estate had relented by now and allowed Morrison to "do them a favour". After this, the Benton song segues into a sinuous alto-sax and scat instrumental before a closing song, "Tell Me What You Want", indicating once more that the singer feels somewhat put-upon.

The album has by this time made a varied musical journey from the opening, title track, "Too Long in Exile". This is not the happy homecoming that the title might suggest, because Morrison suggests that "you can never go home again". Instead, he identifies himself with a list of expatriates, and seems to be coming to the depressing conclusion that the rolling stone who stays away too long will always be in exile, even if he moves physically back home. James Joyce, Samuel Beckett, Oscar Wilde, Alex Higgins – and Morrison, doomed to rootlessness.

Festival appearances studded the rest of summer 1993: in August he was billed to star at a Cornish WOMAD event near St Austell, on the same day that the *Ulster Newsletter* predicted that he would be appearing at Londonderry's Octoberfest 93, billed as Ireland's Festival of Festivals. After Cornwall he topped the bill at the Wiltshire Festival held in Lydiard Park, near Swindon, and in September he was back in Dublin, performing at Slane Castle.

His litigious side emerged when a respectful and lavishly illustrated biography was published at this time: Steve Turner's *Too Late to Stop Now*. "Lies, exaggerations and innuendo," proclaimed the paranoid star. "The fact that I may be successful at what I do does not mean that I accept that anyone can come along and publish details of my private life for other people to read purely for their personal enjoyment." Turner revealed that Morrison's management had made enquiries about buying up the entire print run. "Of course it was out of the question," said Turner. "It would have been an admission of guilt."

"That book is about somebody else," claimed Morrison, sending the author a list of 36 alleged inaccuracies. "Two thirds of the criticisms were simply opinions he didn't agree with," responded Turner. "I really don't understand why he's reacting like this. The truth was far worse than what I actually wrote. There were some very wild stories that I left out. He can be grumpy, he can be drunk. But I didn't go out to drag up mud."

Meanwhile, it was ten years since the last live album, and so it was time for Morrison to produce another exhilarating "state of play" bulletin. The mobile trucks assembled at the Mystic Theater in Petaluma, north of San Francisco, on 12 December 1993, and six days later at the Masonic Auditorium in the city itself. The rhythm section consisted of those who had provided the core of the last album, bassist Nicky Scott and drummer Geoff Dunn, along with guitarist Ronnie Johnson and vibes player Teena Lyle. Georgie Fame's organ was complemented by Jonn Savannah on keyboards, Kate St John played saxes and oboe, while Haji Ahkba came in as flugel-horn player and master of ceremonies. Brian Kennedy was now working with Morrison as featured second vocalist, along with James Hunter, singing and playing guitar, while altoist Candy Dulfer, though part of the band, was billed as a "special guest" for contractual reasons. Morrison's daughter Shana was featured on "Beautiful Vision" and there were guest appearances by three of the greatest names in the blues: John Lee Hooker, of course; harmonica master Junior Wells and veteran singer Jimmy Witherspoon. Morrison has privately deemed the results, released in May 1994 as a double set, as one of his favourites among all his albums.

The form of the album is of a two-and-a-half hour musical revue of the type familiar in black show business, so it is appropriate that the informing style of the concerts is that of the blues, and that the guest heroes are also from this world. There is the "let's hear it for Van Morrison" MC, the second lead singer to take over when the star takes a break, the back-up chorus, spotlight solos for all the musicians, frequent name checks and party pieces by the guest stars.

In contrast to the Belfast album a decade earlier, Morrison is now happy to draw on his entire career – back beyond Them, even, in that the final work-out featuring John Lee Hooker mixes "Gloria" with one of Morrison's earliest band influences, Johnny Kidd and the Pirates' "Shakin' All Over". Such medleys are the norm here, with only a dozen songs given undivided attention. More typically, the band work their way through an arrangement that can take any number of references, quotes and verses on board. The 15-minute sequence billed as "Lonely Avenue/4 O'Clock in the Morning", for example, does indeed begin and end with the Doc Pomus song and includes the Morrison blues in the title, but also wheels on Jimmy Witherspoon for his own medley and throws in passing quotes from "Be Bop a Lula", Sly Stewart's "Family Affair" (with Jonn Savannah contributing a fine falsetto) and even Roy Orbison's "Down the Line" among other references. In another musical joke, a long version of Sonny Boy Williamson's "Help Me" is adorned with the Booker T Jones organ solo and Steve Cropper's guitar break from "Green Onions", a number that shares the same underlying riff.

As with James Brown's band, the impression is of jazz musicians playing ensemble r'n'b, displaying an empathy that can only start with charts and rehearsal, but must grow way beyond such formality. Morrison, not a man who finds it easy to put thoughts into words, is known to get very frustrated in the studio when the music fails to gel as he wants it. But when the music overcomes this initial cold awkwardness the results can be sublime – Morrison's tunes, after all, are almost always straightforward, leaving room for the musical flights so often demonstrated here.

Diehard Morrison fans are divided over the contributions of Brian Kennedy to recent stage shows – after all, some say, they don't pay for the star to rest in the wings. An item in Scotland's tabloid *Daily*

Record of 26 April 1995 is typical of this school of thought: "...there's only one Van Morrison. His Glasgow show last week was superb. But I was miffed when two guest singers took over during his 'rests'. When some unknown launched into the classic 'Have I Told You Lately', we all felt cheated. At £18 a head you expect Van the Man – not Van's other man."

But when they work together, Kennedy's pure tenor and Morrison's improvised, explosive vocal swoops form an effective bond. There is little new light cast on Morrison originals during *A Night in San Francisco* – it is above all a show – but there are some intriguing nuggets. The repetitive mantric chant of "No guru, no method, no teacher" is an example, deliberately divorcing the line from its context within the song "In the Garden". And Kennedy's clarity of voice, when singing the opening to "Tupelo Honey", doubles one's focus on the song, a lone country-inflected number in a sea of blues.

The final element making the project such a success, and no doubt helping to explain its triumph as an ensemble piece, is the good humour that pervades it – not always a quality to be found at Morrison gigs. When Jimmy Witherspoon sings "When Will I Be a Man?" Morrison ad-libs "It's up to you." "Some decorum, please," he requests at the end, while Kate St John enunciates G-L-O-R-I-A as if giving an elocution lesson. The sleeve design promises "ballads, blues, soul, funk & jazz," and Morrison delivers.

Morrison's relationship with Rocca had one obvious effect during this time: the recluse was becoming a man about town, whether that town be Dublin, London or New York. He was, in her company of course, an unlikely guest at showbiz events, gigs and awards ceremonies that left to himself he would have shunned. And, at last, in April 1995 the *Sunday Independent* headline trumpeted: "Michelle says 'Yes' to Van".

"The engaged couple kept their secret at the IRMA awards on

Friday night," bubbled the paper in the accompanying story, "but their very public commitment was there for all to see. Indeed if the liggers and PR people hadn't been so self-absorbed, they would have seen the signs writ large.

"Van's rendering of 'Have I Told You Lately That I Love You' with Sinead O'Connor and Paul Brady was dedicated to Michelle. Of course, it's not unusual for the singer to invoke his brown-eyed girl, but this rendering sent frissons down the spines and was described as 'unforgettable' by all who heard it. Secondly, the radiant Michelle in stunning blue had swapped her old diamond solitaire for Van's Celtic-designed gold band (which Van had secretly made for Michelle on Thursday – the beautiful diamond earrings Michelle wore were also an engagement present from Van). And thirdly, when Van and Michelle left their table to pose for this engagement picture (when has Van ever before left a table to pose for anyone?) he was cheerful and relaxed and looked quite satisfied. Obviously that old hunger for love no longer dogs him. He need wait no more. 'I'm very happy,' he told me and left it to his joyous fiancée to fill in the details. This will be Van Morrison's second marriage. He has one daughter Shana by his first marriage to Janet Planet. It will also be second nuptials for Michelle, who has two daughters, Natasha and Danielle, by her marriage to John Devine, and her youngest daughter Claudia by Cathal Ryan to whom she was engaged.

"Although the Rocca/Morrison romance [a striking order of names] has been high profile, the couple have actually taken the relationship slowly. They have been friends and business partners for over three years. No wedding date is set, but a long engagement is not envisaged… "

Meanwhile, as well as a guest performance on the Chieftains' new album *The Long Black Veil* and one-off gigs, Morrison worked on the next solo release. When *Days Like This* came out in June 1995 the first track, "Perfect Fit", confirmed Morrison's new-found happiness in the form of a tight, r'n'b/funk love song, though subsequent songs on the set indicated that life is never that simple. The atmospheric cover photograph showed the happy couple walking their dogs along a dark back alley, Morrison in his new "uniform" of black suit, pate-hiding hat and shades, Rocca dressed more like an ex-Miss Ireland than someone taking the dogs for a walk, particularly in a dark alley.

Georgie Fame was no longer on board but saxophonist and arranger Pee Wee Ellis returned to augment the most recent "hard core" of Morrison's band – bassist Nicky Scott and drummer Geoff Dunn, guitarist Ronnie Johnson, saxophonist Kate St John doubling on oboe, multi-instrumentalist Teena Lyle and second singer Brian Kennedy. Kennedy's harmony singing is again effective, though too often he is simply asked to repeat each line after Morrison has sung it, as if acting as an aural subtitle to Morrison's sometimes semi-coherent delivery. Among additional names, old Belfast friend Phil Coulter played piano and co-produced some of the tracks.

Optimism is a mood that Morrison returns to in the title track, which is about days when everything goes right, and in the closing song "In the Afternoon", a time of day made for love. But, inevitably, the album explores alternatives to contentment. "Russian Roulette" expresses unease, possibly in the press curiosity and rumours about his relationship with Rocca: "None of them really know just who that you are," he sings, with more feeling than syntax.

"Raincheck" is defiant, with Morrison back to his put-upon self, and in its repeated "Won't let the bastards grind me down" he probably had in mind a recent political scandal where Tory government minister Michael Mates, who held the Northern Ireland portfolio, was forced to resign having sent the disgraced entrepreneur Asil Nadir a watch which had been inscribed "Don't let the bastards grind you down."

"No Religion" is a complex, somewhat opaque song. "I cleaned up my diction," sings Morrison (a claim not fully borne out by some tracks on the album), "I had nothing left to say, except there's no religion… " This stumble of faith is supported by other lines, such as, "So cruel to expect the saviour to save the day." Cruel? And what else would a saviour be for? The song, addressing the death of Christian faith, is an intriguing enigma.

The Coulter influence is apparent in two straight country standards, austerely effective. In singing "You Don't Know Me" with his daughter Shana, Morrison adds a new dimension to the lyric, given that Shana stayed in the USA with her mother Janet after the divorce. It is worth ignoring the more direct references in the song's bridge to sexual love to see the majority of the song as a meditation between estranged father and daughter. "I'll Never Be Free", a 1950 country hit for superstar duo Kay Starr and Tennessee Ernie Ford, is a similar pleasure.

The titles of two songs indicate that Morrison is constitutionally incapable of undiluted happiness. "Underlying Depression" is the more effective of the two (the other is "Melancholia") in that Morrison can distance himself from the affliction, avoiding the trap of self-pity in such lines as "and these times ain't even so hard": he recognises that depression is an illness, not an indulgence. "Songwriter" is another of his exercises in demystifying what he does, while the closest the collection comes to mysticism is in "Ancient Highway". Significantly, the highway is now full of cars, and the mountain shares the horizon with the overpass, while "there's a roadside jam playin' on the edge of town." In days when towns don't have edges, just another overspill housing estate, this is a deliberately romantic image.

The *Sunday Independent* piece referred to the business relationship between Morrison and Rocca, and the most obvious manifestation of this was that she now controlled his promotional interviews by the simplest possible means – she did them herself. The record com-

pany video accompanying the release of *Days Like This* consisted of
the two in conversation; *Mojo* magazine was granted an interview
text for publication in their August 1995 issue, headlined "Pillow
Talk!" and copyrighted to Morrison's company Exile Productions
Limited. Morrison repeats his claim that he never plans the concept
of an album – he simply writes songs until he's got enough – reflects
that the process of recording has becoming more long-winded over
the years, and rejects the idea that pop music is a poetic art rather
than simple entertainment. Significantly, he admits to having "run
out of steam" as far as the mystical approach to subject matter is
concerned. Once again he denies that the life depicted in his songs
is his life, that the emotions described are his emotions. He confirms
his distaste for the music business and the star system.

Looking to the future, Morrison mentioned his Honorary
Doctorate from Ulster University and added, "If I was offered a position I'd do it tomorrow." The University saw the interview and took
him at his word, as Eamonn McCann reported in *The Observer* on
20 August. "Belfast-born Morrison is considering three options from
the university's Department of Language and Literature which
would involve giving lectures and taking seminars… The suggestions put to Morrison cover creativity and ideology in the modern
world and would slot into degree courses in humanities, politics and
philosophy, as well as business and management. Sources at the university say Morrison has responded positively but has ideas of his
own to discuss before making a decision."

By the time *Days Like This* was released Morrison was involved
in working with a jazz line-up led by trumpeter Guy Barker, reuniting
him with Georgie Fame, and had switched his attention to the
resulting album, *How Long Has This Been Going On?*: during gigs in
autumn 1995 he would plug the imminent new collection. At the
end of October he played the Cork Jazz Festival with the musicians
on the album, billed as Van Morrison and the Jazz Set – Barker and

Fame, tenor-players Alan Skidmore and Leo Green, pianist Robin Aspland, bassist Alec Dankworth and drummer Ralph Salmins.

On 30 November 60,000 people were crammed into Belfast city centre, in front of City Hall, singing "Days Like This". The occasion was the visit of President Bill Clinton to Belfast. Van Morrison was his "warm-up act", and the title song from his latest album had become the official anthem of the peace process, which was to come to such an unexpected and brutal end two months later. At the end of 1995, however, optimism was still high, and Belfast had been transformed, revealed once again as an elegant and friendly city. "Days Like This" had been licensed by the Northern Ireland Office to be the soundtrack to a television advertising campaign, designed to reinforce the "feel-good factor" after 15 months of peace. And the Irish rover was back in town, singing to his own people.

One of the year's least likely cultural events occurred in December, at the UK Year of Literature Closing Festival in Swansea. Morrison was on stage, talking about his work to a former schoolmate, the poet Gerald Dawe. Given the nature of the event, Dawe's brief was to probe the literary influences behind Morrison's work. While Morrison remained in a polite mood, it gradually became apparent that he wasn't going to change the habit of a lifetime, and the conversation died. After an interval he turned with relief to doing what he does best – singing his songs instead of talking about them.

Days Like This had continued to prove very successful and Morrison had a higher profile than of late. The jazz album appeared shortly before Christmas 1995, on Polygram's Verve/Polygram Jazz imprint. In a small-combo setting displaying immaculate musicianship Morrison re-examines many of his lyrics, often excitingly, but without ever convincing the listener that he has been a jazz singer all along. Twenty-five years earlier *Moondance* probably took his technique of white r'n'b phrasing as close to the discipline of jazz as it could comfortably go: now, returning to the song, any depths it might have had have been obscured by hurried vocal gymnastics, not enough in themselves.

Whether or not he will ever prove to be a jazz singer – or a university lecturer for that matter – the breadth of Morrison's achievements in a 35-year career is stunning. Helped neither by his own ungracious behaviour nor by the tendency of music fans to load too much weight on to their heroes, he has nothing left to prove. His musical and spiritual journey, rewardingly that of someone who asks more questions than provides answers, is unique in popular music. And if, as seems likely, he can do nothing but continue the journey, there must be further rewards to come.

One promise to himself has been kept of late – he has moved away from the big album-promoting tours that proved such a treadmill. Although it leaves many of his admirers somewhat at a loss to know when to expect him, he now prefers "weekend gigs", announced only a week or so in advance, sometimes at low-key club venues. In February 1996, for example, he, Georgie Fame and the band turned up in Exeter – a world away from the Masonic Auditorium, San Francisco. And what was in his repertoire? "Madame George", "Ballerina", "Slim Slow Slider"… ! Van Morrison in a tiny provincial club singing songs from *Astral Weeks*: all's right with the world.

TEN

The Angel and the Devil,
Riding Side by Side

In the unreal world of show business bad manners are too often tolerated. Even tinpot little "starlets" are allowed to misbehave and keep people waiting: their publicists will despise them in private but they will keep the gravy train on the rails. And the journalists, required to return to the office with their ration of words, will go along with it. The public is peddled a myth that "being difficult" is a by-product of the strains caused by working in the crazy world of entertainment. One of the world's leading opera singers takes pleasure in humiliating those who are instructed, on pain of dismissal, to humour him, is sexually unpleasant towards female colleagues, and spits at people. Because he can.

Morrison can bruise people like that, and yet he has never seemed to be a prima donna. Certainly his boorishness cannot be condoned, any more than it would be if circumstances had forced him to do a "real job". He was once a window cleaner – would his East Belfast customers have tolerated truculence, unreliability and insults? No, but nor would a publisher have commissioned a biography of him.

Nick Lowe once wrote a powerful song of repentance, "The Beast in Me". "God help the beast in me," growls his former father-in-law Johnny Cash, in a spare, reverberating reading on his 1994 album *American Recordings*. As the Man in Black ponders his sin, one takes a mental step backwards just in case the Almighty doesn't respond in time to cage the beast. This collision between the spiritual and the earthly, the dynamic struggle between a private angel and devil, seems to be at the core of Van Morrison's art.

In the life and work of Jerry Lee Lewis this conflict is more nakedly apparent, because such matters are more clear-cut in the deep South. Lewis knows that he's heading for Hell, because this can be the only destination for a blaspheming, hard-drinking, womanising, violent rock'n'roll singer. But no matter how many times he brushes up against the law, no matter how many times he abuses the codes of personal and marital conduct, no matter how many bits of his internal plumbing he leaves in the surgeon's aluminium dish, Lewis knows that he can only go down fighting. He has no choice.

Unlike Lewis, Morrison does not break the law, has rarely sought a fight and never brandishes a gun. Nor has he ever thumped the Bible and predicted Hellfire. Eternal punishment, in fact, is not one of his concerns. The two sides of his character are engaged in a more subtle battle. The fuel for his lifelong journey is spiritual curiosity, as he attempts to tap into the eternal mystery. At the same time he can be a discourteous lout.

Many of us would admit that our shyness and social awkward-ness can sometimes be manifested as abruptness, or even unintended rudeness, but that doesn't mean that we turn ill-temper into an art form. Nor do we sit down and write "Madame George", "Into the Mystic", "In the Garden" or "Avalon of the Heart". The devil and the angel strike sparks, and Morrison turns the reaction between them into decade on decade of great music. The full force gale of his work has even led many of those bruised by his gracelessness to forgive the unforgiveable.

One of the themes of this book has been Morrison's curiosity over spiritual matters, which has found its most coherent, inspirational form in a pantheistic response to landscape and climate. In general, however, he has been an intellectual and emotional grasshopper, hopping through a library of religions and philosophies, taking down something new from the shelves, dipping into it, replacing it. Paul Jones, a committed though far from uncritical Christian – and an admirer of Morrison's work as a fellow blues-singing, harmonica-playing white performer – feels that Morrison's spiritual journey "has never progressed beyond that of the dilettante". This seems undeniable: it is a harsh verdict but it is also a truthful one, on Morrison's own confession that he can never "arrive". And while this remains the case, the wrestling match between angel and devil must continue.

In 1983 a Somerset teacher, Andy Lock, and his partner Trina arranged to be married in the parish church of Stogumber, a small picture-postcard village in the north of the county, just west of the Taunton-to-Minehead road. Since neither were admirers of traditional church organ music they asked the vicar, Roger Spurr, if they could provide their own music. "Have whatever you like," he replied. "Some people have 'Annie's Song'." Lock had Van Morrison, rather than John Denver, in mind.

"I was working in Leicester at the time," says Lock, "and somebody up there said I ought to write to *Jim'll Fix It*, to see if I could get him to come and play at the wedding. So I got the address of his record company and wrote to him there saying that we were getting married in Stogumber, 'down by Avalon', do you mind if we use your music? I left it like that and I didn't hear anything.

"Just before the wedding I told my wife I'd written to him and hadn't heard. We got married at half past nine in the morning. Trin went down the aisle to 'Connswater'. We had 'Full Force Gale', 'Forever Young' by Dylan, a few things by other people. We had the reception back here at the house. And about 1.30 there was a phone call. Trin went to answer it and said that Van Morrison was coming. I said: "Don't be bloody silly, what'll he do, fly over?" It was just a big joke. I was sure she was messing about, so it became a running joke – he's coming, he's coming.

"About quarter to four my mother-in-law walked in and said that 'That man's here.' Apparently he'd never heard his music played in church – he'd actually wanted to come to the wedding but he only got the letter the day before. I think that the woman he was with at the time, Cathy McGhee, said: 'Let's go.' They got a train down from London to Bristol, where she had friends. Train to Taunton, taxi out. He stayed about an hour, very shy and nervous. We went in and talked to him for about 40 minutes, about anything, all sorts. Then he went. About a month later he turned up on a Saturday night, stayed about two-and-a-half hours. Talked about all sorts of things. Quite difficult – how do you talk to somebody like that when you've been listening to their music for years?

"I didn't see him again and then, in 1989, I went up to see him at a concert. I'd just got *Beautiful Vision*, things like that, and I thought they'd sound really good in church. So I left him a note saying, 'I don't know if you remember coming to our wedding, but how do you fancy playing in the church?' He rang up and said he thought it was a good idea. I asked him how much he wanted and he said just expenses. He came down on the following Wednesday and I took him to meet the vicar. We sorted it out for 17 January 1990.

"I sold the tickets in two days. I just rang up people I knew. The church held 300 and I wanted people who really wanted to come to get in so we only charged £10. He was down here at midday which seemed pretty amazing, because he usually just turns up and does it. He was sound-checking all afternoon...

"They had an interval in the middle of the concert – he walked out with the audience and walked back with them. That's how good a mood he was in. Afterwards when we went back to the hotel he said it was the best concert he'd ever done. You could literally hear a pin drop in there.

"I thought it would be nice to have something specific that we could say the money from the Van Morrison concert was spent on. So I thought of the wall painting in the church, which was really tatty, needed restoration. He thought that was fine. It got in the papers that he was doing the concert to save the painting. He wasn't, that was incidental, just some way of using the money. I've learned since that he was thinking of playing in a church, he was interested to know what his music would sound like, so I obviously wrote to him at the right time. He said that if I found him 20 churches he'd do a tour of Somerset. I did, and he didn't."

Although no Van Morrison gig would be complete without a brush with the press, in this case a local television crew, and a display of bad temper – he stormed off in the afternoon because Haji Ahkbar had got lost and missed the rehearsal – no one could doubt the "rightness" of hearing Morrison's music in the setting of a village church. This would not be true of a more obviously Christian, evangelistic, "happy clappy" performer: instead, the fit is perfect because of the mysterious spirituality informing so many of Morrison's finest songs. "I was looking through the visitors' book in the church," says Lock, "and I found an entry for New Year's Day, 1990. 'Van Morrison, Belfast and London, looking forward to the gig.' So he must have come down on his own, looked around the church, didn't talk to anybody, went away again. I think he's on a higher plane than basic Christianity. I don't even think he's particularly religious. At Stogumber he was trying to get a sense of meditation, of relaxation, over to the audience."

On 6 October 1993 Morrison was playing in South Wales at the King's Hotel, Newport, a place he'd played before, in keeping with his clear preference in recent years for the more intimate atmosphere that is afforded by such venues. "It started off as a really good concert," recalls Graham Barrett. "About 90 minutes into the set he said it was Jerry Lee Lewis' birthday [it had actually been seven days earlier] and he did a raunchy 25-minute rock'n'roll set. Then his mood seemed to change."

At this point, while the band doodled on with increasing awkwardness, Morrison began to lecture the audience. "This is not rock, this is not pop, this is called soul music. So instead of all the mother-fucking bastards who say something different, this is what it is..."

He made several attempts to start singing, never getting beyond "I'm on a trans-Euro train," with Brian Kennedy gamely repeating the phrase. Since this was clearly going nowhere one of the members of the audience called for "Brown Eyed Girl". Not a good idea.

"'Brown Eyed Girl' was lunchtime. This is dinnertime. 'Brown Eyed Girl' never was. Never is. It's an affliction of somebody's imagination. Had to do something for the fucking French people. Which means in other words the Yanks, you know..." After another aborted attempt to sing he began to warm to his theme:

"I'm talking about soul... I'm a soul singer. I'm more a mother-fucking soul singer than some mother-fucking mother-fucker. I'm a soul singer. I sing soul songs. Blues. Fuck the pop charts... I don't want to play 'Brown Eyed Girl'. Because I don't have to. Thank God, I don't have to. If I had to I'd commit suicide. I don't have to play 'Brown Eyed Girl' no more. I'm a soul singer. Fuck the assholes. I'm a soul singer..."

"He does seem to include a lot of swearing," observes Graham Barrett with commendable understatement. "Some people can swear and it's funny. But with him it just seems to be a vulgarity. As if he doesn't really like what he's doing." This, of course, has echoes of Cliff Richard's comment about self-loathing – the devil that is at war with his spirituality, his angel. Between them they are at the heart of the enigma.

Sources of quotes

INTRODUCTION

'Springsteen's definitely ripped me off...': Van Morrison in
   conversation with Stephen Davis, Boston, 17 May 1985.

'From the journalistic point of view...': Van Morrison, interview
   with Jackie Flavelle, Downtown Radio Ulster, 28 February 1983.

'I'm not really interested...': Van Morrison, interview with John
   Tobler, BBC Radio Oxford, 1983.

'...incorporated the Irish ballad...': Shay Healy, interview with
   author.

'I don't think of myself as a songwriter...': Van Morrison, interview
   with Paul Vincent, KMEL Radio, California, 1981.

'We were playing a young farmers' dance...' and further quotes:
   Harry Bird, interview with author.

'He's a cryptic person...': Donall Corvin, source unknown.

'He stormed in 35 minutes late...': Liam Fay, interview with author.

'Never had a cross word...': Shay Healy, as above.

'I was never part of the record business...': Van Morrison, interview
   with Mick Brown, *The Interview Album* (Mercury promotional
   release), 1986.

'I heard a story once...': Harry Bird, as above.

A CHILDHOOD IN EAST BELFAST

'I can't win...': Leslie Brennan, *Sunday Life*, 1 December 1991.

'Those houses at the back...': George Jones, interview with author.

'Solly just couldn't understand...': Dougie Knight, interview with
   author.

'My father had records...': Van Morrison, interview with Paul Jones,
   BBC Radio 2, 1991.

'For a while... a brief encounter...': Van Morrison in conversation with Stephen Davis, Boston, 17 May 1985.

'He was my guru...': Van Morrison, interview with Jonathan Cott, *Rolling Stone*, 1978.

'Sonny Terry, Muddy Waters...': Van Morrison, interview with Mick Brown, *The Interview Album* (Mercury promotional release), 1986.

'I heard a lot of blues records...': Van Morrison, interview with Happy Traum, *Rolling Stone*, 1970.

'There was a guy down the street...': Van Morrison, interview with Mick Brown, as above.

'He was a little isolated...': Rod Demick, interview with author.

'I heard this cat...': Carl Perkins, interview with author.

'What I connected with...': Van Morrison, quoted by Steve Turner, *Too Late to Stop Now*, 1993.

'The skiffle thing...': Van Morrison, interview with Mick Brown, as above.

A MUSICAL APPRENTICESHIP

'The Thunderbirds...': Van Morrison, interview with Mick Brown, *The Interview Album* (Mercury promotional release), 1986.

'We were originally the Thunderbolts...' and following quotes: George Jones, interview with author.

'The Javelins was...': Billy McAllen, interview with Steve Turner, *Too Late To Stop Now*, 1993.

'I had a window cleaning business...': Van Morrison, interview with Sean O'Hagan, *Select*, October 1990.

'Hospital stage productions...': Van Morrison, interview with Mick Brown, as above.

'We did US bases...' and following quote: Van Morrison, interview with Mick Brown, as above.

'Heidelberg...': Van Morrison, diary entry quoted by Ritchie Yorke, *Into the Music*, 1975.

'It was a really bad song...': Van Morrison, interview with Ritchie Yorke, as above.

'That's the sort of group...': Herbie Armstrong, quoting Van Morrison, interviewed by Steve Turner, as above.

'There was quite a bit...': Harry Bird, interview with author.

'...the first person I saw...': Van Morrison, quoted by Steve Turner,
as above.

'We'd had Ruby Murray...': Rod Demick, interview with author.

ANGRY YOUNG THEM

'The band was started...' and following quotes: Billy Harrison,
interview with author.

'...quite a lot of work...' and following quotes: Eric Wrixon,
interview with author.

'...with a jazz showband...': Dougie Knight, interview with author.

'I grew up...': Van Morrison, quoted in BBC Radio Ulster
documentary *Maritime Blues*, 1991.

'We were into...': Alan Henderson, interview with Steve Turner, *Too
Late to Stop Now*, 1993.

'Violins, spoons...': Jerry McCurvey, *Maritime Blues*, as above.

'There wasn't much r'n'b...': Van Morrison, interview with Paul
Jones, Radio 2, 1991.

'There were quite a few jazz things...': Van Morrison, interview with
Jackie Flavelle, Downtown Radio Ulster, 28 February 1983.

'Here is a room...': John Wilson, *Maritime Blues*, as above.

'The image was fine...': John Trew, quoted by Vincent Power, *Send
'Em Home Sweatin'*, 1990.

'They were pelted...': Vincent Power, as above.

'We did gigs...': Van Morrison, interviewed by Ritchie Yorke, *Into
the Music*, 1975.

'Morrison was electric...': Peter Lloyd, *Maritime Blues*, as above.

'My first recollection...': Mervyn Solomon, *Maritime Blues*, as above.

'He was handling...' and following quotes: Jim Armstrong,
interview with author.

'I didn't want Them...': Dick Rowe, interview with Johnny Rogan, *A
Portrait of the Artist*, 1984.

'By that time the whole r'n'b thing...': Van Morrison, interview with
Mick Brown, *The Interview Album* (Mercury promotional record),
1986.

'We never had the group...': Jimmy Conlon, *Maritime Blues*, as
above.

'Dublin was more pop...': Rory Gallagher, *Maritime Blues*, as above.

'I happened because of that scene…': Van Morrison, *Maritime Blues*, as above.

A TRANSITIONAL PERIOD

'I wanted to get more into…': Van Morrison, interview with Mick Brown, *The Interview Album* (Mercury promotional record), 1986.

'He's not a professional…': Philip Solomon, interview by Johnny Rogan, *A Portrait of the Artist*, 1984.

'We were drinking…': Rod Demick, interview with author.

'I was working in Belfast…': Van Morrison, interview with Mick Brown, as above.

'After everyone else had left…': Dougie Knight, interview with author.

'Bert wanted me…' and further quotes: Van Morrison, interview with Happy Traum, *Rolling Stone*, 1970.

'I knew he was a good r'n'b producer…': Van Morrison, interview with Mick Brown, as above.

'Morrison's rambling…': Bob Sarlin, *Turn It Up - I Can't Hear the Words*, 1973.

'The signature track…': Greil Marcus, *The Rolling Stone Illustrated History of Rock & Roll*, 1976.

'That was just a mistake…': Van Morrison, interview with Paul Vincent, KMEL Radio, California, 1981.

'…the Top 40 thing' and following quotes: Van Morrison, interview with Happy Traum, *Rolling Stone*, 1970.

'I'm writing TB Sheets Part II…': Van Morrison, interview with John Grissim Jr, *Rolling Stone*, 22 June1972.

'It wasn't really an album…': Van Morrison, interview with Mick Brown, as above.

'It was one day…' and following quote: Van Morrison, interview with Sean O'Hagan, *Select*, October 1990.

STELLAR HEIGHTS

'I didn't really want to be in…': Van Morrison, interview with Mick Brown, *The Interview Album* (Mercury promotional record), 1986.

'People like Jimi Hendrix…': Van Morrison, quoted by Ritchie Yorke, *Into the Music*, 1975.

'You must remember...': Joe Smith, interview by Ritchie Yorke, as
   above.
'At the time...' and following quotes: Bob Schwaid, interview in
   Mojo magazine, August 1995.
'In those days...': Jay Berliner, as above.
'I was kind of...': Van Morrison, interview with Happy Traum,
   Rolling Stone, 1970.
'...probably the most spiritually...': Van Morrison, various sources.
'I remember reading...' and any further Van Morrison quotes in the
   chapter not attributed below: Ritchie Yorke, as above.
'It sounds as if...': John Payne, interview with Steve Turner, *Too Late
   to Stop Now*, 1993.
'Guys like Richard Davis...': Van Morrison, Happy Traum, as above.
'It was a success musically...' and following quote: Van Morrison,
   interview with Mick Brown, as above.

MOONDANCING
'I definitely don't fit...': Van Morrison, interview with Richard
   Williams, *Melody Maker*, 28 July 1973.
'I met Jack Schroer...' and following quotes: Van Morrison,
   interview with Ritchie Yorke, *Into the Music*, 1975.
'It seemed as though...': Graham Blackburn, interview with Steve
   Turner, *Too Late To Stop Now*, 1993.
'I suppose I was about...': Van Morrison, interview with Steve
   Turner, 13 December 1985, quoted in *Too Late to Stop Now*, 1993.
'It's just about...' and following quotes: Van Morrison, Ritchie
   Yorke, as above, with the exception of the next attribution.
'It started out as a saxophone solo...': Van Morrison, interview with
   Sean O'Hagan, *Select*, October 1990.
'It was originally...' and following quotes: Van Morrison, interview
   with Richard Williams, *Melody Maker*, 28 July 1973.

WEST FROM WOODSTOCK
'Woodstock was getting...': Van Morrison, interview with Richard
   Williams, *Melody Maker*, 28 July 1973.
'He didn't want to leave...': John Platania, interview with Steve
   Turner, *Too Late to Stop Now*, 1993.

'I'm extremely wasted…': Van Morrison, quoted by Johnny Rogan,
  A Portrait of the Artist, 1984.
'When I went on the West Coast…' and following quote: Van
  Morrison, interview with Sean O'Hagan, *Select*, October 1990.
'I'd never work with Van Morrison again…': Ted Templeman,
  interviewed in *Bam* magazine, early 1980s.
'He doesn't like a lot of people around…': Janet Planet, interviewed
  by Shay Healy, *Spotlight*, 25 June 1972.
'The vibes here…': Van Morrison, interview with John Grissim Jr,
  Rolling Stone, 22 June 1972.
'The picture was taken…' and following quotes: Van Morrison,
  quoted by Ritchie Yorke, *Into the Music*, 1975.
'That came with just…': Van Morrison, interview with Sean
  O'Hagan, as above.
'…was difficult to live with': Janet Planet, quoted by John Platania
  in Steve Turner's *It's Too Late to Stop Now*, 1993.
'It was a combination…': Van Morrison, interview with Sean
  O'Hagan, as above.
'…statement that you…': Van Morrison, quoted by Ritchie Yorke, as
  above.
'Just picking things up…' and following quote: Van Morrison,
  interview with Sean O'Hagan, as above.
'I would say that…': John Platania, interview with Steve Turner, as
  above.
'I am getting more into performing…': Van Morrison, quoted by
  Ritchie Yorke, as above.
'Sometimes Van would suddenly decide…': Pete Wingfield,
  interview in *Beat Instrumental*.
'From 1964 right through to about 1974…': Van Morrison, interview
  with Sean O'Hagan, as above.
'We got a few tracks out of it…': Van Morrison, interview with Ian
  Birch, *Melody Maker*, 25 June 1977.
'There was never a Crusaders session…': Van Morrison, interview
  with Stephen Davis, Boston, 17 May 1985.

ON A NEW WAVELENGTH
'When I started out I was in dance bands…': Van Morrison,
  interview with Jonathan Cott, *Rolling Stone*, 30 November 1978.

'I mean, people who go to work…': Van Morrison, interview with Dermot Stokes, *Hot Press*, March 1978.

'What is behind all this stuff…': Van Morrison, interview with Paul Vincent, KMEL Radio, California, 1981.

'I've cut down to the minimum…' and following quotes: Van Morrison, interview with Jackie Flavelle, Downtown Radio Ulster, 28 February 1983.

'It isn't true…' and following three quotes: Van Morrison, interview with Stephen Davis, Boston, 17 May 1985.

'I'm not doing anything special…' and following quotes: Van Morrison, interview with Seamus Creagh, *Hot Press*, 5 December 1985.

'There have been many lies put out about me…': Van Morrison, interview with Anthony Denselow, *The Observer*, 3 August 1986.

' I take you through the meditation programme…' and following quotes: Van Morrison, interview with Mick Brown, *The Interview Album*, Mercury promotional release, 1986.

'This is my job…': Van Morrison, interview with Anthony Denselow, as above.

'I think there's a lot of illusions…': Van Morrison, interview with Mick Brown, as above.

'I started off making a jazz album…': Van Morrison, interview with Bill Morrison, Polygram video, 12 August 1987.

IRISH HEARTBEAT

'Going away and coming back…': Van Morrison, interview in *The Irish Times*, 1989.

'I started touring very young…': Van Morrison, interview with Sean O'Hagan, *Select*, October 1990.

'Since hooking up with Georgie Fame…': Van Morrison, interview with Paul Jones, BBC Radio 2, 1991.

'Georgie's very open…': Richie Buckley, quoted by Harry Browne in *The Irish Times*, 15 December 1990.

'I didn't have anything to do…': Van Morrison, interview with Sean O'Hagan, as above.

'…four very intense days…': Paul Durcan, quoted by Harry Browne, as above.

'Being in the studio with Van Morrison...': Tom Jones, quoted in *Vox*, April 1991.

'It was the most hectic session...': Alan Douglas, as above.

'...filled with self-loathing': Cliff Richard, talking to Joe Jackson, *The Irish Times*.

'Lies, exaggerations and innuendo...': Van Morrison, quoted in *The Belfast Telegraph*, 24 September 1993.

'Of course it was out of the question': Steve Turner, as above.

'That book is about somebody else': Van Morrison, quoted in *Today*, 28 October 1993.

'Two thirds of the criticisms...': Steve Turner, as above.

THE ANGEL AND THE DEVIL...

'...has never progressed...': Paul Jones, in conversation with the author.

'I was working in Leicester at the time...': Andy Lock, interview with author.

'It started off...': Graham Barrett, interview with author.

Discography

This is an attempt to compile the most complete annotated list to date of Van Morrison's official, bootlegged and promotional releases, with the Monarchs, Them and as a solo artist, together with compilations and guest appearances, songs written by Morrison but recorded only by other artists, film soundtracks, and appearances on film, television and video. The sources were my own collection and research, and previous biographies (see bibliography) in the first instance. The Internet produced valuable Morrison pages compiled by Michael Hayward, but all additional work, together with checking existing sources, was done by Graham Barrett. The Van Morrison Newsletter was the initial source of the film, TV and video appearances. In spite of Graham's expert help I alone must take responsibility for inevitable omissions, incomplete annotations and, I confess, whatever inaccuracies have crept in. No one person could possibly give absolute chapter and verse on everything included here, but we have attempted to check wherever possible. Many bootlegs, for instance, give incorrect sources and musician details – we have caught and corrected whatever we can. Some unofficial recordings, usually on audio tape, will have been copied and circulated privately without coming to our attention, and are therefore not included. How many copies before it becomes a bootleg? The bootleg industry never sleeps, and so in between completing this manuscript and publication there will be one or two additions to the list. And so it goes on. But I return to my original claim: this is the most complete list to date.

JOHN COLLIS

FIRST-EVER RECORDING:
Boozoo Hully Gully/Twingy Baby (CBS Germany only)
The Monarchs (Van Morrison on sax)

ALBUMS WITH THEM:
Them (Decca) (UK EP) February 1965
    Philosophy/Baby Please Don't Go/One Two Brown Eyes/Don't
    Start Crying Now
Them (Decca) (UK) June 1965
    Mystic Eyes/If You and I Could Be As Two/Little Girl/Just a
    Little Bit/I Gave My Love a Diamond/Gloria/You Just Can't
    Win/Go On Home Baby/Don't Look Back/I Like It Like That/I'm
    Gonna Dress in Black/Bright Lights, Big City/My LittleBaby/(Get
    Your Kicks on) Route 66
Them (Parrot) (US) July 1965
    Mystic Eyes/If You and I Could Be As Two/Little Girl/Gloria/Go
    On Home Baby/Don't Look Back/I Like It Like That/I'm Gonna
    Dress in Black/(Get Your Kicks on) Route 66/One Two Brown
    Eyes/One More Time/Here Comes the Night
Them Again (Decca) (UK) January 1966
    Could You Would You/Something You Got/Call My Name/Turn
    On Your Love Light/I Put a Spell on You/I Can Only Give You
    Everything/My Lonely Sad Eyes/I Got a Woman/Out of
    Sight/It's All Over Now, Baby Blue/Bad or Good/How Long
    Baby/Hello Josephine/Don't You Know/Hey Girl/Bring 'Em On
    in
Them Again (Parrot) (US) April 1966
    Could You Would You/Something You Got/Call My Name/Turn
    On Your Love Light/I Can Only Give You Everything/My Lonely
    Sad Eyes/Out of Sight/It's All Over Now, Baby Blue/Bad or
    Good/How Long Baby/Don't You Know/Bring 'Em On In
Untitled (Dutch EP) 1967
    Times Getting Tougher Than Tough/Stormy Monday/Baby What
    You Want Me to Do/Friday's Child
Them (London) (UK/US) 1988: CD reissue of UK album *Them*
Them Again (Deram) (UK/US) 1989: CD reissue of UK album *Them
    Again* plus US version of One More Time

THEM ANTHOLOGIES:

The World of Them (Decca) (UK) 1970

Here Comes the Night/Baby Please Don't Go/I'm Gonna Dress in
 Black/Richard Cory/I Put a Spell on You/Bring 'Em On in/
 Gloria/Mystic Eyes/Turn On Your Lovelight/It's All Over Now,
 Baby Blue/One Two Brown Eyes/Don't Start Crying Now

Them Featuring Van Morrison (Parrot) (US) 1972

Mystic Eyes/If You and I Could Be As Two/Little Girl/Gloria/
 Don't Look Back/I Like It Like That/(Get Your Kicks on) Route
 66/One Two Brown Eyes/One More Time/Here Comes the
 Night/Could You Would You/Something You Got/Turn On Your
 Lovelight/I Can Only Give You Everything/My Lonely Sad Eyes/
 Out of Sight/It's All Over Now, Baby Blue/Bad or Good/How
 Long Baby/Bring 'Em On in

Backtrackin' (London) (US) October 1974

Richard Cory/I Put a Spell on You/Just a Little Bit/I Gave My
 Love a Diamond/Half As Much/Baby Please Don't Go/Hey
 Girl/Don't Start Crying Now/All for Myself/Mighty Like a Rose

Rock Roots: Them (Decca) (UK) 1976

Don't Start Crying Now/I'm Gonna Dress in Black/(Get Your
 Kicks on) Route 66/How Long Baby/Bright Lights, Big City/
 Don't You Know/Call My Name/The Story of Them, Parts One
 and Two/Mighty Like a Rose/Times Getting Tougher than
 Tough/Stormy Monday/Baby What You Want Me To Do/Friday's
 Child

The Story of Them Featuring Van Morrison (London) (US) March 1977

The Story of Them, Parts One and Two/Times Getting Tougher
 Than Tough/Stormy Monday/Baby What You Want Me to Do/
 Bright Lights, Big City/My Little Baby/I Got a Woman/
 Philosophy/Friday's Child

Them Featuring Van Morrison (London) (UK/US CD) 1987

Gloria/The Story of Them/Stormy Monday/Mystic Eyes/Hey
 Girl/Baby Please Don't Go/Here Comes the Night/My Lonely
 Sad Eyes/Richard Cory/(It Won't Hurt) Half As Much/Turn On
 Your Love Light/I Put a Spell on You/Don't Look Back

THEM SINGLES:

(Released on Decca in the UK and Parrot in the US, where
    appropriate)

One Two Brown Eyes/Don't Start Crying Now (UK/US) September
    1964

Baby Please Don't Go/Gloria (UK/US) November 1964

Here Comes the Night/All for Myself (UK/US) March 1965

One More Time/How Long Baby (UK) (June 1965)

(It Won't Hurt) Half as Much/I'm Gonna Dress in Black (UK/US)
    August 1965

Mystic Eyes/If You and I Could Be As Two (UK/US) November
    1965

Call My Name/Bring 'Em On In (alternate takes) (UK) March 1966

Call My Name/Bring 'Em On In (album cuts) March 1966

I Can Only Give You Everything/Don't Start Crying Now (US) 1966

Richard Cory/Don't You Know (UK/US) May 1966

Gloria/If You and I Could Be As Two (US) August 1972

(Released on Major Minor in the UK)

Stormy Monday (July 1967)

The Story of Them (September 1967)

THEM TRACKS ON OTHER COLLECTIONS:

Little Girl (Uncensored version on *England's Greatest Hitmakers*,
    Decca, 1965)

Baby, Please Don't Go (on *Good Morning, Vietnam*, A&M, 1988)

Baby, Please Don't Go (on *Wild at Heart*, Polydor, 1990)

Baby, Please Don't Go, Gloria (on *History of British Rock Volume 5*,
    Rhino, 1991)

Here Comes the Night, Mystic Eyes (on *History of British Rock
    Volume 6*, Rhino, 1991)

Here Comes the Night (on *British Sixties*, undated)

ALBUMS CREDITED TO VAN MORRISON, WITH US RELEASE
    DATES:

Blowin' Your Mind (Bang) September 1967

    Goodbye Baby/Spanish Rose/He Ain't Give You None/TB
    Sheets/Who Drove the Red Sports Car/Ro Ro Rosey/Brown Eyed

Girl/Midnight Special
Astral Weeks (Warner Brothers) November 1968
   Astral Weeks/Beside You/Sweet Thing/Cyprus Avenue/The Way
   Young Lovers Do/Madame George/Ballerina/Slim Slow Slider
Moondance (Warner Brothers) March 1970
   And It Stoned Me/Moondance/Crazy Love/Caravan/Into the
   Mystic/Come Running/These Dreams of You/Brand New Day/
   Everyone/Glad Tidings
The Best of Van Morrison (Bang) November 1970
   Spanish Rose/It's All Right/Send Your Mind/The Smile You Smile/
   The Back Room/Brown Eyed Girl/Goodbye Baby/Ro Ro Rosey/
   He Ain't Give You None/Midnight Special
His Band and the Street Choir (Warner Brothers) December 1970
   Domino/Crazy Face/Give Me a Kiss/I've Been Working/Call Me
   Up in Dreamland/I'll Be Your Lover, Too/Blue Money/Virgo
   Clowns/Gypsy Queen/Sweet Jannie/If I Ever Needed Someone/
   Street Choir
Tupelo Honey (Warner Brothers) November 1971
   Wild Night/(Straight to Your Heart) Like a Cannonball/Old Old
   Woodstock/Starting a New Life/You're My Woman/Tupelo
   Honey/I Wanna Roo You (Scottish Derivative)/When That
   Evening Sun Goes Down/Moonshine Whiskey
Saint Dominic's Preview (Warner Brothers) July 1972
   Jackie Wilson Said (I'm in Heaven When You Smile)/Gypsy/I Will
   Be There/Listen to the Lion/Saint Dominic's Preview/ Redwood
   Tree/Almost Independence Day
Hard Nose the Highway (Warner Brothers) July 1973
   Snow in San Anselmo/Warm Love/Hard Nose the Highway/
   Wild Children/The Great Deception/Bein' Green/Autumn Song/
   Purple Heather
TB Sheets (Bang) January 1974
   He Ain't Give You None/Beside You/It's All Right/Madame
   George/TB Sheets/Who Drove the Red Sports Car/Ro Ro
   Rosey/Brown Eyed Girl
It's Too Late to Stop Now (Warner Brothers) February 1974
   Ain't Nothin' You Can Do/Warm Love/Into the Mystic/These
   Dreams of You/I Believe to My Soul/I've Been Working/Help

Me/Wild Children/Domino/I Just Wanna Make Love to You/
Bring It on Home to Me/Saint Dominic's Preview/Take Your
Hand out of My Pocket/Listen to the Lion/Here Comes the
Night/Gloria/Caravan/Cyprus Avenue

Veedon Fleece (Warner Brothers) October 1974
Fair Play/Linden Arden Stole the Highlights/Who Was That
Masked Man/Streets of Arklow/You Don't Pull No Punches, But
You Don't Push the River/Bulbs/Cul de Sac/Comfort You/Come
Here My Love/Country Fair

Two Originals of Van Morrison (Warner Brothers) October 1975
British re-package of *His Band and Street Choir* and *Tupelo Honey*

A Period of Transition (Warner Brothers) April 1977
You Gotta Make It Through the World/It Fills You Up/The
Eternal Kansas City/Joyous Sound/Flamingos Fly/Heavy
Connection/Cold Wind in August

This Is Where I Came in (Bang) September 1977
Spanish Rose/Goodbye Baby (Baby Goodbye)/He Ain't Give You
None/Beside You/Madame George/TB Sheets/Brown Eyed
Girl/Send Your Mind/The Smile You Smile/The Back Room/Ro
Ro Rosey/Who Drove the Red Sports Car/It's All Right/Joe
Harper Saturday Morning/Midnight Special

Wavelength (Warner Brothers) September 1978
Kingdom Hall/Checkin' It Out/Natalia/Venice USA/Lifetimes/
Wavelength/Santa Fe/Beautiful Obsession/Hungry for Your
Love/Take It Where You Find It

Into the Music (Warner Brothers) August 1979
Bright Side of the Road/Full Force Gale/Stepping Out
Queen/Troubadours/Rolling Hills/You Make Me Feel So Free/
Angeliou/And the Healing Has Begun/It's All in the Game/You
Know What They're Writing About

Common One (Warner Brothers) August 1980
Haunts of Ancient Peace/Summertime in England/Satisfied/
Wild Honey/Spirit/When Heart Is Open

Beautiful Vision (Warner Brothers) February 1982
Celtic Ray/Northern Muse (Solid Ground)/Dweller on the
Threshold/Beautiful Vision/She Gives Me Religion/Cleaning
Windows/Vanlose Stairway/Aryan Mist/Across the Bridge

Where Angels Dwell/Scandinavia

Inarticulate Speech of the Heart (Warner Brothers) March 1983
   Higher than the World/Connswater/River of Time/Celtic Swing/
   Rave On, John Donne/Inarticulate Speech of the Heart No. 1/Irish
   Heartbeat/The Street Only Knew Your Name/Cry for Home/
   Inarticulate Speech of the Heart No. 2/September Night

Live at the Grand Opera House, Belfast (Mercury) February 1984
   Introduction: Into the Mystic (Instrumental)/Inarticulate Speech
   of the Heart/Dweller on the Threshold/It's All in the Game/You
   Know What They're Writing About/She Gives Me Religion/
   Haunts of Ancient Peace/Full Force Gale/Beautiful Vision/
   Vanlose Stairway/Rave On, John Donne/Rave On, Part Two/
   Northern Muse (Solid Ground)/Cleaning Windows

A Sense of Wonder (Mercury) December 1984
   Tore Down a la Rimbaud/Ancient of Days/Evening Meditation/
   The Master's Eyes/What Would I Do/A Sense of Wonder/
   Boffyflow and Spike/If You Only Knew/Let the Slave
   (incorporating The Price of Experience)/A New Kind of Man

No Guru, No Method, No Teacher (Mercury) July 1986
   Got to Go Back/Oh the Warm Feeling/Foreign Window/A Town
   Called Paradise/In the Garden/Tir Na Nog/Here Comes the
   Knight/Thanks for the Information/One Irish Rover/Ivory Tower

Poetic Champions Compose (Mercury) September 1987
   Spanish Steps/The Mystery/Queen of the Slipstream/I Forgot
   that Love Existed/Sometimes I Feel like a Motherless Child/Celtic
   Excavation/Someone Like You/Alan Watts Blues/Give Me My
   Rapture/Did Ye Get Healed?/Allow Me

Irish Heartbeat (with the Chieftains) (Mercury) June 1988
   Star of the County Down/Irish Heartbeat/Ta Mo Chleamhnas
   Deanta/Raglan Road/She Moved Through the Fair/I'll Tell Me
   Ma/Carrickfergus/Celtic Ray/My Lagan Love/Marie's Wedding

Avalon Sunset (Polydor) June 1989
   Whenever God Shines His Light/Contacting My Angel/I'd Love
   to Write Another Song/Have I Told You Lately/Coney Island/I'm
   Tired Joey Boy/When Will I Ever Learn to Live in God/
   Orangefield/Daring Night/These are the Days

The Best of Van Morrison (Polydor) March 1990
  Bright Side of the Road/Gloria/Moondance/Baby Please Don't
  Go/Have I Told You Lately/Brown Eyed Girl/Sweet Thing/
  Warm Love/Wonderful Remark/Jackie Wilson Said (I'm in
  Heaven When You Smile)/Full Force Gale/And It Stoned Me/
  Here Comes the Night/Domino/Did Ye Get Healed?/Wild
  Night/Cleaning Windows/Whenever God Shines His Light/
  Queen of the Slipstream/Dweller on the Threshold
Enlightenment (Polydor) October 1990
  Real Real Gone/Enlightenment/So Quiet in Here/Avalon of the
  Heart/See Me Through/Youth of 1,000 Summers/In the Days
  Before Rock 'n' Roll/Start All Over Again/She's My Baby/
  Memories
Hymns to the Silence (Polydor) September 1991
  Professional Jealousy/I'm Not Feeling It Anymore/Ordinary
  Life/Some Peace of Mind/So Complicated/I Can't Stop Loving
  You/Why Must I Always Explain/Village Idiot/See Me Through
  Part Two (Just a Closer Walk with Thee)/Take Me Back/By His
  Grace/All Saints Day/Hymns to the Silence/On Hyndford
  Street/Be Though My Vision/Carrying a Torch/Green Mansions/
  Pagan Streams/Quality Street/It Must Be You/I Need Your Kind
  of Loving
Bang Masters (Epic) 1991
  Brown Eyed Girl/Spanish Rose (with additional verses)/Goodbye
  Baby (Baby Goodbye)/Ro Ro Rosey/Chick-a-Boom/It's All
  Right/Send Your Mind/The Smile You Smile/The Back Room/
  Midnight Special/TB Sheets/He Ain't Give You None (alternate
  take)/Who Drove the Red Sports Car/Beside You/Joe Harper
  Saturday Morning (additional verses)/Madame George/Brown
  Eyed Girl (alternate take)/I Love You (the Smile You Smile)
The Best of Van Morrison Volume Two (Polydor) January 1993
  Real Real Gone/When Will I Ever Learn to Live in God/
  Sometimes I Feel Like a Motherless Child/In the Garden/A Sense
  of Wonder/I'll Tell Me Ma/Coney Island/Enlightenment/Rave
  On, John Donne/Rave On Part Two (Live)/Don't Look Back/It's
  All Over Now, Baby Blue/One Irish Rover/The Mystery/Hymns
  to the Silence/Evening Meditation

Too Long in Exile (Polydor) June 1993

Too Long in Exile/Big Time Operators/Lonely Avenue/Ball and Chain/In the Forest/Till We Get the Healing Done/Gloria/Good Morning Little Schoolgirl/Wasted Years/The Lonesome Road/ Moody's Mood for Love/Close Enough for Jazz/Before the World Was Made/I'll Take Care of You/Instrumental/Tell Me What You Want

Payin' Dues (Charly) 1994

Brown Eyed Girl/He Ain't Give You None/TB Sheets/Spanish Rose/Goodbye Baby (Baby Goodbye)/Ro Ro Rosey/Who Drove the Red Sports Car/Midnight Special/Beside You/It'sAll Right/ Madame George/Send Your Mind/The Smile You Smile/The Back Room/Joe Harper Saturday Morning/Chick-a-Boom/I Love You (The Smile You Smile)/Brown Eyed Girl (alternate take)/ Twist and Shake/Shake and Roll/Stomp and Scream/Scream and Holler/Jump and Thump/Drivin' Wheel/Just Ball/Shake It Mable/Hold On George/The Big Royalty Check/Ring Worm/ Savoy Hollywood/Freaky If You Got This Far/Up Your Mind/ Thirty Two/All the Bits/You Say France and I Whistle/Blow in Your Nose/Nose in Your Blow/La Mambo/Go for Yourself/Want a Danish/Here Comes Dumb George/Chickee Coo/Do It/Hang On Groovy/Goodbye George/Dum Dum George/Walk and Talk/The Wobble/Wobble and Ball

In Portugal (1992) these tracks were released on two CDs, as here, except that each contained some of the "real" Bang tracks plus half of the "contractual obligation" stuff. The title was *The Lost Tapes, Volume 1* and *Volume 2*, subtitled *The Bang Masters* and *Previously Unreleased Takes*

A Night in San Francisco (Polydor) May 1994

Did Ye Get Healed?/It's All in the Game/Make It Real One More Time/I've Been Working/I Forgot That Love Existed/Vanlose Stairway/Trans-Euro Train/Fool for You/You Make Me Feel So Free/Beautiful Vision/See Me Through/Soldier of Fortune/ Thank You Falettinme Be Mice Elf Again/Ain't That Loving You Baby?/Stormy Monday/Have You Ever Loved a Woman?/No Rollin' Blues/Help Me/Good Morning Little Schoolgirl/Tupelo Honey/Moondance/My Funny Valentine/Jumpin' with

Symphony Sid/It Fills You Up/I'll Take Care of You/It's a Man's,
Man's Man's World/Lonely Avenue/4 o'Clock in the Morning/So
Quiet in Here/That's Where It's At/In the Garden/You Send
Me/Allegheny/Have I Told You Lately That I Love You?/Shakin'
All Over/Gloria

Blowin' Your Mind (Gold Mastersound/Sony) February 1995
Brown Eyed Girl/He Ain't Give You None/TB Sheets/Spanish
Rose/Goodbye Baby (Baby Goodbye)/Ro Ro Rosey/Who Drove
the Red Sports Car/Midnight Special/Spanish Rose (alternate
take)/Ro Ro Rosey (alternate take)/Goodbye Baby (Baby
Goodbye) (alternate take)/Who Drove the Red Sports Car
(alternate take)/Midnight Special (alternate take)

Days Like This (Polydor) June 1995
Perfect Fit/Russian Roulette/Raincheck/You Don't Know Me/No
Religion/Underlying Depression/Songwriter/Days Like This/I'll
Never Be Free/Melancholia/Ancient Highway/In the Afternoon

Cuchulain (Molex) 1991: A reading from Irish mythology released by
Moles Records, Bath, Avon, UK

BOOTLEG ALBUMS BY VAN MORRISON:

Since some of these records are undated, others cover many years
and yet others were released years after the recordings were made,
they are listed alphabetically by title. Details of these bootleg
releases are included because they are an important and revealing
part of the Van Morrison story, but this does not imply any particular stance by author or publisher on the ethics of bootlegging. In
this case any argument is surely an artistic one – does a performer
have a right to present his music as he, and/or his record company,
chooses, through a planned sequence of record releases, or does the
Morrison junkie have a greater right to feed his or her habit in any
way possible? They are also an indication of songs by other artists
that have caught Morrison's fancy, for example Bo Diddley's "Who
Do You Love" and Johnny Kidd and the Pirates classics, "Shakin' All
Over" and "Shot of Rhythm and Blues".

JC

Amsterdam's Tapes (with Doctor John) (Phonocomp) 1991
Fever/I'll Go Crazy/Baby Please Don't Go/Santa Rosalia/I Just

Want to Make Love to You/Shakin' All Over/I Believe/Into the
Music
Recorded live at the Vara Studios, Amsterdam, 24 June 1974. Van
Morrison (vocals, acoustic guitar), Dr John (keyboards, back-up
vocals, percussion), Mick Ronson (lead guitar, back-up vocals),
Leo Nocentelli (rhythm guitar), Art Neville (organ), Jo Modeliste
(drums), George Porter Jr (bass). Assumed to be recorded from a
radio show

Bluesology 1963-73 (Musichien) Undated
Stormy Monday/Don't Start Crying Now/Here Comes the
Night/All for Myself/Gloria/One More Time/I Shall Sing/
Hound Dog (live)/You Move Me/Misty (live)/When I Deliver/
Come On Child/Goodnight Irene/All Around the World/The
Street Only Knew Your Name/BooZooh/Oh Twingy Baby
The first two tracks are from Them's first recording session for
Decca, 1964; tracks 3 and 4 from a BBC Radio session, March 1965;
tracks 5 and 6 from Them's next BBC Radio session, June 1965;
tracks 7-15 are studio out-takes or live versions; the last two tracks
are the Monarchs single recorded in German, given slightly
different (but equally silly) titles

Can You Feel the Silence (Great Dane) 1989
Go to the Hide-Place in Your Mind/Into the Mystic/Moondance/
Wavelength/Full Force Gale/Bright Side of the Road/It's All in
the Game/She Gives Me Religion/Northern Muse/Vanlose
Stairway/Help Me/When I Come Home/Celtic Ray/Dweller on
the Threshold/Satisfied/Cleaning Windows/ Summertime in
England/Scandinavia
Italian bootleg recording taken from the *Rockpalast* tv special
concert in Essen, Germany, 3 April 1982 (also transmitted on
BBCtv). This is the same record as the *Live in Essen* bootleg (see
below) with some variations in track timings

The Church of Our Lady St Mary (Kiss the Stone) 1991
Did Ye Get Healed/Whenever God Shines His Light/It's All in the
Game/Orangefield/When Will I Ever Learn?/Full Force Gale/
Beautiful Vision/Dweller on the Threshold/Vanlose Stairway/
Give Me My Rapture/Bright Side of the Road/So Quiet in
Here/Thank God/Into the Mystic/She Gives Me Religion/

Northern Muse/Down by the Riverside
This is the concert referred to in the text, when Morrison and his
band played at the Church of Our Lady St Mary, Stogumber,
Somerset on 17 January 1990: Van Morrison (vocals, saxophone,
guitar, keyboards), Georgie Fame (keyboards, back-up vocals),
Bernie Holland (lead guitar), Brian Odger (bass), Haji Ahkbar
(flugelhorn) and Dave Early (drums, percussion). This is an
incomplete recording of the concert, omitting "In the Garden".
Copycats Ripped off My Soul (Skeleton) 1991
Moondance/Celtic Swing/Tore Down a la Rimbaud/Warm
Feeling/Here Comes the Night/Domino/I Will Be There/Gloria/
Sense of Wonder/And the Healing Has Begun/In the Garden/
Rave On John Donne
Recorded in concert in Frankfurt, 1986 (though it claims to be from
a Belgian performance)
Dark Knight of the Soul (with the Chieftains) (Moontunes) Undated
Tore Down a la Rimbaud/In the Garden/Rave On John Donne/
Did Ye Get Healed/Star of the Down/She Moved Through the
Fair/Ta Mo Chleamhnas Deanta/Tell Me Ma/Carrickfergus/
Celtic Ray/Marie's Wedding/Boffyflow and Spike/Goodnight
Irene/Moondance/T for Texas/When I Was a Cowboy/Sense of
Wonder/Celtic Ray/In the Garden/Raglan Road/Send In the
Clowns
The first 14 tracks come from a concert at Belfast's Ulster Hall, 15
September 1988, tracks 15-20 from a concert at Coleraine
University, 20 April 1988, and the final track was recorded at
Ronnie Scott's club in Frith Street, London on 6 June 1986. Tracks
1-4 are with the Van Morrison Band, tracks 5-14 with the
Chieftains, tracks 15-20 "unplugged" with Derek Bell and track 21
with Chet Baker. The bootleg emanates from the Czech Republic
Desert Land (Flashback World Productions) Undated
Brown Eyed Girl/Moonshine Whisky/Moondance/Wild
Night/Ballerina/Blue Money/Buona Sera Senorita
Recorded at Pacific High Studios on 19 September 1971. This was
a live radio programme and Morrison performed to an invited
audience of 200 people. No musician credits. The bootleg comes
from Luxembourg. See also (below) *The Inner Mystic* (also *Into the*

Mystic, referred to there), and *This is Van Morrison*, other bootlegs
taken from this same radio session

From the Coast of Barcelona (Razor's Edge) 1995 Bob Dylan 2 CD set
Recorded on Dylan's 1984 European tour, it includes two duets
with Van Morrison at Slane Castle, Ireland, on 8 July 1984, "It's All
Over Now, Baby Blue" and "Tupelo Honey". Morrison is pictured
with Dylan on the enclosed booklet

Gets His Chance To Wail series: there was originally one US release
under this title, listed here first. Following its release, a series of
(to date) three European bootlegs on the Gold Standard label
nicked the *Gets His Chance to Wail* tag, but used it as a sub-title. So
they are all included here for convenience, but in terms of origin
there is no connection between the first one and the following
three, though there is a lot of duplication of material

Gets His Chance To Wail (unknown label) Undated
Ballerina/Domino/If I Ever Needed Someone/These Dreams of
You/And It Stoned Me/Come Running/Bit By Bit/Hey Where
Are You (Lean On Me?)/Lorna/I Need Your Kind of Loving/Rock
& Roll Band (Wasn't That a Time?)/Funny Face/Wild Night/
Brand New Day/When the Evening Sun Goes Down/Nobody
Really Knows/Caravan/The Way Young Lovers Do
The tracks date from 1969-71, and are mainly demo versions of
songs destined for *Moondance, His Band and Street Choir* and *Tupelo
Honey*

Laughing in the Wind (*Van Morrison Gets His Chance To Wail Volume 1*)
(Gold Standard) Undated
Ballerina/Domino/If I Ever Needed Someone/These Dreams of
You/And It Stoned Me/Come Running/Bit By Bit/Hey Where
Are You (Lean On Me?)/Lorna/I Need Your Kind of Loving/Rock
& Roll Band (Wasn't That a Time?)/Funny Face/I Shall Sing/
Laughing in the Wind/Street Theory/Foggy Mountain Top (T For
Texas?)/There There Child/It Hurts To Want It So Bad/Feedback
on Highway 101
The first 12 tracks are studio demos 1969-71, and are also on the
first,'real,' *Gets His Chance To Wail* bootleg, followed by seven
studio demos 1974-75. On the CD itself the title is given, even
more confusingly, as *Naked in the Jungle Volume 1*

Naked in the Jungle (Van Morrison Gets His Chance To Wail Volume 2)
(Gold Standard) Undated
Wild Night/Brand New Day/When the Evening Sun Goes
Down/Nobody Really Knows/Caravan/The Way Young Lovers
Do/Spare Me a Little/You've Got the Power/Try For Sleep/
Naked in the Jungle/And the Streets Only Knew Her Name/Grits
Ain't Groceries/Don't Change On Me/Down to Earth/
Mechanical Bliss/Real, Real Gone/Foreign Window
The first six tracks are studio demos 1969-71, and are also on the
first *Gets His Chance To Wail*, plus ten tracks 1974-76 and "Foreign
Window" with Bob Dylan, late 1980s. "Spare Me a Little" features
Jackie DeShannon

Rocks His Gypsy Soul (Van Morrison Gets His Chance To Wail Volume 3)
(Gold Standard) Undated
Moondance/Glad Tidings/Crazy Love/Come Running/The Way
Young Lovers Do/Everyone/Brown Eyed Girl/And It Stoned
Me/These Dreams Of You/Caravan/Cyprus Avenue/Into the
Mystic/Stormy Monday Blues/Don't Start Crying Now/All By
Myself/Caledonia/What's Up, Crazy Pup?
The first 12 tracks were recorded live at Fillmore West, 26 April
1970, plus two studio demos from 1964, a Them track broadcast
live on BBC Radio, 1965, and two 1973 tracks with the Caledonia
Soul Orchestra. Eleven of the Fillmore West numbers are those on
Into the Man (see below), and all of the Fillmore material is on
Moonlight Serenade and *Live in San Francisco 1970*

Gospels for the Ocean (Lobster) 1990
Moondance/Wavelength/Into the Mystic/Checkin' It Out/Brown
Eyed Girl/Kingdom Hall/Hungry for Your Love/Natalia/Wild
Night/Caravan
An Italian bootleg taken from the *King Biscuit Flower Hour* radio
broadcast at New York's Bottom Line Club, 15 May 1978. The
section on promo releases (below) comments on the 'flower'
spelling

Haunts of Ancient Peace (Templar) 1991
Inarticulate Speech of the Heart I & II/Medley: Baby Please Don't
Go; Gloria; Here Comes the Night; Brown Eyed Girl/I Will Be
There/Jackie Wilson Said/Saint Dominic's Preview/It's All in the

Game/Vanlose Stairway/Hard Nose the Highway/If You Only
Knew/Northern Muse/Haunts of Ancient Peace/She Gives Me
Religion/Ballerina/Summertime in England/Celtic Swing
Recorded at Montreux, 1984. Van Morrison (vocals, guitar, piano,
saxophone), Richie Buckley (saxophone, back-up vocals on
"Summertime in England"), Martin Drower (trumpet), Kenny
Craddock (keyboards), Artie McGlynn (guitar), Jerome Rinson
(bass), Terry Popple (drums).

I Can't Go On… But I'll Go On (GSCD) 1990
Inarticulate Speech of the Heart I/Baby Please Don't Go/Gloria/
Here Comes the Night/Brown Eyed Girl/I Will Be There/Jackie
Wilson Said/Saint Dominic's Preview/It's All in the Game/
Vanlose Stairway/She Gives Me Religion/Ballerina/Summertime
in England/Celtic Swing/Jazz Session/What Would I Do
Italian bootleg recorded at the Montreux Jazz Festival, 11 July
1984, presumably partly duplicating the previous listing. The
musicians are the same, plus (on "Jazz Session") Freddie Hubbard
(trumpet), Joe Henderson (saxophone), Billy Hart (drums)

If You Don't Like It, Go Fuck Yourself (LifeLine) 1991
It's Not the Twilight Zone/I Like It Like That/T For
Texas/Bulbs/Boffy Flow/Heathrow Shuffle/Naked in the
Jungle/Street Choir/Instrumental/Since I Fell for You
Recorded live at Montreux, 30 June 1974, with Van Morrison
(vocals, guitar, harmonica), Pete Wingfield (keyboards, back-up
vocals), Dallas Taylor (drums), Jerome Rimson (bass). The title
comes from a suggestion made by Morrison to a heckler in the
audience

Pure (Multi-Coloured Music) Undated
Included here, out of alphabetical order, because it is the previous
record with the addition of a version of "Send in the Clowns" with
Chet Baker (trumpet), Michel Grailler (piano), Ricardo Del Fra
(bass). This is the Ronnie Scott's Club track also on *Dark Knight of
the Soul*, recorded on 6 June 1986

The Inner Mystic (Oh Boy) 1990
Into the Mystic/I've Been Working/Friday's Child/Hound Dog/
Ballerina/Tupelo Honey/Wild Night/Just Like a Woman/
Moonshine Whiskey/Dead or Alive/You're My Woman/These

Dreams Of You/Domino/Call Me Up in Dreamland/Blue
Monday/Bring It On Home To Me/Buona Sera Senorita
A two-CD set taken from the live radio session, with an invited
audience of 200, at Pacific High Studios, California, on 19
September 1971 (see *Desert Land*, above). Musicians unknown.
Released in Luxembourg. Also available as *Into the Mystic*
(Scorpio) as a double CD with an extra track, "Caledonia Soul
Music"
Into the Man (Wild Bird Records) 1991
Moondance/Glad Tidings/Crazy Love/Come Running/The Way
Young Lovers Do/Everyone/Brown Eyed Girl/And It Stoned
Me/These Dreams of You/Caravan/Cyprus Avenue/Into the
Mystic
Recorded live at Fillmore West, 26 April 1970. The tracks are also
included on *Rocks His Gypsy Soul (Van Morrison Gets His Chance to
Wail Volume 3)*. This Italian release was mixed at Planet Sound
Studios, Florence, in February 1991. Van Morrison (vocals, rhythm
guitar, saxophone), Jeff Labes (keyboards), John Platania (guitars),
Jack Schroer (saxophones), Collin Tillton (tenor sax, flute), John
Klingberg (bass), Elias Shaar Dahaud (drums). With the exception
of the drummer this is the *Moondance* band
Irish Soul (Oh Boy) 1990
Moondance/Wavelength/Into the Mystic/Checkin' It Out/Brown
Eyed Girl/Kingdom Hall/Hungry for Your Love/Natalia/Wild
Night/Caravan
A Luxembourg bootleg, taken from a recording made at the
Bottom Line Club, New York, on 15 May 1978. Van Morrison
(vocals, piano), Peter Bardens (keyboards), Bobby Tench (guitar),
Herbie Armstrong (guitar), Mickey Feat (bass), Peter Van Hooke
(drums), Katie Kissoon (back-up vocals), Linda Dillard (back-up
vocals)
It Ain't Why, It Just Is (Big Music) 1993
I've Been Working/The Way Young Lovers Do/Purple Heather/
Come Running/Sweet Thing/Blue Money/Green/Wild Night/
Caravan/Cyprus Avenue/It's Not the Twilight Zone/Foggy
Mountain Top/Heathrow Shuffle/Naked in the Jungle
Up to and including "Cyprus Avenue" recorded live at the Los

Angeles Troubadour, 26 May 1973, the remainder live in USA, precise location unknown, 1974. These are out-takes from the double abum *It's Too Late To Stop Now*, which was originally envisaged as a triple, and these cuts are taken from the acetates. With the Caledonia Soul Orchestra. An Italian bootleg

It's Never Too Late (Dynamite Studios) Undated

I've Been Working/The Way Young Lovers Do/These Dreams Of You/Wild Mountain Thyme/Come Running/Into the Mystic/Domino/Sweet Thing/Blue Money/Bring It On Home/Being Green/I Believe to My Soul/Wild Night/I Just Want to Make Love to You/Cyprus Avenue

The notes say "All tracks were taken from the original acetates recorded during Van Morrison and the Caledonia Soul Orchestra's World Tour, 1973." There is much duplication both with *It Ain't Why, It Just Is* (above) and with the official Warner Brothers release of the tour, *It's Too Late to Stop Now*. A Luxembourg bootleg

Leatherette (Three Cool Cats) Frank Zappa 2 CD set

Van Morrison is featured as vocalist on the track "Dead Girls of London"

Listen to the Lion (Van Morrison and Denmark's Radio Big Band) (Three Cool Cats) 1991

A New Kind of Man/Haunts of Ancient Peace/Listen to the Lion/Vanlose Stairway/Got to Go Back/I Will Be There/Vanlose Stairway/Here Comes the Night

Recorded live in Copenhagen on 28 February 1987, except the last two, recorded on 15 October 1986

Live at the Roxy (Seagull) 1989

Brown Eyed Girl/Wavelength/And It Stoned Me/Checkin' It Out/Hungry for Your Love/Kingdom Hall/Crazy Love/Tupelo Honey/Caravan/Cyprus Avenue

Van Morrison (vocals, saxophone, guitar, keyboards), Bob Tench (guitar), Peter Van Hooke (drums), Mickey Feat (bass), Herbie Armstrong (guitar) Katie Kassoon (back-up vocals, lead on "Crazy Love"), Anne Peacock (back-up vocals), John Allair (keyboards). Recorded live in September 1979

Live in Edinburgh at the Playhouse (Yellow Cat Records) 1993

Celtic Swing/Northern Muse (Solid Ground)/Vanlose Stairway/

Dimples/It's All in the Game/Foreign Window/Cleaning Windows/Dweller on the Threshold/A Sense of Wonder/And the Healing Has Begun/Here Comes the Knight/In the Garden/ Gloria/Shakin' All Over/It's All Over Now, Baby Blue

An Italian release. The Edinburgh tracks are those up to and including "In the Garden", recorded in 1986. The medley of "Gloria" and "Shakin' All Over" is performed by Morrison with Bono of U2, and for the final, Dylan, song he is joined by Dylan himself, Bono, Chrissie Hynde, Elvis Costello, Kris Kristofferson and Steve Winwood. These tracks come from a gig at The Point, Dublin, on 6 February 1993

Live in Essen, 1982 (Golden Stars) 1990

Go to the High Place in your Mind/Into the Mystic/Moondance/ Wavelength/Full Force Gale/Bright Side of the Road/It's All in the Game/She Gives Me Religion/Northern Muse/Vanlose Stairway/Help Me/When I Come Home (Love to You?)/Celtic Ray/Dweller on the Threshold/Satisfied/Can You Feel the Silence/Cleaning Windows/Summertime in England/ Scandinavia

An Italian bootleg recorded live in Essen, Germany, on 4 April 1982, at the Rockpalast TV show, and also released under the title *Can You Feel the Silence* on the Great Dane label, with minor differences to track timings. Van Morrison (vocals, guitar, piano on "Scandinavia"), Pee Wee Ellis (saxophone, vocals on "Love to You" and "Summertime in England"), Chris Michie (lead guitar), John Allair (organ, lead vocals on "Go to the High Place in your Mind"), Peter Van Hooke (drums), Tom Dollinger (drums), Bianca Thornton (back-up vocals, lead vocals on "Love To You"), Pauline Lozano (back-up vocals), Annie Stocking (back-up vocals), David Hayes (bass), Mark Isham (trumpet, synthesiser), Sean Fulsom (probably) (pipes on "Northern Muse" and "Celtic Ray")

Live in Montreux (Swingin' Pig Records) Undated

Yeh Yeh/Did Ye Get Healed/It's All in the Game/Here Comes the Night/Baby Please Don't Go/Domino/Jackie Wilson Said/Sweet Thing/Star of the County Down/Northern Muse – When Heart Is Open/Whenever God Shines His Light/Summertime in England/ Caravan/In the Garden

Recorded live at Montreux, Switzerland, in July 1990, with special
guest Georgie Fame, who sings "Yeh Yeh"

Live in San Francisco 1970

This would seem to be the same as *Into the Man* (above). Although
the venue for that is given as Fillmore West there is some
confusion here: it could be Fillmore East

Live in the USA (Live & Alive) Undated

Moondance/Glad Tidings/Crazy Love/Come Running/The Way
Young Lovers Do/Everyone/Brown Eyed Girl/And It Stoned
Me/These Dreams Of You/Caravan/Cyprus Avenue/Into the
Mystic/It's Not the Twilight Zone/I Like It Like That/T for
Texas/Bulbs/Boffyflow and Spike/Naked in the Jungle/
Heathrow Shuffle/Street Choir/Since I Fell for You/Celtic
Swing/Tore Down a la Rimbaud/Oh the Warm Feeling/I Will Be
There/A Sense of Wonder

A German two-CD set. Up to and including "Into the
Mystic"recorded live in San Francisco, 1970; the remainder given
as "live in the USA 1974 and 1986". Musicians unknown

Moondance: Live in New York 1978

This record has the same content as *Irish Soul* (above), and is taken
from a *King Biscuit* radio broadcast

Moonlight Serenade (Teddy Bear Records) Undated

Moondance/Glad Tidings/Crazy Love/Come Running/The Way
Young Lovers Do/Everyone/Brown Eyed Girl/And It Stoned
Me/These Dreams of You/Caravan/Cyprus Avenue/Into the
Mystic

Recorded live at Fillmore West, San Francisco, 26 April 1970.
Music from this show is also available on *Live in San Francisco
1970*, *Rocks His Gypsy Soul (Gets His Chance To Wail Volume 3)* and
the first disc of *Live in the USA*. Van Morrison (vocals, rhythm
guitar, saxophone), Jeff Labes (keyboards), John Platania (guitars),
Jack Schroer (saxophones), Collin Tillton (tenor saxophone, flute),
John Klingberg (bass), Elias Shaar Dahaud (drums)

My Name Is Raincheck (Smoking Crocodile) 1994

Did Ye Get Healed/Tore Down a la Rimbaud/Vanlose Stairway/
Wonderful Remark/Crazy Love/My Name Is Raincheck/See Me
Through/Ain't That Lovin' You Baby/Don't Cry No More/

Stormy Monday/Help Me/Good Morning Little Schoolgirl/
Moondance/I'll Take Care of You/Tupelo Honey/You Don't
Know Me/Lonely Avenue/In the Garden/Have I Told You
Lately/Shakin' All Over/It's All Over Now, Baby Blue/Foreign
Window/Buona Sera Senorita

This two-CD set was largely recorded at the Manchester Apollo on
4 March 1994, and bears comparison with the "official" release of
the same period, *A Night in San Francisco*. "Foreign Window",
however, comes from the Oxford Apollo, 25 February 1994, and
"Buona Sera Senorita" from the Edinburgh Playhouse, 5 May 1994

Pagan Streams (BIG) 1992 (2 CD set)

Out of Sight/The Girl Can't Help It/Ain't That Lovin' You Baby/
Satisfied/Who Do You Love/And the Healing Has Begun/See Me
Through/Moondance/Some Peace of Mind/It's All in the Game/
Enlightenment/Whenever God Shines His Light/It Must Be You/
Help Me/Northern Muse (Solid Ground)/It Fills You Up/So
Complicated/The Fayre of County Down/Orangefield/
Summertime in England/Have I Told You Lately That I Love
You/Caravan/In the Garden/Send In the Clowns/Gloria –
Shakin' All Over/I Can't Stop Loving You/Baby Please Don't Go -
Who Do You Love – What'd I Say

An Italian release recorded live in Utrecht/Vredenburg, Holland,
on 1 April 1991

St Patrick's Day (Beech-Marten) 1991 2 CD set

Moondance/Vanlose Stairway/Here Comes the Night/Gloria/
Domino/She Gives Me Religion/It's All in the Game/Into the
Mystic/Cry For Home/Haunts of Ancient Peace/Celtic Swing/
Cyprus Avenue/No Guru/Dweller on the Threshold/Caravan/
Tura-Lura-Lural/Rave On John Donne/Send in the Clowns

Italian bootleg recording of the *Radio Today* radio special (1989),
performance at the Greek Theatre, Berkeley (25 July 1986) and
tracks from *It's Too Late To Stop Now*

Soul Labyrinth (Kiss the Stone Records) 1992

Out of Sight/Ain't That Lovin' You Baby/Baby Please Don't Go/
Who Do You Love/When the Healing Has Begun/See Me
Through/Some Peace of Mind/Enlightenment/Caravan/In the
Garden/You of a Thousand Summers/Whenever God Shines His

Light/Vanlose Stairway/Full Force Gale/Moondance
An Italian bootleg recorded live at the Concertgebouw, the Hague, Holland on 31 March 1991. Van Morrison (vocals, saxophone, guitar), Neil Drinkwater (piano, synthesiser, accordion), Arty McGlynn (guitar), Clive Culberton (bass), Roy Jones and Dave Early (percussion, drums). Some sources, apparently incorrectly, give venues as the Fleadh in Finsbury Park, London, and in Eire, 1991

Sounding in the Clouds (Living Legend Records) 1991
Moondance/Vanlose Stairway/It's All in the Game/Into the Mystic/Like a Song/Haunt of Ancient Peace/Celtic Swing/ Cyprus Avenue/In the Garden/Caravan/Tura Lura/Rave On, John Donne/Sounding in the Clouds
An Italian bootleg recorded live in Berkeley, California on 25 July 1986. Van Morrison (vocals, guitar, saxophone, harmonica), John Platania (guitar), David Hayes (bass), Dahaud Shaar (drums), Jeff Labes (piano), Pee Wee Ellis (saxophones, flute), Terry Adams (violin), Bob Doll (trumpet), Susie Davis (back-up vocals), Carol Kenyon (back-up vocals). Strings arranged and conducted by Jeff Labes. Some of the tracks may well not be from the Berkeley gig, however

This Is Van Morrison (Traditional Line)
Dead or Alive/Moonshine Whiskey/You're My Woman/These Dreams (of You)/Domino/Call Me Up in Dreamland/Blue Money/Buona Sera Senorita/Into the Mystic/I've Been Working/ Friday's Child/Hound Dog/Just Like a Woman
A West German release recorded live in California, 19 September 1971: the same radio gig as is released on *Desert Land*, *The Inner Mystic* and *Into the Mystic* (see above)

Van Morrison Meets Bob Dylan and John Lee Hooker (Living Legend) 1992
Crazy Love (with Bob Dylan)/Baby Please Don't Go (with John Lee Hooker)/Wednesday Evening Blues (with Hooker)/Vanlose Stairway (with the Danish Radio Big Band)/I Will Be There (with the Danish Radio Big Band)/Foreign Window (with Dylan)/One Irish Rover (with Dylan)/Raglan Road (with the Chieftains)/ Don't Look Back (with Hooker)/Enlightenment/So Complicated/

Star of the County Down/Just Like a Woman/Caledonia Soul
Music (the final five tracks with his band)
Italian bootleg taken from the soundtrack of the BBCtv special *One
Irish Rover*, plus tracks from the September 1971 Pacific High
Studios session referred to elsewhere plus a studio out-take
Van the Man (Insect) 1994
Inarticulate Speech of the Heart/Medley: On Hyndford Street;
Baby Please Don't Go/Crawling King Snake/I'm Not Feeling It
Anymore/Ordinary Life/Why Must I Always Explain?/Haunts
of Ancient Peace/She Moves on Solid Ground/All Saints Day/
Cleaning Windows/Be Bop a Lula/Hey Hey (What'd I Say)/
Vanlose Stairway/It's All Over Now, Baby Blue/Youth of 1000
Summers/Nightshirt (Help Me)/Enlightenment/See Me
Through/It's All in the Game/No Guru (In the Garden)
Italian bootleg recorded at the Glastonbury Festival, 28 June 1992
Wild Night (Silver Rarities) 1994
I'm Not Feeling It Anymore/Why Must I Always Explain?/See
Me Through/Domino/Cleaning Windows/Vanlose Stairway/
Moondance/Haunts of Ancient Peace/So Quiet in Here/That's
Where It's At/Wild Night/Medley: Route 66; Shake, Rattle and
Roll/Shot of Rhythm and Blues/Irish Heartbeat/Wavelength/
Tore Down a la Rimbaud/Youth of 1000 Summers/A Town Called
Paradise/Did Ye Get Healed/It's All in the Game/Lonely
Avenue/Medley: In the Garden; Daring Night; Real Real
Gone/Medley: Solid Ground;, When Heart is Open/Brown Eyed
Girl/Star of the County Down/What's I Say/Medley: Gloria,
Shakin' All Over/It's All Over Now, Baby Blue
A two-CD set, possibly originating from West Germany, of live
concert performances. The first seven tracks are possibly from the
Hammersmith Apollo, 22 March 1993, and the rest of the first CD
from Bristol, 23 January 1993
Wild Night in California: the Easy Rider Generation in Concert (no
details available)

SINGLES BY VAN MORRISON:
(US releases, with variations elsewhere indicated):
Brown Eyed Girl/Goodbye Baby (Bang) 1967

Ro Ro Rosey/Chick-a-Boom (Bang) 1967

Spanish Rose/Midnight Special (Bang) 1968

Spanish Rose/Who Drove the Red Sports Car (Holland) (Pink Elephant) 1968

Brown Eyed Girl/Midnight Special (Hip Pocket) 1968

Come Running/Crazy Love (Warner Brothers) 1970

Domino/Sweet Jannie (Warner Brothers) 1970

Domino/Come Running (Spain) (Warner Brothers) 1970

Blue Money/Sweet Thing (Warner Brothers) 1971

Call Me Up in Dreamland/Street Choir (Warner Brothers) 1971

Wild Night/When That Evening Sun Goes Down (Warner Brothers) 1971

Tupelo Honey/Starting a New Life (Warner Brothers) 1972

(Straight to Your Heart) Like a Cannonball/Old Old Woodstock (Warner Brothers) 1972

Jackie Wilson Said (I'm in Heaven When You Smile)/You've Got the Power (Warner Brothers) 1972

Redwood Tree/St Dominic's Preview (Warner Brothers) 1972

Redwood Tree/Jackie Wilson Said (I'm in Heaven When You Smile) (Germany) (Warner Brothers) 1972

Gypsy/St Dominic's Preview (Warner Brothers) 1973

Warm Love/I Will Be There (Warner Brothers) 1973

Bein' Green/Wild Children (Warner Brothers) 1973

Gloria/? (Warner Brothers) 1973

Gloria/Warm Love (Germany) (Warner Brothers) 1974

Ain't Nothin' You Can Do/Wild Children (Warner Brothers) 1974

Bulbs/Cul de Sac (Warner Brothers) 1974

Bulbs/Who Was that Masked Man? (UK) (Warner Brothers) 1974

Caledonia/What's Up Crazy Pup? (UK, France, Germany, Italy: credited to Van Morrison and the Caledonia Soul Express) (Warner Brothers) 1974

Joyous Sound/Mechanical Bliss (Warner Brothers) 1977

Cold Wind in August/Moondance (Warner Brothers) 1977

The Eternal Kansas City (edited version)/Joyous Sound (UK) (Warner Brothers) 1977

Wavelength (edited version)/Checkin' It Out (Warner Brothers) 1978

Natalia (edited version)/Lifetimes (Warner Brothers) 1979

Kingdom Hall/Checkin' It Out (Warner Brothers) 1979

Bright Side of the Road/Rolling Hills (Warner Brothers) 1979

Full Force Gale/Bright Side of the Road (Holland) (Warner Brothers) 1979

Full Force Gale/Troubadours (Holland) (Warner Brothers) 1979

You Make Me Feel So Free/Full Force Gale (Warner Brothers) 1980

Cleaning Windows/Scandinavia (Warner Brothers) 1982

Cleaning Windows/It's All in the Game (UK) (Mercury) 1982

Cleaning Windows/Aryan Mist (Spain) (Mercury) 1982

Scandinavia/Dweller on the Threshold (UK) (Mercury) 1982

Cry for Home/Summertime in England (12" version includes All Saint's Day. Live at Ulster Hall, Belfast) (UK) (Mercury) 1983

Celtic Swing/Mr Thomas (12" version includes Rave On, John Donne) (UK) (Mercury) 1983

Dweller on the Threshold/Northern Muse (Solid Ground) (UK) (Mercury) 1984

A Sense of Wonder/Haunts of Ancient Peace (live) (UK): 12" version (US) (Mercury) 1984

Tore Down a la Rimbaud/Haunts of Ancient Peace (live) (UK) (Mercury) 1985

Ivory Tower/New Kind of Man (UK 12" version added A Sense of Wonder and Cleaning Windows) (Mercury) 1986

Got to Go Back/In the Garden (UK) (Mercury) 1986

Did Ye Get Healed?/Allow Me (UK) (Mercury) 1987

Someone Like You/Celtic Excavation (UK) (Mercury) 1987

Queen of the Slipstream/Spanish Steps (UK) (Mercury) 1987

I'll Tell Me Ma/Ta Mo Chleamhnas Deanta (credited to Van Morrison and the Chieftains: 12" and CD versions added Carrickfergus) (UK) (Mercury) 1988

Have I Told You Lately/Contacting My Angel (12" version adds Listen to the Lion, CD version adds Irish Heartbeat) (UK) (Polydor) 1989

Whenever God Shines His Light (edited version) (credited to Van Morrison with Cliff Richard)/I'd Love to Write Another Song (12" and CD single has full version of Whenever God Shines His Light and adds Cry For Home) (UK) (Polydor) 1989

Orangefield/These Are the Days (12" version adds And the Healing
   Has Begun, CD version further adds Coney Island) (UK) (Polydor)
   1989

Coney Island/Have I Told You Lately (12" single adds A Sense of
   Wonder, CD single also adds Spirit) (UK) (Polydor) 1989

Gloria/Rave On, John Donne (12" single adds Vanlose Stairway, CD
   single also adds Bright Side of the Road) (UK) (Polydor) 1990

Real Real Gone/Start All Over Again (12" and CD singles add
   Cleaning Windows) (UK) (Polydor) 1990

In the Days Before Rock 'n' Roll/I'd Love to Write Another Song
   (12" and CD singles add Coney Island) (UK) (Polydor) 1990

Enlightenment/Avalon of the Heart (12" and CD singles add Jackie
   Wilson Said…) (UK) (Polydor) 1991

I Can't Stop Loving You/All Saints Day (A-side credited to Van
   Morrison and the Chieftains: 12" and CD singles add Carrying a
   Torch) (UK) (Polydor) 1991

Why Must I Always Explain?/So Complicated (12" and CD singles
   add Enlightenment) (UK) (Polydor) 1991

Gloria (with John Lee Hooker)/It Must Be You (Live) (Double CD
   single adds live versions of Whenever God Shines His Light, Star
   of the County Down/It Fills You Up/And the Healing Has
   Begun/See Me Through) (UK) (Exile) 1993

The live tracks are from the Utrecht/Vredenburg, Holland gig (1
   April 1991), apparently taken by Morrison himself from the Pagan
   Streams bootleg CD (see above)

OFFICIAL VAN MORRISON RELEASES:
radio station discs, promotional records etc:
Van Morrison Live at the Roxy (WB Music Show – promotional
   release) 1979
   Brown Eyed Girl/Wavelength/And It Stoned Me/Checkin' It
   Out/Hungry For Your Love/Kingdom Hall/Crazy Love/Tupelo
   Honey/Caravan/Cyprus Avenue
King Biscuit Flower Hour (DIR Broadcasting) 1989
   A single CD of the concert recorded at the Bottom Line, New York,
   on 15 May 1978, distributed to radio stations for use in a specific

week in 1989. "Flower" is indeed spelt like this, as it is on other radio-only releases. In 1941, in Helena, Arkansas, Max S Moore's Interstate Grocer Company, producer of King Biscuit Flour, began to advertise their product on the newly-formed local radio station Radio KFFA, and on their show they employed two of the greatest local blues artists of the day, guitarist Robert Lockwood Jr and Rice Miller (who took the name Sonny Boy Williamson in a deliberate attempt to confuse his identity with that of the existing Chicago perfomer of that name). The decision to call another, later, enterprise by a name that sounds the same but is spelt differently is a mystery.

The Interview Album (Mercury 830 222-1) Vinyl only
   Van Morrison is interviewed by journalist Mick Brown, in May 1986, on a record distributed as part of the promotion for the *No Guru* album. It contains the track "Ivory Tower" as a sampler
Radio Today Entertainment (New York) Radio only disc
St Patty's Day Special: Turn Up Your Radio - An Evening with Van Morrison (1989)
   A 2 CD set containing the concert recorded at the Greek Theatre, Berkeley, 25 July 1986, together with tracks from *It's Too Late to Stop Now* and voice-overs by Graham Nash, Robbie Robertson and Huey Lewis
Avalon Sunset (Polydor) Radio station promotion
   Contains the album in CD and cassette form, pen, two colour slides, an 8x10 black-and-white photograph and a biography
Hymns to the Silence (Polydor, US only) 1991
   A deluxe version of the album issued in a cloth-bound folder: 2 CDs and a booklet in a fold-out sleeve
Professional Jealousy/Quality Street (Van 12 DJ) 1991
   UK-only promotional CD tied to the album *Hymns to the Silence*

VAN MORRISON TRACKS ON OTHER COLLECTIONS:
in almost all cases film soundtrack albums:
Hungry for Your Love (on *An Officer and a Gentleman*, Polygram, 1982)
Wonderful Remark (on *King of Comedy*, 1983)
Here Comes the Knight (on *Live for Ireland*, MCA, 1987) from the

1986 Self Aid concert

Boffyflow and Spike (on *A Chieftains Celebration*, RCA, 1989)

Brown Eyed Girl (on *The Wonder Years*, Warner Brothers, 1989)

Brown Eyed Girl (on *Born on the Fourth of July*, MCA, 1989)

Wonderful Remark (on *Nobody's Child*, Warner Brothers, 1990)

TB Sheets (on *Dogfight*, Nouveau, 1991)

Someone Like You (on *Only the Lonely*, Varese, 1991)

Jackie Wilson Said (I'm in Heaven When You Smile) (on *Queen's Logic*, Columbia, 1991)

Brown Eyed Girl (on *Sleeping with the Enemy*, Columbia, 1991)

That's Where It's At (with the Holmes Brothers) (on *A Week or Two in the Real World*, Real World Records, 1994)

Brown Eyed Girl (on *Mellow Sixties*, undated)

GUEST APPEARANCES ON OTHER ARTISTS' ALBUMS:

The Band, *Cahoots* (Capitol) 1971

John Lee Hooker, *Never Get out of These Blues Alive* (Crescendo) 1972

John Lee Hooker, *Born in Mississippi, Raised Up in Tennessee* (ABC) 1973

Bill Wyman, *Stone Alone* (Rolling Stones) 1976

The Band, *The Last Waltz* (Warner Brothers) 1978

Jim Capaldi, *Fierce Heart* (Warner Brothers) 1983

Chet Baker, *Live at Ronnie Scott's, London* (Hendring/Wadham) 1987

Georgie Fame, *Cool Cat Blues* (Bluemoon) 1990

Roger Waters, *The Wall: Live in Berlin 1990* (Mercury) 1990

Mick Cox, *Compose Yerself* (SBM) 1990

John Lee Hooker, *Mr Lucky* (Silvertone) 1992

The Chieftains, *The Long Black Veil* (BMG) 1995

John Lee Hooker, *Chill Out* (Pointblank) 1995

SINGLES PRODUCED BY VAN MORRISON FOR OTHER ARTISTS:

Jackie DeShannon, Sweet Sixteen, Atlantic, 1973

Herbie Armstrong, Real Real Gone, Avatar, 1980

Tom Jones, Carrying a Torch, Dover, 1991

UNRELEASED VAN MORRISON SONGS RECORDED BY OTHER ARTISTS:

Roy Head, Bit by Bit

Art Garfunkel, I Shall Sing (on Angel Clare, CBS, 1973)
Johnny Winter, Feedback on Highway 101 (on Saints and Sinners, 1974)
Buckwheat Zydeco, Bayou Doll (on Five Card Stud, Island, 1994)
Brian Kennedy, Tell Me All About Your Love (on EP CD Intuition)
   1995

FILMOGRAPHY:
Ready Steady Go!, ITV, 1964
   Volume 1 of Original Performances (Dave Clark International
   Video) includes Them performing "Baby Please Don't Go"
Top Pop Gold, Dutch TV, Deventer, 1967
   Morrison with Cuby and the Blizzards, performing "Mystic Eyes"
   (4 minutes)
Randall's Island, July 1970
   A five-minute film of "Come Running"
San Francisco Scene Video
   Includes a clip of Morrison performing "Domino", early 1970s
Don Kirschner's In Concert, US TV, April 1973
   Caravan/Gloria/Flamingoes Fly/Cyprus Avenue (24 minutes)
Rainbow Theatre, London, 23 July 1973
   Warm Love/Take Your Hand Out of My Pocket/Here Comes the
   Night/I Just Wanna Make Love to You/Brown Eyed Girl/
   Moonshine Whiskey/Moondance/Help Me/Domino/Caravan/
   Cyprus Avenue (BBCtv). When shown on RTE the songs also
   included I Paid the Price/Wild Night/St Dominic's
   Preview/Gloria
Old Grey Whistle Test
   Interview on the BBC2 show, 1973
Talk About Pop
   Conversation with Donall Corvin, plus performance of Wild
   Children/Slim Slow Slider/Warm Love/Drumshanbo Hustle/
   Autumn Song (RTE)
Hammersmith Odeon, London, Spring 1974
   In performance, shown on BBCtv
Montreux Jazz Festival, Switzerland, 30 June 1974
   Boffyflow & Spike/Heathrow Shuffle/Naked in the Jungle/Street
   Choir

Musik Laden, Bremen, West Germany, 10 July 1974
Heathrow Shuffle/Warm Love/I Like It Like That/Bulbs (West German TV show) "Bulbs" was also shown on *The Best of the Beat Club* (ITV) in 1988

The Orphanage, San Francisco, August 1974
Morrison in concert with Soundhole, plus interview with Tom Donahue. Heathrow Shuffle/Ain't Nothing You Can Do/Street Choir/I Believe To My Soul/Snow in San Anselmo/Moondance/Into the Mystic/Foggy Mountain Top (42 minutes)

Midnight Special, NBC Studios, Los Angeles, 28 March 1977
Featuring Morrison with George Benson, Carlos Santana, Tom Scott, Etta James, Dr John and Stanley Banks performing Moondance/Bring It On Home to Me/Misty. With John Platania, Jeff Labes, Ollie Brown and Dr John, Morrison also performs Heavy Connection/Cold Wind in August/The Eternal Kansas City/Joyous Sound. Transmitted on NBC 22 April 1977 (20 minutes)

Promotional Appearance, Maunkberry's, Granada TV, 15 June 1977
Morrison with Dr John, Mick Ronson, Mo Foster and Peter van Hooke performing Venice/The Eternal Kansas City/an untitled instrumental/Joyous Sound (18 minutes)

Wonderland, Vara Studios, 1977
Morrison and Dr John perform three songs

The Last Waltz, US, 1978
Martin Scorsese's film is a record of the farewell performance by The Band at San Francisco's Winterland in 1976, together with documentary footage and interviews. Morrison was one of the guest performers along with Bob Dylan, Joni Mitchell, Neil Diamond, Emmylou Harris, Neil Young, Muddy Waters, Dr John and Ronnie Hawkins. Available on MGM/UA Home Video

Our Times: Promotional Video for Warner Brothers, Denver, 1978
Wavelength/Brown Eyed Girl/Checkin' It Out/Kingdom Hall/Caravan (30 minutes)

Midnight Special, US TV, 1978
Morrison performs "Kingdom Hall" (4 minutes)

Saturday Night Live, US TV, 1978
Morrison performs "Wavelength" and "Kingdom Hall", a clip

repeated several times in the 1990s on MTV (10 minutes)
Good Evening Ulster, Ulster TV, 1979
Interview with Gloria Hunniford on local news magazine
Whitla Hall, Belfast, Northern Ireland TV, February 1979
News report including concert clip and interview with George
Jones, formerly of the Monarchs (2 minutes)
Van Morrison in Ireland, 1979
Recording of live performances in Dublin and Belfast, 1979,
released by Hendring Ltd
Moondance/Checking It Out/Moonshine Whiskey/Tupelo
Honey/Wavelength/Saint Dominic's Preview/Don't Look Back/
I've Been Working/Gloria/Cyprus Avenue. Performance intercut
with "band on the bus" footage, shots of Hyndford Street, Cyprus
Avenue etc. The Band is Peter Bardens (keyboards),Bobby Tench
(guitar), Micky Feat (bass), Peter van Hooke (drums), Herbie
Armstrong (rhythm guitar), Pat Kyle (saxophone), John Altham
(saxophone), Toni Marcus (violin), Katie Kissoon, Anna Peacock
(back-up vocals). 57 minutes
Live at the Capitol Theatre, Passaic, New Jersey, 1979
Unreleased black-and-white concert footage. Kingdom Hall/
Bright Side of the Road/Here Comes the Night/Into the Mystic/
You Make Me Feel So Free/Warm Love/Call Me Up in
Dreamland/It's All in the Game/You Know What They're
Writing About/Ain't Nothing You Can Do/Angeliou/Full Force
Gale/ Moondance/Moonshine Whiskey/Wavelength/Tupelo
Honey/ I've Been Working/Troubadours/Brown Eyed Girl
(90 minutes)
Paris, 1979
French TV show: Wavelength/Tupelo Honey/Natalia/Cyprus
Avenue (18 minutes)
Montreux Jazz Festival, Switzerland, 10 July 1980
Morrison performs Summertime in England/Moondance/Haunts
of Ancient Peace/Wild Night/Ballerina, shown on tv 5 in Europe,
17 February 1988 (30 minutes)
Rotterdam, 1981
A Dutch TV set
Rockpalast, Grugahalle, Essen, 3 April 1982

Go to the High Place in Your Mind/Into the Mystic/Moondance/
Wavelength/Full Force Gale/Bright Side of the Road/It's All in
the Game/She Gives Me Religion/Solid Ground/Vanlose
Stairway/Help Me/Love to You/Celtic Ray/Dweller on the
Threshold/Satisfied/Cleaning Windows/Summertime in
England/Scandinavia. Shown on BBCtv. 74 minutes. Also report
and clip of the event shown on *Rockpalast Postbox* on West German
TV (3 minutes)
Celtic Swing (Phonogram promotion) 1983
Late Late Show (RTE) February 1983
    Morrison performs "Cry for Home" on Gay Byrne's long-running
    chat show
Werchter Festival, 1983
    Fragment of performance of "Cry For Home", details unknown
Rockpalast, MIDEM, Cannes (RAI, Italy) 28 January 1984
    She Gives Me Religion/Help Me/Beautiful Vision/Solid Ground/
    Bright Side of the Road/Celtic Ray/Higher than the World/River
    of Time/The Street Only Knew Your Name/Cry for Home/
    Haunts of Ancient Peace/Cleaning Windows/Summertime in
    England/Full Force Gale
Eight Days a Week, BBC2, 15 June 1984
    Review of Morrison's concerts at the Dominion Theatre, London,
    on short-lived rock magazine
MTV Special 1984
    Concert performance from Wembley Stadium, London, on 7 July
    1984, with Bob Dylan, Carlos Santana and Chrissie Hynde.
    Morrison guests with Dylan on "It's All Over Now, Baby Blue" (5
    minutes)
Mary O'Hara Show (BBCtv) 19 August 1984
Old Grey Whistle Test (BBC2) 13 November 1984
    Morrison performs "A Sense of Wonder"
BBC Northern Ireland Commemoration Show, 1 November 1984
    Morrison and band perform "What Would I Do" on a show
    compered by Phil Coulter
Pavilion Theatre, Glasgow, 15 November 1984
    A BBC Scotland performance of "Celtic Swing" and "Cry for
    Home" with the Battlefield Band (6 minutes)

Entertainment Centre, Sydney, Australia, Australian TV, February 1985
   Morrison performs "A Sense of Wonder" and "Tore Down a la
   Rimbaud" (10 minutes)
The Tube, Channel 4, 29 March 1985
   Tore Down a la Rimbaud/His Master's Eyes/If Only You Knew
   (12 minutes)
Self Aid, Dublin (RTE) 17 May 1986
   Thanks for the Information/Here Comes the Knight/A Town
   Called Paradise (15 minutes)
Chet Baker at Ronnie Scott's, London, 6 June 1986
   Morrison sings "Send in the Clowns". Hendring Video/Channel
   4, 1990 (5 minutes)
Wogan, BBC1, 27 June 1986
   Performance of "Ivory Tower" on BBCtv chat show
Northern Irleand News (BBC1 Northern Ireland) 3 November 1986
   News feature interview with Liam Creagh
Festival Report, 12 November 1986
   TV Belfast Festival preview including Morrison interview (8
   minutes)
Nimajazz, Whitla Hall, Queen's University, Belfast, 13 November
   1986
   Guest appearance by Morrison with the big band of the Northern
   Ireland Music Association conducted by Dave Gold. I Will Be
   There/A New Kind of Man/ Here Comes the Knight/Vanlose
   Stairway/Haunts of Ancient Peace/Bright Side of the Road
Saturday Review, BBC2, 15 November 1986
   Feature on Morrison including interview and performance of "The
   Healing Has Begun" and "In the Garden" from the Belfast
   concerts (above) (15 minutes)
Polydor promotional video
   An interview with Morrison, 12 August 1987, and performance of
   "Did Ye Get Healed?" and "The Mystery" filmed at Hammersmith
   Odeon, 7 July 1987 (24 minutes). The clip of "Did Ye Get Healed?"
   was shown on ITV (4 minutes)
As I Roved Out, October 1987
   Morrison sings with the Chieftains on a 40-minute special shown
   jointly on RTE (4 March 1988) and BBC (17 March 1988), recorded

at Balmoral Studios of BBC (Northern Ireland). Raglan Road/Star of the County Down/My Lagan Love/Celtic Ray

Ulster TV News, December 1987

A feature on upcoming events including rehearsal footage of Morrison singing "The Mystery"

The Late Late Show: Tribute to the Chieftains, RTE, March 1988

Includes a guest appearance by Morrison singing "Star of the County Down" and "Marie's Wedding". Available on an RTE video

Van the Man, University of Ulster Literary Society, Coleraine, May 1988

Interview and discussion recorded at the Riverside Theatre, Coleraine, Northern Ireland, and including six acoustic songs: Western Plain/Foggy Mountain Top/A Sense of Wonder/Celtic Ray/In the Garden/Raglan Road. Shown on Ulster Television, July 1988 (55 minutes)

Songs of Innocence: Van Morrison and the Chieftains at the Ulster Hall, 15 September 1988

Tore Down a la Rimbaud/In the Garden/Rave On John Donne/Did Ye Get Healed? (with band)/Star of the County Down/She Moved Through the Fair/Ta Mo Chleamnas Deanta/I'll Tell Me Ma/Celtic Ray/Marie's Wedding/Boffyflow & Spike/Goodnight Irene/Moondance (with the Chieftains). Shown on Channel 4 on 17 March 1989 (60 minutes)

Have I Told You Lately

Polydor promotional video

The Prince's Trust 1989 Rock Gala, National Exhibition Centre, Birmingham

Shown on ITV, including Morrison performance

Montreux Jazz Festival, Switzerland, 17 July 1989 (shown August 1990), BBC2

Morrison, Georgie Fame and the Dallas Jazz Orchestra perform "Vanlose Stairway" (5 minutes). A longer recording (23 minutes) was shown on Italian TV

Inside Ulster, BBC Northern Ireland, 25 August 1989

Interview with Liam Creagh at the Grand Opera House, Belfast, shown on local news magazine (3 minutes)

Edinburgh Nights, August 1989
   Van Morrison and Georgie Fame discuss the film *Let's Get Lost* (10
   minutes)
Montreux Jazz Festival, Switzerland, 17 July 1989 (shown August
   1990), BBC2
   Morrison, Georgie Fame and the Dallas Jazz Orchestra perform
   "Vanlose Stairway" (5 minutes). A longer recording (23 minutes)
   was shown on Italian TV
Eco Rock, 24 July 1988
   Fife Aid, Craigtoun Park, St Andrews, Scotland. A Sense of
   Wonder/Mairie's Wedding/Cleaning Windows. Released on
   Castle/Hendring video, 1990
Killer: Jerry Lee Lewis at the Hammersmith Odeon, November 1989
   (shown on BSB 1991)
   Morrison performs "Goodnight Irene" and "What'd I Say", plus
   interview. Only "What'd I Say" is included on the MCA video
   release of the concert, *Jerry Lee Lewis and Friends*
Van Morrison: the Concert
   Recorded at the Beacon Theater, New York, 30 November 1989,
   released on Polygram video 1990.
   Morrison with guests Mose Allison and John Lee Hooker. I Will Be
   There/Whenever God Shines His Light/Cleaning Windows/
   Orangefield/When Will I Ever Learn to Live in God/Thank God
   for Self Love/Raglan Road/Carrickfergus/Summertime in
   England/Caravan/Moondance/Fever/Star of the County Down/
   In the Garden/Have I Told You Lately/Gloria/It Serves Me Right
   to Suffer/Boom Boom/She Moved Through the Fair (90 minutes)
Late Night with Letterman, New York 1 December 1989
   Chat-show host claimed that Morrison's 10-minute appearance
   was his first on US TV since 1977's *Midnight Special* (1978 is given
   above)
Whenever God Shines His Light
   Polydor promotional video
Wogan, December 1989, BBC1
   Morrison and Cliff Richard sing "Whenever God Shines His Light"
Top of the Pops, December 1989, BBC1
   Morrison and Cliff Richard sing "Whenever God Shines His Light"

Arena Special: Slim Gaillard's Civilisation, late 1989-early 1990, BBC2
  A series on the veteran jazzman, resident in London, in which
  Morrison and Gaillard perform "Arabian Boogie" and, in another
  sequence, Gaillard plays piano, accompanying Morrison reading
  excerpts from Jack Kerouac's *On the Road*
NBC Today, 11 January 1990
  Interview and film clips (7 minutes)
San Remo Festival, Super Channel, 24 February 1990
  Morrison sings "Have I Told You Lately" live to backing track
Rock Steady Special, February 1990, Channel 4
  Van Morrison and Mose Allison in Bristol (15 minutes)
The Show, 17 March 1990, BBC1 Northern Ireland
  Morrison and band at the Joker Club, Belfast. Have I Told You
  Lately/These are the Days/Carrickfergus/Whenever God Shines
  His Light (20 minutes)
The Wall, 21 July 1990, Channel 4
  Roger Waters's performance at the Berlin Wall, during which
  Morrison sings "Comfortably Numb" and "The Tide is Turning"
Real Real Gone
  Polydor promotional video
The Late Show, 13 November 1990, BBC2
  Performance of Enlightenment/Avalon of the Heart/So Quiet in
  Here (15 minutes)
The South Bank Show: Clear Cool Crystal Streams, LWT, 21 October
  1990
  ITV's major arts strand (60 minutes)
Showtime: Coast to Coast, US TV, 22 October 1990
Morrison performs "Moondance" and "How Long Has This Been
  Going On?" in a Los Angeles TV studio with Herbie Hancock,
  Freddie Hubbard, Chick Corea, Larry Carlton and Georgie Fame
Van Morrison and Tom Jones, February 1991
  Promotional video of a Tom Jones recording session, with
  performance of "Carrying a Torch" and "I'm Not Feeling It
  Anymore"
Polydor promotional video
  Unreleased performance of "I Can't Start Loving You" with the
  Chieftains, recorded at the Mean Fiddler, London, 6 March 1991

Coney Island of the Mind, 12 March 1991, Channel 4
  Morrison and Irish poets filmed in Wicklow and Belfast (30
  minutes)
One Irish Rover, 16 March 1991, BBC2
  An *Arena Special*, also transmitted on the A&E cable channel.
  Morrison performs with John Lee Hooker in Mississippi, Bob
  Dylan in Athens, the Danish Radio Big Band in Copenhagen, the
  Chieftains in Belfast and with his band at Ronnie Scott's, London.
  Crazy Love/Baby, Please Don't Go/Wednesday Evening Blues/
  Help Me/It's All in the Game/You Know What They're Writing
  About/Did Ye Get Healed?/Vanlose Stairway/I'd Love to Write
  Another Song/Haunts of Ancient Peace/Whenever God Shines
  His Light/I Will Be There/Foreign Window/One Irish Rover/
  Raglan Road/Summertime in England/Moondance/Don't Look
  Back/Celtic Swing. (75 minutes)
Omnibus, 29 March 1991, BBC1
  Appearance on Tom Jones special
EMA Awards, March 1991, BBC1 Northern Ireland
  Performance of "You're the One" in awards show sponsored by
  the *Belfast Telegraph*
A River of Sound, Irish TV, 1995
  Morrison performs "My Lagan Love" with piano backing
David Letterman Show: Letterman in London, BBC2, 17 May 1995
The American chat-show host brought his programme to London:
  Morrison performed "Have I Told You Lately" as a duet with
  Sinead O'Connor, with the Chieftains
Album of the Year – Live, 23 September 1995
Morrison performs songs from *Days Like This* with Guy Barker on
  trumpet

FILM SOUNDTRACKS
Three American Albums (Wim Wenders, West Germany, 1970) A short
  film with music by Harvey Mandel, Creedence Clearwater
  Revival and Van Morrison ("Slim Slow Slider")
Slipstream (Canada, 1970) "Astral Weeks"
An Officer and a Gentleman (Taylor Hackford, USA, 1982) "Hungry
  for Your Love"

An American Werewolf in London (John Landis, USA, 1982)
   "Moondance"
King of Comedy (Martin Scorcese, USA, 1983) "Wonderful Remark"
The Schooner (Bill Muscally, Eire, 1983) A film for RTE, with
   Morrison's original soundtrack recorded at Cucumber Studios
The Outsiders (Francis Ford Coppola, USA, 1983) "Gloria"
Lamb (Colin Gregg, UK, 1985) Original soundtrack by Morrison
Good Morning Vietnam (Barry Levinson, USA, 1987) "Baby Please
   Don't Go"
Wild at Heart (David Lynch, USA, 1990) "Baby Please Don't Go"
Sleeping with the Enemy (USA, 1991) "Brown Eyed Girl"

Bibliography

Van Morrison: Into the Music by Ritchie Yorke (Charisma/Futura 1975)

Van Morrison: A Portrait of the Artist by Johnny Rogan (Elm Tree Books/Hamish Hamilton Ltd 1984)

Van Morrison: Too Late to Stop Now by Steve Turner (Bloomsbury 1993)

Send 'Em Home Sweatin' by Vincent Power (Kildanore Press 1990)

Turn It Up! (I Can't Hear the Words) by Bob Sarlin (Simon and Schuster 1973)

The Rolling Stone Interviews Vol 2 (Warner Paperback Library 1973)

Irish Rock by Tony Clayton-Lea and Richie Taylor (Sidgwick and Jackson 1992)

The Rolling Stone Illustrated History of Rock & Roll (Rolling Stone Press 1976)

Making Tracks by Charlie Gillett (W H Allen 1975)

British Beat by Chris May and Tim Phillips (Socion Book 1974)

Index

PICTURE CREDITS
The publishers would like to thank the following for supplying the photos used in this book:
Graham Barrett: 9 (b), 10 (tl & bl), 12 (both)
London Features International: 8, 9 (t), 13 (t), 16 (both)
Redferns: 1 (all), 2/3, 3, 4, 5 (both), 6/7, 7, 10/11, 13 (cr & br), 14, 14/15, 15